PTSD FREE

PTSD FREE

A Ten-Week Self-Help Guide to Overcome Post-Traumatic Stress Disorder

DR. DAVE FERRUOLO

Dr. Dave Books

Dr. Dave Books
PO BOX 6421
Laconia, NH 03247
drdavebooks.com

PTSD FREE: A Ten-Week Self-Help Guide to Overcome Post-Traumatic
Stress Disorder

ISSBN: 978-1-963834-99-4 (hard cover)

Printed in the United States of America
0 1 2 3 4 5 6 7 8 9

First Printing, 2024

DISCLAIMER

It is essential to emphasize that this PTSD self-help guidebook does not replace professional mental health or psychiatric care. For those living with PTSD, professional help is recommended. The journey through PTSD can be challenging and deeply personal, often necessitating specialized, professional guidance for effective treatment and safe healing.

If you experience a mental health or medical emergency, immediately call emergency services.

CONTENTS

PART III

PART I

PTSD FREE INTRODUCTION & OVERVIEW

| 1 |

Welcome to Your Guide

Welcome to your PTSD guidebook, a structured and supportive tool designed to aid individuals living with PTSD. This book is structured into three parts: an introduction to PTSD and the therapies used, the 10-week self-help guided program for PTSD, and information on moving forward and sustaining a PTSD free life.

Part I: Introduction to PTSD and Therapies

In the first part, we provide a foundational understanding of PTSD, its symptoms, causes, and prevalence. We introduce various therapeutic modalities like Cognitive Processing, TF-CBT, IFS, Transpersonal Psychology, Positive Psychology, and Solution-Focused Therapy. This section is educational, offering a holistic understanding of PTSD and the approaches to its treatment.

Part II: The 10-Week Self-Help Program – Embracing the Challenge

At the heart of this guidebook lies the 10-week self-help program, a meticulously structured journey designed for individuals coping with PTSD. This program is more than just a series of chapters or weekly themes; it is a comprehensive, step-by-step process to foster deep, personal healing and growth. The program's structure is intentional, with each week building on the last, ensuring a progressive, comprehensive, and ecological approach to PTSD management.

Understanding that PTSD is not just a condition but a challenging journey that affects every aspect of one's life is crucial. This program recognizes the complexity and the often nonlinear nature of healing from trauma. The road to recovery can be arduous, filled with emotional hurdles and moments of self-doubt. Therefore, the 10-week challenge is about reading, understanding, and immersing yourself fully in the guided process.

Each week of the program brings specific tasks and daily exercises designed to engage you in active self-discovery and healing. These tasks are not arbitrary; they are carefully crafted to address various aspects of PTSD, from understanding and processing traumatic memories to rebuilding a sense of self and enhancing emotional resilience. By committing to these daily exercises, you are taking active steps toward confronting and managing the symptoms of PTSD.

This program's true challenge and essence is to commit wholeheartedly to this process. It requires more than passive reading; it demands active participation, consistent effort, and an open heart and mind. The daily exercises are designed to be integral to your healing journey, each contributing to a gradual but significant transformation.

As you navigate through this program, it's important to remember that healing from PTSD is a deeply personal and unique experience. Progress may come in various forms and at different paces for everyone. There might be days when the exercises feel particularly challenging or progress seems stagnant. Your commitment to fully engaging in the process is paramount during these times.

Embracing this 10-week challenge means allowing yourself to experience and work through difficult emotions, to reflect deeply on your experiences, and to actively engage in practices that foster healing. It's about giving yourself the space and permission to heal, one day at a time, one exercise at a time.

This 10-week program is not just a guide but a companion in your journey toward healing from PTSD. It is a call to invest in yourself, to engage with each task with sincerity, and to recognize that while the journey may be challenging, it is also a path to reclaiming your strength and resilience. Remember, this program is a part of your support system, designed to accompany you as you take these essential steps toward recovery and empowerment.

Part III: Moving Forward

Finally, we provide strategies for sustaining progress, preventing relapse, and managing future challenges. This section emphasizes long-term wellness and growth, emphasizing self-care and ongoing support.

Important Note to the Reader

This book is intended to be a brief overview and a self-help guide, not a comprehensive or standalone treatment for PTSD. While it offers valuable information and structured support, it does not replace professional mental health or psychiatric care. We highly recommend and encourage individuals who have PTSD or any other mental health issue to seek professional care. Although *PTSD FREE* can be effective as a standalone self-help guide, it would be incredibly beneficial alongside therapy as a supplementary resource.

Embarking on Your Journey

As you begin this journey, remember that healing from PTSD is a personal and often nonlinear process. This book aims to support and guide you through that journey, providing tools, skills, and knowledge to aid your recovery. Use this guide as a companion for healing, empowerment, and growth.

| 2 |

Understanding PTSD and Its Complexities

Welcome to your journey toward understanding and managing post-traumatic stress disorder (PTSD). PTSD is a mental health condition triggered by experiencing or witnessing a terrifying event. The symptoms can be overwhelming and may include flashbacks, severe anxiety, uncontrollable thoughts about the event, and more. Understanding PTSD is the first step in learning how to navigate its complexities and find a path toward healing.

Post-traumatic stress disorder is a condition that emerges in the wake of experiencing or witnessing a deeply traumatic, life-threatening event. It is characterized by persistent and intense thoughts, emotions, and physical sensations that endure long after the traumatic incident has passed. These symptoms can disrupt daily life, affecting relationships, work, and one's sense of self. We'll briefly explore the common symptoms of PTSD, which are typically grouped into four primary categories. Later in this chapter, we will go into more depth.

1. Intrusive Memories

- Recurrent, Unwanted Distressing Memories: Individuals with PTSD often find themselves reliving the traumatic event in their minds, leading to significant distress. These memories can intrude unexpectedly during waking hours, causing considerable distress.
- Flashbacks are instances where a person perceptually relives or reexperiences the traumatic event in real-time. During a flashback, it might seem like the trauma is happening repeatedly, blurring the line between past and present.
- Nightmares: Traumatic events can manifest in dreams, leading to frequent, vivid nightmares related to the trauma. These can significantly disrupt sleep patterns and lead to a fear of going to sleep.

1. Avoidance

- Avoiding Reminders: There's a strong inclination to steer clear of discussions, thoughts, or anything that serves as a reminder of the traumatic event. This avoidance can extend to activities, places, and even people linked to the trauma.
- Emotional Numbing: As part of the avoidance mechanism, individuals might attempt to numb their emotions or disconnect from their experiences. This might include lacking interest in activities they once enjoyed or avoiding forming new relationships.

1. Negative Changes in Thinking and Mood

- Feelings of Hopelessness: A sense of despair about the future and a pervasive feeling that things will never improve or that life will never return to 'normal.'
- Memory Problems include difficulty remembering essential aspects of the traumatic event and general memory lapses.

- Negative Self-Perception: Persistent negative beliefs about one-self, such as thinking one is 'broken,' 'bad,' or 'worthless.' There may also be unjustified feelings of guilt or shame related to the event.
- Detachment: Feeling estranged from family and friends leads to isolation and disconnecting from social circles.

1. Changes in Physical and Emotional Reactions

- Hyperarousal involves constantly being on edge or guarded, always anticipating danger, even in safe environments. This heightened arousal can make it difficult to relax or feel at ease.
- Self-Destructive Behavior: Engaging in risky or harmful activities, possibly as a means of coping or expressing underlying distress.
- Trouble Sleeping: Difficulty falling or staying asleep, often due to nightmares or heightened alertness.
- Irritability and Angry Outbursts: Experiencing sudden, intense bursts of anger or irritability over minor issues, often with little to no provocation.

Understanding these symptoms is important for recognizing PTSD in oneself or others and is the first step toward seeking appropriate treatment and support. Acknowledging that these reactions are normal responses to abnormal events can also be a part of the healing process.

In the following sections, we will explore the causes, risk factors, and treatments for PTSD, offering a comprehensive view of how this complex disorder affects individuals and how they can regain control over their lives.

Causes and Risk Factors

Post-traumatic stress disorder is not limited to any one demo-graphic or experience; it is a condition that can arise in anyone who has encountered severe trauma. This section aims to demystify the causes of PTSD and delve into the risk factors that can influence its development.

Post-traumatic stress disorder can stem from a wide array of traumatic events. These events often involve a threat to life or safety, but any situation that overwhelms an individual with feelings of helplessness, horror, or intense fear can lead to PTSD. Some common causes include:

- *Combat Exposure*: Commonly seen in military personnel, PTSD can develop after exposure to war or combat situations.
- *Natural Disasters*: Events like earthquakes, floods, and hurricanes, which can be unpredictable and devastating, often leave lasting psychological impacts.
- *Serious Accidents*: Car crashes, industrial accidents, or other life-threatening incidents can be traumatic enough to trigger PTSD.
- *Personal Assaults*: Experiences such as robbery, mugging, physical attack, sexual assault, or child abuse are deeply emotional traumas that can lead to PTSD.
- *Other Life-Threatening Medical Situations*: Serious health issues, particularly those involving intense treatments like surgery or intensive care, can be traumatic.
- *Witnessing Trauma*: Sometimes, simply witnessing a traumatic event, such as a violent crime, a serious accident, or the atrocities of war, can lead to PTSD. This is called vicarious trauma.

While trauma is the primary activator for PTSD, not everyone who experiences trauma will develop symptoms or impairments. Various factors can increase the likelihood of developing PTSD following a traumatic event:

- *Previous Traumatic Experiences*: People who have experienced other traumas, especially early in life, are at a higher risk.

- *Existing Mental Health Conditions*: Those with a history of mental health disorders, such as anxiety or depression, may be more susceptible.
- *Family History*: A family history of mental health conditions can be a risk factor.
- *Lack of Support System*: Limited social support after a traumatic event can increase the risk. Supportive family and friends can buffer the effects of trauma.
- *Nature and Severity of the Trauma*: The more severe and prolonged the trauma, the higher the risk of developing PTSD.
- *Individual Resilience Factors*: Personal coping skills and resilience can influence the likelihood of developing PTSD. Those with more robust coping mechanisms may be less likely to develop the disorder.
- *Personality Traits*: Certain personality traits, like neuroticism or a tendency to avoid dealing with problems, can increase vulnerability.
- *Gender*: Women are statistically more likely to develop PTSD than men, although the reasons for this disparity are complex and multifaceted.

Understanding these causes and risk factors will assist in recognizing the signs of PTSD and pointing to appropriate support and treatment. It's important to remember that developing PTSD is not a sign of weakness. Many factors, both internal and external, can influence the development of this disorder. In the next section, we will explore the prevalence of PTSD, shedding light on how widespread this condition is and how it can affect various demographics.

The Brain and PTSD

The intricate relationship between the brain and post-traumatic stress disorder is pivotal in understanding how PTSD manifests and endures. Traumatic events can precipitate profound brain structure and function changes, particularly in regions associated with emotion regulation, memory processing, and threat detection. This section will explore the neurobiological underpinnings of PTSD, shedding light on why symptoms occur and why they can be so persistent.

Hyperactivation of the Amygdala: In PTSD, the amygdala, which is central to the brain's mechanism for identifying and responding to fear, operates at an elevated level of activity. This condition of hyperactivation does more than just sharpen the senses; it essentially recalibrates the body's threat detection system, making it overly sensitive to real and imagined dangers. As a result, individuals with PTSD live in a state of constant vigilance, as if their internal security system is perpetually sounding an alarm, even in the absence of actual threats. This heightened state of alert can lead to a surge in anxiety levels and provoke strong emotional reactions to stimuli that would normally be considered non-threatening.

The implications of an always-active amygdala extend beyond just an increased readiness for perceived dangers; it fundamentally alters how individuals with PTSD perceive and react to the world. Everyday situations can become emotionally charged, leading to disproportionate responses to the actual events. This constant misalignment between perception and reality can make daily life exceptionally challenging.

Recognizing the role of amygdala hyperactivation in PTSD can inform effective treatment methods. By targeting this overactivity, therapeutic strategies can aim to recalibrate the brain's fear response system, helping individuals with PTSD reduce their heightened state of alertness and realign their emotional responses with their current reality.

Hippocampal Changes: The hippocampus is responsible for forming and processing memories, acting as a sort of librarian that helps categorize and store our experiences. In the context of PTSD, the trauma experienced can have a significant impact on this part of the brain, leading to observable changes. Specifically, research has highlighted that individuals with PTSD often show a reduction in hippocampal volume. This physical alteration has profound implications for how those with PTSD interact with their memories.

A smaller hippocampus struggles with effectively distinguishing between the past and the present. This difficulty is not just a matter of mistaking one memory for another; it's the brain's inability to place memories in the correct timeline. As a result, individuals with PTSD might find themselves reliving traumatic events as if they are happening in the present. This manifests through nightmares that disrupt sleep, flashbacks that intrude upon daily life, and intrusive memories that pop up without warning. These symptoms are distressing and interfere with the ability to live a normal, uninterrupted life.

Understanding the role of the hippocampus in PTSD sheds light on why memory related symptoms are so prominent in the disorder. It also highlights the importance of treatments that address these brain changes, aiming to help those with PTSD find a way to place their memories in the past, where they belong, and reduce the intrusion of these memories into their present lives.

Prefrontal Cortex Dysfunction: In PTSD, the prefrontal cortex, which orchestrates high-level functions such as decision-making, planning, and regulating impulsive actions, often operates below its optimal capacity. This area of the brain manages our responses to fear and controlling emotions, moderating the amygdala's alarm signals. When the prefrontal cortex is compromised, as seen in individuals with PTSD, this essential regulatory function is disrupted.

This disruption manifests in several challenging ways. Individuals may find it hard to quell the intense fear and anxiety triggered by the amygdala, leading to an inability to calm down after experiencing stress. Moreover, the dysfunction in the prefrontal cortex can make it difficult to make rational decisions or control impulses effectively, further complicating their ability to navigate everyday situations. The impaired functioning of the prefrontal cortex thus heightens emotional responses and undermines the ability to manage these responses healthily.

The impact of prefrontal cortex dysfunction on emotional regulation and decision-making can cause significant distress and impairments in people suffering with PTSD. Therapeutic strategies that focus on enhancing the functioning of this brain region can offer significant benefits, helping individuals regain control over their emotional responses and improve their ability to handle stress. By targeting these neural circuits, treatment can be tailored to address the specific challenges faced by those with PTSD, paving the way for more effective management of the condition.

Altered Stress Hormone Response: Trauma can potentially disturb the body's standard regulation of cortisol, a key stress hormone. In those with PTSD, this disruption manifests as an altered cortisol response, deviating from typical patterns observed in stress management. This irregularity in cortisol levels can significantly influence both physiological and psychological responses to stress, often amplifying the severity of PTSD symptoms.

The altered cortisol response can lead to an imbalance in how the body and brain manage and react to stress. For example, it may hinder the ability to return to a state of calm after a stressor has passed or increase susceptibility to being triggered by reminders of trauma. Additionally, these changes in cortisol levels can affect other bodily systems, contributing to a range of symptoms from sleep disturbances to heightened anxiety.

Understanding this altered stress hormone response is critical for addressing the complex nature of PTSD. It underscores the need for treatments that can normalize these hormonal imbalances, thereby helping to mitigate the impact of stress on those with PTSD and improve their overall symptom management.

Post-traumatic stress disorder is often characterized by an exaggerated fight, flight or freeze response, which is the body's natural reaction to perceived threats. The brain's altered processing of threat cues can lead to an overactive or inappropriate activation of this response, manifesting in symptoms like hypervigilance, avoidance, and numbing.

Despite the significant impact trauma can have on the brain, it's important to highlight the brain's ability—a concept known as neuroplasticity. This adaptability provides a basis for the effectiveness of various PTSD treatments, which can help to rewire the brain's response to trauma.

Understanding the neurobiological impact of PTSD not only helps in comprehending the persistence of symptoms but also guides effective treatment strategies. Therapies like Cognitive Behavioral Therapy (CBT) and Eye Movement Desensitization and Reprocessing (EMDR) are designed to modify these neural pathways, thereby alleviating symptoms.

The exploration of the brain's response to trauma reveals the complexity of PTSD as more than just a psychological reaction; it is also physiological. This understanding underscores the importance of comprehensive treatment approaches that address the mind and the brain.

In the next section, we will delve into the co-occurring conditions often found alongside PTSD, further illuminating the multifaceted nature of this condition.

Co-occurring Conditions

Individuals with post-traumatic stress disorder often face additional emotional and psychological challenges. These co-occurring conditions can complicate the clinical picture and influence the course and treatment of PTSD.

Depression: Depression is a common comorbidity in individuals with PTSD, affecting a substantial number of those diagnosed. This dual presence of PTSD and depression complicates the emotional landscape, as symptoms of deep sadness, a marked decrease in pleasure from previously enjoyable activities, and profound feelings of worthlessness or inadequacy add layers to the already challenging symptoms of PTSD. The overlap of these conditions can intensify the emotional distress experienced, making treatment more intricate.

The co-occurrence of depression with PTSD calls for interventions that address the specific aspects of PTSD, such as hyperarousal and flashbacks, and the pervasive symptoms of depression. This combination necessitates a careful balancing of treatment modalities to effectively target the broad spectrum of symptoms present, ensuring that care is tailored to the complex needs of those facing both PTSD and depression. Recognizing this intersection will help develop comprehensive treatment plans that can more effectively aid recovery.

Anxiety Disorders: Anxiety disorders, such as generalized anxiety disorder (GAD), panic disorder, and various phobias, often coexist with PTSD, creating a compounded effect on the individual's mental health. This heightened anxiety state can amplify the body's stress response, further exacerbating key PTSD symptoms, including an exaggerated state of alertness (hypervigilance) and difficulties with sleep (insomnia).

The interplay between anxiety disorders and PTSD intensifies the overall distress and symptom severity, making the management and treatment of PTSD more complex. For instance, the pervasive worry characteristic of GAD can deepen the fear responses associated with PTSD. At the same time, panic disorder can lead to sudden and overwhelming feelings of terror, heightening the sense of unpredictability and lack of control. Similarly, specific phobias can trigger intense fear and avoidance behaviors, which overlap with PTSD's avoidance symptoms.

This overlap requires strategies that address the acute symptoms of anxiety disorders and the underlying trauma-related aspects of PTSD. This dual focus ensures a more holistic approach to therapy, aiming to reduce anxiety levels while also tackling the trauma at the core of PTSD, thereby offering a pathway to improved well-being for those affected by both conditions.

Substance Use Disorders: Substance Use Disorders are notably common among individuals with PTSD, with many turning to alcohol or drugs to escape the distressing symptoms they experience. This approach may offer short-term relief from the intense anxiety, flashbacks, and sleep disturbances characteristic of PTSD. However, reliance on substances frequently escalates into a cycle of physiological and psychological dependency, where the long-term consequences outweigh the temporary escape they provide.

This cycle not only complicates the treatment of PTSD but can also exacerbate the condition, leading to a deterioration in mental health. Substance use can mask symptoms, delay the pursuit of effective treatments, and ultimately intensify the challenges of managing PTSD. Moreover, dependency introduces additional health risks, including the potential for developing new mental health disorders or worsening existing ones.

Integrated Treatment Approach: An integrated treatment approach becomes essential when PTSD coexists with other mental health conditions. This strategy ensures that both PTSD and the accompanying conditions are treated concurrently, providing a more holistic and effective method of care. By addressing the complexities of each disorder together, this approach aims to improve overall mental health outcomes, reduce symptoms more effectively, and enhance the individual's quality of life.

The integrated treatment model acknowledges the interrelated nature of mental health conditions and tailors therapy to encompass all aspects of the individual's psychological well-being. It often combines various therapeutic modalities, such as cognitive-behavioral therapy (CBT), which also is used for conditions like depression, anxiety, or substance use disorders. This comprehensive approach seeks to alleviate symptoms and address underlying issues contributing to the co-occurrence of disorders.

Medication Management: When managing co-occurring conditions such as depression, anxiety, and PTSD, an assessment for pharmacological interventions is always recommended. To ensure the most effective and safe use of psychotropic medications, consultation with a psychiatrist or psychiatric nurse practitioner. These specialists can provide expert guidance on medication management, tailoring the choice of psychotropics and dosages to the individual's specific needs and health profile.

Psychiatric consultation is a necessity for navigating the complexities of treating multiple conditions simultaneously. It enables a more precise assessment of which medications can offer relief from symptoms across different disorders, considering factors like potential side effects and interactions with other medications. This personalized approach to medication management is a key component of a comprehensive treatment plan.

Therapy Adjustments: Therapy adjustments are often necessary to effectively address the complexities of co-occurring conditions, such as when PTSD is present alongside substance use disorders. In such cases, treatment plans must incorporate additional components tailored to these conditions' specific needs and challenges. For instance, individuals dealing with both PTSD and substance use disorders may require initial detoxification processes to manage withdrawal symptoms safely. Following detoxification, therapy might include relapse prevention strategies designed to help individuals recognize and cope with triggers in a healthy manner.

Incorporating these specialized components into the overall treatment plan acknowledges the interconnected nature of PTSD and substance use disorders. It allows for a more holistic approach, aiming to address not only the psychological impact of trauma but also the patterns of substance use that may have developed as a coping mechanism.

Education: It is important to understand the complex relationship between PTSD and any co-occurring conditions you might be facing. By learning how these conditions interact, you'll be better able to spot patterns in your symptoms and take a more active role in your treatment.

This knowledge isn't just empowering—it's transformative. It demystifies the reasons behind the comprehensive treatment plans and the integrated approaches your healthcare team suggests. More importantly, recognizing how your symptoms interweave can inspire you to engage more deeply with all facets of your treatment, from therapy sessions and medication to important lifestyle adjustments.

With this understanding, you can communicate more effectively with your healthcare providers, ensuring your treatment is collaborative and tailored to your needs. Educating yourself about the dynamics of PTSD and other conditions fosters a sense of control and optimism, key allies in navigating the path to wellness.

The Spectrum of Trauma Responses

The experience of trauma and its aftermath can vary significantly from one person to another, leading to a wide range of responses and coping mechanisms. This diversity is what forms the spectrum of trauma responses. Understanding this spectrum is essential in recognizing the individualized nature of PTSD and tailoring treatment approaches accordingly.

Physiological Responses: Understanding the physiological responses to PTSD is essential. This condition can manifest in various bodily reactions, from elevated alertness to severe exhaustion. It's not uncommon for individuals to experience a rapid heartbeat and hypervigilance, where they are constantly on edge, scanning for potential threats. This heightened state of arousal can significantly interfere with daily activities and overall well-being.

Conversely, some individuals may find themselves feeling physically numb or extremely fatigued. This fatigue isn't just about feeling tired; it's a profound exhaustion that rest doesn't seem to alleviate, impacting one's ability to engage in routine tasks and enjoy life.

Moreover, PTSD can lead to somatic symptoms, a phenomenon where psychological distress is expressed through physical pain or discomfort. These symptoms are not just "in the head" but are real, painful experiences that can vary greatly in intensity and form, from headaches and stomachaches to unexplained aches and pains throughout the body.

Recognizing these physiological responses is the first step toward addressing them. Understanding that these physical manifestations are linked to PTSD can help individuals and their caregivers develop more effective treatment plans.

Emotional Reactions: Navigating the emotional landscape after a traumatic event is a deeply personal journey, marked by a spectrum of emotional reactions that can significantly affect one's quality of life. Trauma can elicit a range of intense feelings, from fear and anger to profound sadness and guilt. These emotions may not only arise in response to specific triggers but can also occur unexpectedly, overwhelming the individual at moments when they least expect it.

Fear is a common response, manifesting as an ongoing sense of dread or panic, often accompanied by anxiety about potential future threats. Anger, too, can surface, directed either outwardly toward others or inwardly, turning into self-blame or frustration over feeling powerless. Sadness may envelop individuals, leading to episodes of crying, despair, or a persistent melancholy that hampers one's ability to find joy in life.

Guilt is another emotion that frequently burdens those with PTSD, stemming from thoughts of what they could have done differently or the belief that they are somehow to blame for what happened. This guilt can be debilitating, affecting one's self-esteem and sense of worth.

On the other end of the emotional spectrum is numbness, a defense mechanism where individuals detach from their feelings, leading to a sense of disconnection from both themselves and the world around them. This emotional detachment can make it challenging to form or maintain personal relationships and leave individuals isolated and alone.

Recognizing and understanding these varied emotional responses will help in the treatment of PTSD. Acknowledging and validating these emotions as normal reactions to abnormal events can pave the way for healing. It highlights the need for a tailored approach to therapy that respects the individual's emotional experience and provides them with the tools to navigate and process these complex feelings.

Cognitive Processing: Trauma profoundly affects cognitive functioning, altering how individuals interpret and interact with their surroundings. The impact on cognitive processing can manifest in several ways, significantly affecting daily life and overall mental well-being. Individuals might find themselves grappling with confusion or experiencing impaired concentration ability. These challenges can make routine tasks and decision-making more difficult, leading to frustration and decreased productivity.

Intrusive thoughts are another common cognitive symptom of PTSD. These are unwelcome, often distressing memories of the traumatic event that can suddenly invade a person's mind without warning. They can be intense and vivid, disrupting daily activities and contributing to heightened stress and anxiety levels.

Some individuals might resort to denial as a way to cope with the reality of their trauma. By refusing to acknowledge the event or its impact, they temporarily shield themselves from the pain and distress associated with their memories. However, this coping mechanism can hinder the healing process, as it prevents individuals from confronting and processing their trauma.

Dissociation is another coping strategy where individuals detach from their thoughts, feelings, memories, or sense of identity. This can range from mild detachment to more severe dissociation, like depersonalization or derealization, where one feels disconnected from one's body or the world around them. While dissociation can provide temporary relief from emotional pain, it can also contribute to a sense of alienation and difficulty in forming or maintaining personal relationships.

Recognizing and addressing these cognitive challenges is a vital component of PTSD treatment. Through therapeutic interventions, individuals can learn strategies to manage intrusive thoughts, improve concentration, and gradually confront and process their trauma. This cognitive work is essential for recovery, enabling individuals to reshape their perceptions and regain control over their lives.

Behavioral Changes: the behavioral impact of PTSD reflects a spectrum of changes that can significantly disrupt an individual's life and relationships. One of the most common behaviors is avoidance, where individuals steer clear of places, people, or activities that remind them of the traumatic event. This avoidance can serve as a protective measure, attempting to prevent the reexperiencing of trauma-related distress, but it can also lead to isolation and a narrowed life experience.

Social withdrawal is another behavior frequently observed in those dealing with PTSD. Individuals may pull away from friends, family, and social gatherings, finding it difficult to relate to others or fearing others won't understand their experience. This withdrawal can compound feelings of loneliness and alienation, exacerbating the condition.

Conversely, some may engage in increased risk-taking behaviors. This could manifest as reckless driving, substance abuse, or other activities that put the individual or others at risk. These behaviors might temporarily distract from trauma-related pain or numb emotional distress but ultimately lead to further complications and potential harm.

On the other end of the spectrum, some individuals with PTSD may seek solace in routines and structure. Adhering to a strict schedule or engaging in repetitive behaviors can provide a sense of control and predictability in a chaotic and unsafe world. While beneficial to some extent, an overreliance on rigid structures can become limiting and restrict opportunities for healing and growth.

Erratic or impulsive behaviors are also common, reflecting a struggle with self-regulation. These behaviors can strain relationships, impact work or academic performance, and lead to a cycle of guilt and self-recrimination.

It's important to approach these behaviors empathetically, recognizing them as coping mechanisms rather than personal failings. Therapy can help individuals develop healthier coping strategies, rebuild social connections, and gradually confront the trauma in a supportive and controlled environment. By addressing these behavioral changes, individuals can work toward regaining a sense of agency and rebuilding their lives post-trauma.

Nature of the Trauma: The nature of the trauma experienced plays a pivotal role in shaping the individual's response and recovery process. Traumas vary widely in their type, severity, and length of exposure, each leaving a unique imprint on those affected. Chronic exposure to traumatic situations, such as sustained abuse, warfare, or long-term neglect, tends to have a profound and enduring impact. Individuals subjected to prolonged trauma may develop complex PTSD, characterized by more severe symptoms, including deep-seated feelings of shame, persistent distrust in others, and difficulties in regulating emotions.

Conversely, a single traumatic event, while still potentially devastating, may lead to a different trajectory of symptoms and recovery. These individuals might primarily struggle with flashbacks, nightmares, and acute stress reactions. The intensity of these responses can vary, but the limited exposure may allow for a more straightforward treatment process, focusing on specific traumatic memories and their immediate psychological impacts.

The severity of the trauma also significantly influences the response. High-intensity traumas, such as natural disasters, violent assaults, or life-threatening accidents, can lead to more pronounced psychological distress. The shock and horror experienced during such events can overwhelm an individual's coping mechanisms, leading to more severe manifestations of PTSD.

Chronic traumas often require more complex and multifaceted therapeutic interventions, focusing on building safety, processing deep-seated emotions, and reconstructing a sense of identity. Treatments for those impacted by single-event traumas may concentrate on trauma-focused therapies that work to desensitize the individual to the traumatic memory and reduce its power to elicit distress.

Acknowledging the differences in trauma experiences is essential for effective treatment, emphasizing that recovery is not one-size-fits-all. By considering the type, severity, and duration of the trauma, mental health professionals can better support individuals on their path to healing, offering hope and tailored strategies to navigate the challenges of PTSD.

Personal History: An individual's history is a critical determinant in how they respond to and recover from traumatic events. This history encompasses a range of experiences, including any previous traumas, their upbringing, and the coping mechanisms they've developed over time. Individuals with a history of prior trauma may find themselves more susceptible to PTSD following new traumatic incidents. This heightened vulnerability can be attributed to an already sensitized stress response system, making it more challenging to process subsequent traumas.

Furthermore, the environment in which one is raised plays a substantial role. For instance, those who grew up in supportive, stable environments may have had the opportunity to develop healthier coping strategies. This foundation can provide a measure of resilience when facing future traumas, offering a repertoire of emotional and psychological resources to draw upon.

Conversely, individuals raised in environments marked by instability, neglect, or abuse may have developed coping mechanisms that, while adaptive in their original context, may prove maladaptive in the face of new traumas. These might include avoidance, denial, or substance use, which can complicate and prolong the recovery process.

The cumulative impact of an individual's life experiences, including how they've learned to cope with stress, emotions, and adversity, significantly influences their response to trauma. It allows for a more in-depth understanding of the individual's current challenges and facilitates the development of personalized treatment plans. These plans can address the recent trauma and the deeper historical layers of vulnerability and resilience.

Social Support & Cultural and Societal Factors: Social support and cultural and societal influences are pivotal in shaping an individual's journey through trauma and recovery. A robust support system, characterized by understanding and empathetic friends, family, or community members, can significantly bolster resilience in the face of trauma. Such networks offer emotional sustenance, practical assistance, and a sense of belonging, all vital for healing. Supported individuals are more likely to share their experiences, seek help, and engage in treatment, contributing to more favorable outcomes.

Conversely, the absence of support or outright isolation can intensify the adverse effects of trauma. Isolation not only magnifies feelings of loneliness and abandonment but also reinforces the stigma surrounding mental health challenges. Without a support network, individuals may struggle to find the motivation to pursue recovery, potentially leading to a cycle of worsening symptoms and further withdrawal.

Cultural beliefs and societal attitudes do play a role in how trauma and mental health are perceived and addressed. Cultures that recognize and validate the impact of trauma and mental health issues can facilitate healing by fostering environments where individuals feel safe to express their pain and seek assistance. These cultures may offer specific rituals, community support practices, or perspectives on suffering and recovery that provide comfort and a path forward.

On the other hand, societies with stigmatizing views on mental health or those that undervalue the significance of psychological trauma can hinder individuals from acknowledging their pain or accessing care. Stigma can lead to shame, secrecy, and a reluctance to seek help, delaying or complicating the recovery process. Additionally, cultural misunderstandings or biases within the healthcare system can further alienate those in need, making treatment approaches imperative to be culturally sensitive and inclusive.

Acknowledging the impact of social support, cultural beliefs, and societal attitudes is essential in the context of PTSD treatment. It underscores the need for a holistic approach to care that considers these external factors. Building strong support systems, challenging stigmatizing beliefs, and promoting culturally competent care are key steps in supporting individuals affected by trauma, facilitating a more inclusive and effective pathway to healing and resilience.

This wide range of trauma responses underscores the necessity for a multifaceted approach to PTSD treatment, emphasizing:

Personalized Treatment Plans: Recognizing the uniqueness of each individual's experience with PTSD is fundamental. It's imperative to craft customized treatment plans to align with each person's specific symptoms, coping mechanisms, and needs. A one-size-fits-all strategy is insufficient for addressing the multifaceted nature of PTSD, necessitating personalized care that adapts to the evolving landscape of an individual's symptoms and recovery process.

Holistic Care: The multifarious manifestations of trauma demand a holistic treatment strategy. This approach should encompass not only the psychological aspect but also the physical, emotional, cognitive, and behavioral dimensions of a person's well-being. Integrating these facets into a comprehensive treatment plan ensures that all areas affected by trauma are addressed, fostering a more complete and sustainable healing process.

Patient-Centered Approach: Placing patients at the heart of the treatment process and actively involving them in developing their care plans significantly enhances therapeutic outcomes. Acknowledging and valuing their lived experiences, preferences, and insights into their needs encourages a more engaged and cooperative therapeutic relationship. This collaborative stance fosters a sense of patient empowerment and agency, aiding effective recovery.

The spectrum of trauma responses illuminates the intricate nature of PTSD, accentuating the critical importance of recognizing and honoring the individuality of each person's experience and path to recovery. As we delve deeper into various facets of PTSD, including its treatment and management, we maintain a steadfast focus on the personal nuances that characterize this journey. This approach not only respects the complexity of PTSD but also champions the resilience and individuality of those navigating their way through recovery.

Understanding PTSD and its complexities is a vital step in the journey toward recovery. This chapter aims to provide you with the knowledge and perspective needed to navigate the challenges of PTSD. As you move forward, remember that this understanding is a powerful tool in your healing process.

In the next chapter, we will build on this foundation and begin exploring effective strategies for managing and overcoming the symptoms of PTSD.

| 3 |

Foundations of Effective Therapy

As we progress in our exploration of psychotherapy for PTSD, Chapter 2 serves as a foundational guide to various therapeutic modalities. This chapter is a brief overview, offering essential insights into each approach rather than a comprehensive guide. The intention is to equip you with basic knowledge to understand the landscape of PTSD treatment. It's important to emphasize that this information is a starting point for those seeking to deepen their awareness and and understanding of the current evidence-base of PTSD treatments. Engaging with qualified professionals or more topic-specific resources can facilitate deeper understanding of the ins and outs of available treatments.

In this chapter, we'll shed light on several key therapeutic modalities such as Cognitive Processing Therapy (CPT), Trauma-Focused Cognitive Behavioral Therapy (TF-CBT), Internal Family Systems (IFS) Therapy, Transpersonal Psychology, Positive Psychology, and Solution-Focused Therapy. Additionally, we will touch upon emerging therapies like psychedelic-assisted psychotherapy to provide a glimpse into the evolving field of PTSD treatment. This chapter aims to give you an initial understanding of these varied approaches, encouraging further exploration and, if compelled, seeking additional resources for a deeper plunge.

Evidenced-Based Practices

Cognitive Processing Therapy (CPT): Cognitive Processing Therapy is a specialized form of cognitive behavioral therapy (CBT) tailored for individuals dealing with the aftermath of traumatic events. It operates on the principle that PTSD symptoms are partly maintained by maladaptive beliefs and thought patterns related to the trauma. CPT helps individuals by guiding them to reevaluate and challenge these unhelpful beliefs, particularly around themes of safety, trust, power, esteem, and intimacy. Through this cognitive restructuring, individuals learn to construct a more realistic and empowering narrative of their traumatic experience, facilitating a sense of closure and personal growth.

Trauma-Focused Cognitive Behavioral Therapy (TF-CBT): Trauma-Focused Cognitive Behavioral Therapy, an adaptation of traditional CBT, is specifically designed for younger individuals who have experienced traumatic events. This approach integrates trauma-sensitive interventions with cognitive behavioral techniques. Central to TF-CBT is the gradual and respectful exposure to trauma memories and cues, which is believed to reduce the power these memories hold. The therapy also encompasses teaching coping skills for dealing with PTSD symptoms and emotional distress, thereby fostering resilience in the face of trauma.

Internal Family Systems (IFS): Internal Family Systems presents a unique lens through which PTSD is viewed not just as a set of symptoms but as a reflection of dissonance within an individual's internal system of 'parts' or subpersonalities. Central to IFS is the belief that healing comes from the individual's 'Self,' which possesses qualities like compassion, curiosity, and calmness. Therapy involves identifying and understanding these parts—often protectors and exiles formed due to traumatic experiences—and helping them to release the burdens they carry, thus restoring balance and promoting inner harmony.

Transpersonal Psychology: Transpersonal Psychology transcends traditional psychotherapeutic approaches by integrating spiritual and transcendent aspects of the human experience with the framework of contemporary evidence-based practices. It views healing from trauma as a transformative process involving the mind, body, and spirit. Techniques might include meditation, mindfulness, and exploring altered states of consciousness to foster a deeper connection with oneself and the broader universe.

Positive Psychology: Positive Psychology shifts the focus from pathology and illness to wellness and thriving. In the context of PTSD, it emphasizes identifying and harnessing individual strengths, virtues, and positive experiences. Techniques such as gratitude exercises, identifying personal strengths, and fostering positive relationships are employed to build resilience, improve well-being, and enhance life satisfaction, thereby counterbalancing therapy's trauma-focused aspects.

Solution-Focused Therapy: Solution-focused therapy stands out in its forward-looking approach. Rather than delving into the past trauma, it focuses on envisioning and realizing a future free from the grip of PTSD. The therapy is grounded in the belief that clients have the inherent capacity to overcome their difficulties. The therapist's role is to help the individual identify and amplify existing strengths and resources and construct a clear vision of their desired future, thereby charting a path of recovery that is both hopeful and pragmatic.

Prolonged Exposure Therapy (PE): Prolonged Exposure Therapy is a stalwart in PTSD treatment, embodying a cognitive-behavioral approach. It systematically exposes individuals to trauma-related stimuli or memories they've been avoiding, aiming to desensitize their emotional response. PE is grounded in the understanding that avoidance perpetuates PTSD symptoms. By confronting these avoided memories and emotions in a safe therapeutic setting, individuals can gradually decrease their PTSD symptoms.

Eye Movement Desensitization and Reprocessing (EMDR): Eye Movement Desensitization and Reprocessing represents a fusion of cognitive therapy techniques with rhythmic eye movements. This innovative approach helps individuals process traumatic memories by focusing on external stimuli like eye movements or hand taps. EMDR facilitates the reprocessing of traumatic events, reducing the emotional impact of these memories and thereby alleviating PTSD symptoms.

Medication: Medication, particularly SSRIs and SNRIs, plays a pivotal role in managing PTSD symptoms. These medications can help reduce anxiety, depression, and sleep disturbances, providing a neurochemical balance that supports other therapeutic interventions.

Cognitive Behavioral Conjoint Therapy for PTSD (CBCT for PTSD): CBCT for PTSD brings a relational dimension to PTSD treatment. It is a couple-based therapy that not only addresses individual PTSD symptoms but also aims to enhance relationship functioning. Involving partners in therapy fosters support, understanding, and joint healing.

Narrative Exposure Therapy (NET): Emerging as a promising approach, NET is especially effective for individuals with a history of complex trauma. This therapy involves creating a detailed chronological narrative of the person's life, focusing on traumatic events. NET helps individuals contextualize and integrate these experiences within their life stories.

Virtual Reality Exposure Therapy (VRET): VRET leverages cutting-edge technology to treat PTSD. By creating virtual simulations of traumatic events, VRET allows individuals to confront and process their trauma in a controlled, safe environment, bridging the gap between imagined exposure and real-life situations.

Mindfulness-Based Stress Reduction (MBSR): MBSR introduces mindfulness as a tool for managing PTSD symptoms. By fostering present-moment awareness and acceptance, MBSR helps individuals reduce stress and develop coping mechanisms that enhance their capacity to manage PTSD symptoms.

Dialectical Behavior Therapy (DBT): Initially designed for borderline personality disorder, DBT's adaptation for PTSD shows promise, particularly for individuals struggling with severe emotional dysregulation or self-harm behaviors. DBT emphasizes balancing acceptance and change, enhancing emotional regulation, and improving interpersonal effectiveness.

Acceptance and Commitment Therapy (ACT): ACT represents a shift in PTSD treatment, focusing on acceptance of thoughts and feelings rather than trying to change or avoid them. This approach encourages individuals to embrace their experiences and commit to actions aligned with their values, fostering psychological flexibility.

Compassion-Focused Therapy (CFT): CFT is particularly suited for individuals who experience intense shame and self-criticism associated with their trauma. It aims to cultivate self-compassion, offering a pathway to counteract negative self-perceptions and enhance emotional healing.

Psychedelic-assisted psychotherapy: Psychedelic-assisted psychotherapy represents a cutting-edge approach to the treatment of PTSD, drawing significant attention for its potential in clinical settings. This innovative therapeutic method integrates the use of specific psychedelic substances - notably psilocybin, ketamine, and MDMA (3,4-methylenedioxymethamphetamine) - with conventional psychotherapeutic practices. Each of these substances has unique properties that can facilitate deep psychological exploration and emotional processing, which might be challenging to achieve with traditional therapy alone.

Psilocybin, a compound found in certain species of mushrooms, is being studied for its potential to create profound changes in consciousness and perspective, which can help individuals confront and reframe traumatic memories in a therapeutic setting. Research suggests that psilocybin, when administered in a controlled environment, can lead to significant and lasting reductions in PTSD symptoms.

Ketamine, originally used as an anesthetic, has shown rapid antidepressant effects, including for those with PTSD. Its ability to provide relief from symptoms sometimes within hours of administration is a notable departure from traditional antidepressants, which typically take weeks to show effects. Ketamine's action on glutamate, a neurotransmitter, might offer a unique pathway for healing in PTSD patients who have not responded to other treatments.

MDMA, often known for its use as a recreational drug, is being researched for its therapeutic potential in treating PTSD. Under professional supervision, MDMA can induce a state of heightened emotional receptivity and reduced fear, allowing individuals to process traumatic experiences with greater ease and less psychological resistance. Clinical trials have demonstrated promising results, with many participants experiencing significant and lasting reductions in PTSD symptoms after MDMA-assisted psychotherapy sessions.

These treatments are in various research and clinical trial stages, emphasizing the importance of undertaking them in professionally approved and controlled clinical settings. The integration of these psychedelic substances into therapy sessions is carefully structured, typically including preparation, guided experiences during the drug's effects, and follow-up integration sessions to process and solidify insights. The emerging evidence from these trials suggests that psychedelic-assisted psychotherapy could soon play a crucial role in the effective treatment of PTSD, offering new hope for those for whom traditional therapies have been insufficient.

Alternative Treatments

Alternative treatments for PTSD have gained attention for their potential to provide relief and healing beyond traditional psychotherapeutic approaches. These treatments often integrate holistic and innovative methods, focusing on the mind-body connection and experiential learning. Here are some notable alternative therapies:

Equine-Assisted Psychotherapy (EAP): This therapeutic approach involves interaction with horses under the guidance of a mental health professional. EAP is based on the premise that caring for and communicating with horses can foster emotional growth, improve self-awareness, and enhance social skills.

Outdoor and Adventure-Based Therapies: These therapies use outdoor activities and adventure experiences, such as hiking, rock climbing, or wilderness expeditions, as therapeutic tools. They aim to build confidence, develop coping skills, and foster resilience through overcoming physical challenges in a natural setting.

Acupuncture and Acupressure: Rooted in traditional Chinese medicine, acupuncture involves inserting thin needles into specific points on the body, while acupressure uses pressure instead of needles. Both practices are believed to balance the body's energy flow (Qi) and can help alleviate PTSD symptoms like anxiety, stress, and insomnia.

Yoga and Mindfulness Meditation: Yoga combines physical postures, breathing exercises, and meditation to promote relaxation and mind-body integration. Mindfulness meditation focuses on cultivating a non-judgmental awareness of the present moment, which can help in managing PTSD symptoms.

Art Therapy: Art therapy uses creative expression through mediums like painting, drawing, or sculpting as a therapeutic tool. It allows individuals to express emotions and experiences that may be difficult to articulate verbally, fostering healing and self-discovery.

Music Therapy: This therapy uses music-making and listening to facilitate emotional expression, reduce stress, and improve psychological well-being. Music therapy can be beneficial in accessing and processing emotions related to trauma.

Animal-Assisted Therapy (AAT): AAT involves interaction with animals (such as dogs or cats) as part of the therapeutic process. These interactions can help reduce anxiety, improve mood, and provide emotional support.

Aromatherapy: Aromatherapy uses essential oils and aromatic compounds to influence mood, cognition, and psychological well-being. Certain scents can have calming effects, which may be beneficial for people living with PTSD.

Massage Therapy involves manipulating the body's muscles and soft tissues to relieve stress and tension. It can be particularly beneficial for those with PTSD by reducing physical manifestations of stress and anxiety.

Floatation Therapy (Sensory Deprivation Tanks): This therapy involves floating in a tank filled with saltwater, isolated from external stimuli. It's believed to induce deep relaxation, reduce stress, and improve mood.

Biofeedback and Neurofeedback: These therapies use electronic monitoring to provide feedback on physiological functions, such as heart rate or brain activity. Individuals learn to control these functions, which can help manage stress and anxiety symptoms associated with PTSD.

Herbal Medicine and Supplements: Certain herbs and dietary supplements are believed to have calming and mood-stabilizing properties. While not a replacement for conventional treatments, they can be used as adjunctive therapy for managing PTSD symptoms.

It's important to note that while these alternative treatments can offer benefits, they should be considered complementary to mainstream PTSD treatments and not as standalone solutions. Consulting with healthcare professionals before starting any alternative therapy is essential to ensure safety and effectiveness.

As we conclude Chapter 2, we have journeyed through a landscape rich in diverse therapeutic modalities, each offering unique perspectives and techniques for addressing PTSD. From the structured approach of Cognitive Processing Therapy (CPT) and the child-focused lens of Trauma-Focused Cognitive Behavioral Therapy (TF-CBT) to the introspective journey facilitated by Internal Family Systems (IFS) Therapy and the holistic views of Transpersonal and Positive Psychology, this chapter has provided a basic yet insightful overview of the tools available for healing from PTSD.

We also ventured into the realm of emerging therapies, such as psychedelic-assisted psychotherapy, highlighting the innovative approaches being explored in current research. These glimpses into various therapeutic practices serve as a foundational understanding, a springboard for further exploration and learning.

It is important to reiterate that this chapter, and the book as a whole, is not a comprehensive guide but an introductory overview meant to inform and inspire further inquiry. For those grappling with PTSD or for readers seeking to support others on their healing journey, remember that this book is but a starting point. Engaging with professional mental health providers remains crucial for effective, personalized treatment and care.

As you turn the pages to the next chapter, carry with you the knowledge that the journey of healing from PTSD is as diverse as the therapies available. There is hope in the multitude of pathways to recovery, and each individual's journey is unique. May this chapter serve as a beacon, guiding you toward the path that resonates most deeply with your own experience and encouraging you to seek professional support that can turn these foundational insights into meaningful steps toward healing and growth.

| 4 |

Living with PTSD

Living with post-traumatic stress disorder can often feel like navigating through a relentless storm. The symptoms—anxiety, flashbacks, emotional numbness, and others—can create a world that feels unpredictable and overwhelming. If you're reading this, you might be seeking a path to calmer waters, a way to understand and manage the challenges of PTSD. This 10-week self-help guidebook is designed to be that guiding light.

PTSD is more than just a reaction to a traumatic event; it's a complex condition that can profoundly affect one's emotions, thoughts, relationships, and overall quality of life. It might feel like PTSD has a firm grip on your life, but through this guidebook, you will discover not only the strength to loosen this grip but also the strategies to take back control.

Why This Guidebook?

1. *Evidence-Based Practices*: *PTSD FREE* is founded on a selection of evidence-based treatment modalities, each meticulously selected for its established efficacy in tackling the complex dimensions of PTSD. Grounded in research-supported approaches, *PTSD FREE* is enriched with methodologies that have been rigorously

evaluated and demonstrated to aid individuals in surmounting the symptoms and hurdles associated with PTSD. Embracing these modalities, *PTSD FREE* presents a holistic and multi-faceted approach to the treatment of PTSD. It aims to comprehensively address the psychological, emotional, cognitive, behavioral, and spiritual dimensions of an individual's recovery journey. This ensures that those affected by PTSD have access to a wide array of therapeutic strategies, providing a versatile toolkit to navigate and overcome the challenges posed by PTSD.

2. *Comprehensive Understanding*: Part One of *PTSD FREE* demystifies post-traumatic stress disorder using clear, accessible language. It equips readers with the knowledge to identify, understand, and foresee the various ways PTSD might manifest. This foundational understanding is empowering, offering readers the tools to navigate their experiences with knowledge, insight and confidence.

The content is thorough and meticulously researched, adhering to the highest clinical standards. *PTSD FREE* draws on a wealth of scientific research and best practices in the field of mental health to provide information that is accurate and actionable. By grounding the discussion in evidence-based practices, *PTSD FREE* ensures that readers are receiving reliable and up-to-date information.

3. *Structured Yet Personalized Approach*: Part Two of *PTSD FREE* presents a Ten-Week Self-Help Guide, meticulously designed to provide a structured and evidence-based approach for addressing PTSD. This guide is grounded in clinical research and best practices, with each week dedicated to exploring different therapeutic aspects customized to support your healing journey.

Throughout this ten-week program, you will embark on a path that begins with rebuilding a sense of safety—both physically and emotionally. Recognizing that feeling safe is the foundation upon which all subsequent healing builds, this initial phase is crucial for preparing you to effectively process and work through trauma.

As the weeks progress, you'll be guided through various techniques and exercises aimed at processing your trauma in a manageable and healthy way. This involves confronting and making sense of traumatic memories, rather than avoiding them, in a supportive and structured manner that minimizes the risk of re-traumatization.

In addition to processing trauma, the guide focuses on developing robust coping strategies. These strategies are designed to help you manage the symptoms of PTSD, such as anxiety, flashbacks, and sleep disturbances. You'll learn practical tools for emotional regulation, mindfulness, and stress reduction, empowering you to navigate daily challenges more effectively.

Each week builds upon the last, ensuring a gradual and sustainable approach to recovery. By dedicating time to different therapeutic concepts and practices, this guide offers a comprehensive roadmap to healing. It's an invitation to take proactive steps towards reclaiming your life from PTSD, with the assurance of a clinically supported framework every step of the way.

4. *Empowering You for the Future*: Part Three is about sustaining your progress and preparing for a future where PTSD does not define you or dictate your life. It's about equipping you with tools to maintain your gains and strategies to handle future challenges.

5. *For Everyone*: Whether you're a therapist seeking a structured approach for clients, an individual looking for self-help strategies, or a loved one trying to understand and support someone with PTSD, this guidebook is designed for you.

Living with PTSD is indeed challenging, but it's important to remember that you're not alone on this journey. Countless individuals have navigated these waters before you and have found their way to a more peaceful and fulfilling shores. With each page, you'll be taking a step toward healing and reclaiming your life from PTSD.

This guidebook is not just about coping with PTSD; it's about transforming your relationship with yourself, your past, embracing the present, and confidently stepping into a future where you are in control. Let this be the first step on your path to recovery and empowerment.

PART II

Welcome to Your 10-Week PTSD FREE Self-Help Guide

| 5 |

Worldview, Schema & Meaning

As we embark on the journey of understanding and healing from Post-Traumatic Stress Disorder (PTSD), it is crucial to begin by exploring the foundational elements that shape our perception of the world. This chapter delves into the concepts of worldviews, schemas, and the meaning-making process. These elements play a pivotal role in how we interpret our experiences, particularly in the context of PTSD.

The Essence of Perception

Our journey through life is greatly influenced by how we perceive the world around us. This perception, however, is not a mere mirror reflecting an objective reality. Instead, it is intricately filtered through the multifaceted lenses of our unique personal experiences, emotional responses, and the environmental influences that have touched our lives. From the earliest moments of our existence, each interaction, encounter, and experience we undergo contributes significantly to shaping our worldviews.

This process of perception formation is deeply personal and subjective. It is not just about processing sensory information but also about interpreting and giving meaning to that information based on our past experiences and emotional responses. These perceptions, be they positive or negative, essentially form the bedrock of our self-concept, understanding of the world, and, crucially, our sense of belonging and purpose.

In the context of PTSD, understanding this essence of perception becomes even more critical. The traumatic experiences that lead to PTSD can profoundly alter an individual's perception, often skewing it toward more negative or threatening interpretations of the world and self. This shift in perception is a key component in both the development and the persistence of PTSD symptoms. Therefore, recognizing and addressing these altered perceptions is fundamental to healing and recovery.

As we delve deeper into this exploration, we will uncover how these perceptions, shaped over a lifetime, can be challenged and reformed. This is both an academic exercise and a transformative process that can reshape how we view the world, engage with it, and find our place within it.

Worldviews are intricate, comprehensive frameworks encompassing our deepest beliefs, attitudes, and values. They form the overarching narrative of our lives, akin to a cake made from various ingredients. Each ingredient represents our unique life experiences, cultural background, education, and social interactions. These components blend to create a worldview that influences our perception and interaction with the world.

A worldview is not static; it evolves as we encounter new experiences, information, and people. It shapes how we interpret events around us and guides our responses to these events. Our worldview can act as a lens that magnifies certain aspects of our experiences while minimizing or ignoring others.

Schemas: The Building Blocks

Schemas are the individual ingredients in the cake analogy—they are the cognitive structures that help us process, categorize, and interpret information. Schemas are mental shortcuts developed from past experiences that help us navigate the world's complexities efficiently. They are foundational to our learning processes, enabling us to recognize patterns, make predictions, and respond to new situations based on prior knowledge.

However, schemas can also lead to distortions in perception, especially when they are based on limited or traumatic experiences. They can cause us to filter out information that contradicts our pre-existing beliefs, leading to a narrow or skewed world perspective.

The Three Critical Dimensions of Worldviews

1. Self-Perception: This dimension encompasses our deepest subconscious thoughts about ourselves. It includes beliefs about our abilities, worth, and identity. Self-perception can vary greatly, from highly positive and empowering to negative and limiting. It plays a crucial role in shaping our self-esteem, confidence, and our roles in our personal and professional lives.

2. Perception of the World: This aspect pertains to our underlying beliefs about the nature and workings of the world. It encompasses our views on whether the world is fundamentally safe, dangerous, just or unjust, predictable or chaotic. This perception influences our sense of security, trust in others, and willingness to engage with the world.

3. Self in the World: The intersection of our self-perception and world perception forms this dimension. It relates to how we perceive our place and role in the broader context of the world. Our self-concept colors this dimension and impacts our interactions, relationships, and the choices we make in life. It influences how we align our goals with the external environment and navigate challenges and opportunities.

It is important to understanding these dimensions, particularly in the context of PTSD, where traumatic experiences can profoundly alter one's worldview and schemas. Recognizing and addressing these altered perceptions is essential in the journey toward healing and recovery, as they shape our understanding of the traumatic event and our ongoing responses to ourselves and the world. This chapter aims to provide a foundation for this understanding, setting the stage for the transformative work that lies ahead in the journey of healing from PTSD.

The Dynamic Nature of Worldviews

To understand the human psyche, you must understand the dynamic nature of worldviews. Unlike fixed lenses, our worldviews are fluid and adaptable, changing shape and color based on different contexts and situations. This malleability is a intricate part of the complexity and depth of human cognition and emotion.

For instance, an individual might exhibit a confident and secure demeanor within the familiar confines of their home, where relationships and routines are well-established. In contrast, this same individual could experience feelings of anxiety and uncertainty in a work environment where challenges and interpersonal dynamics differ vastly. Such variations in perception and response across different life domains – home, work, social settings, and even within oneself—highlight the adaptable nature of our worldviews.

External factors like culture, society, and relationships significantly shape and reshape our worldviews. Cultural norms and societal expectations can dictate what is deemed acceptable or successful, influencing how we perceive ourselves and our place in the world. Relationships, whether nurturing or toxic, can significantly impact our self-perception and outlook toward life.

Internally, our psychological state, including the presence of mental health conditions like PTSD, can cause shifts in our worldviews. Traumatic experiences, in particular, can cause a dramatic shift in how one views safety, trust, and personal resilience. For someone with PTSD, a previously benign situation may suddenly be perceived as threatening, or a once-trusted individual may now be seen with suspicion.

The dynamic nature of worldviews also influences adaptation and coping mechanisms. As we navigate different life stages and experiences, our worldviews evolve to accommodate new information, experiences, and understandings. This adaptive capacity is crucial for growth and learning but can pose challenges when maladaptive perceptions or schemas become entrenched.

Understanding the dynamic nature of worldviews is particularly important in PTSD treatment. It suggests that the altered perceptions stemming from trauma are not permanent and can be reshaped and reformed through therapy and self-awareness. This perspective opens the door to hope and change, affirming that the impact of trauma on one's worldview is not an unchangeable fate but a mutable, evolving process.

The dynamic nature of worldviews is a fundamental concept in understanding human behavior and response, especially in the context of PTSD. It underscores the importance of contextual and situational awareness in therapy and self-help, emphasizing the potential for change and growth in the journey toward healing.

The Role of Perception in Shaping Reality

Our journey from perception to reality is a complex and intricate process that lies at the heart of our experience of the world. While our senses play a crucial role in gathering information from our surroundings, our brain interprets this sensory data. This interpretation is not a mere replication of the external world; rather, it is deeply influenced and filtered through the lens of our worldviews.

The brain's interpretation of sensory inputs results in the creation of subjective stories - personalized narratives that we come to accept as our reality. These narratives are a blend of factual information and our personal biases, beliefs, and past experiences. They shape how we perceive situations, events, and interactions. The subjectivity of these stories means that two individuals can perceive the same event in vastly different ways, each creating their version of reality based on their unique worldview.

The stories we create in our minds have a powerful impact on our emotional and cognitive responses. Depending on how we interpret the situation, they trigger a spectrum of emotions, from joy and excitement to fear and anxiety. For instance, a person with a traumatic past may perceive a harmless situation as threatening, triggering fear and anxiety. In contrast, another person might see the same situation as benign and feel calm and secure.

These emotional responses are accompanied by corresponding thoughts, further coloring our perception and interpretation of reality. Our thoughts can reinforce our beliefs and biases or challenge and reshape them.

The culmination of this process is the influence these narratives have on our behavior and decision-making. Our actions are often a direct response to the emotions and thoughts triggered by our subjective interpretation of reality. This means our perception of a situation can significantly influence our reactions.

For those with PTSD, this process can be particularly impactful. Trauma can profoundly alter perception, leading to heightened vigilance, mistrust, or avoidance behaviors. Understanding the path from perception to reality in this context is crucial, as it highlights the importance of addressing and reshaping these perceptions in the journey toward healing.

The transition from perception to reality is a dynamic and deeply personal process. It underscores the significance of our worldviews in shaping our experiences and highlights the potential for change and growth through altering these perceptions. As we delve deeper into understanding this process, we open the door to more effective ways of managing PTSD and fostering a more adaptive and resilient approach to life.

The Subjectivity of Experience

To illustrate the profound influence of perception on our reality, let's consider two common scenarios: a rainy day and the experience of standing at the edge of a bungee jump platform. These examples vividly demonstrate how different individuals can react differently to the same objective situation, shaped entirely by their unique interpretations and the meanings they attribute to these experiences.

Imagine a gentle rain falling outside. One might look at the rain and feel a sense of coziness and contentment, reminded of peaceful indoor days. This individual's perception of rain is likely tied to positive past experiences or a particular mindset that finds comfort in nature's rhythms. For them, rain might symbolize renewal, tranquility, or even nostalgia.

Conversely, another person might perceive the same rainy weather as gloomy and depressing. This reaction could be influenced by negative associations with rain, perhaps linked to past hardships or a predisposition to feel down during overcast weather. In this case, the rain might represent sadness, confinement, or disruption.

The scenario of three individuals standing on the edge of a bridge, poised to bungee jump, offers a vivid illustration of how personal perceptions and internal worldviews shape our experiences. Despite the objective sameness of their situation—the same bridge, the same day, the same bungee equipment—each person's subjective reaction varies dramatically. This divergence stresses the impact of individual psychological processes on how we interpret and emotionally respond to identical external events.

Person one's excitement and enthusiasm likely stem from a positive attribution of the event. This individual may view the jump as an exhilarating challenge or an opportunity for adventure, indicative of an optimistic or thrill-seeking personality. Their anticipation of the experience is colored by a focus on potential positive outcomes, such as the thrill of the leap or the sense of accomplishment afterward.

The second person's neutrality suggests a different internal calculus. This individual might weigh the event's risks and rewards more evenly or possess a more stoic disposition. Their reaction—or lack thereof—

might reflect a balanced assessment of the situation or perhaps a disinterest in the activity's inherent thrill. For them, the jump is neither particularly enticing nor distressing, and their emotional response is accordingly muted.

The third person's fear is a product of negative attribution. They may focus on the potential dangers of the jump, such as the fear of injury or the discomfort of the experience. This apprehension could be influenced by a variety of factors, including past experiences, inherent anxiety about heights or falling, or a general propensity toward cautiousness. Their perception of the event is filtered through a lens that magnifies potential threats, leading to a heightened state of fear.

These disparate reactions illustrate the concept of subjective perceptual experiencing, where our inner worldviews and personal attributions shape our emotional responses. Even when faced with the same objective reality, our unique psychological makeup, personal histories, and prevailing attitudes determine how we interpret and feel about our experiences. This phenomenon highlights the intricate interplay between the external world and our internal processes, underscoring the importance of understanding individual psychological differences in explaining human behavior and emotional responses.

These rain and bungee jumping examples highlight how our brain's interpretation of situations shapes our emotional and behavioral responses. The objective reality—the rain falling or the height of the jump—remains the same, but our subjective experiences of these events can be worlds apart. This divergence in perception underscores the power of our worldviews and schemas in coloring our experiences of the world.

In the context of PTSD, such differences in perception can be even more pronounced, as traumatic experiences can significantly alter how one interprets and reacts to seemingly ordinary situations. Recognizing and understanding this variability in perception is a crucial step in the journey toward managing PTSD, as it opens avenues for reshaping harmful or limiting interpretations into more adaptive and positive ones.

The Mechanism of Confirmation Bias

One of the most fascinating aspects of human cognition is how our brain functions as a confirmation machine, constantly seeking evidence to support our existing beliefs and worldviews and actively dismissing contrary information. This phenomenon, known as confirmation bias, is fundamental to processing information and making sense of the world around us. It represents our brain's tendency to favor information that aligns with our pre-existing beliefs and discount or ignore information that contradicts them.

This bias is not just an abstract concept; it has concrete implications in our daily lives and decision-making processes. For instance, if individuals believe they are unworthy of love or happiness, they are likelier to notice and focus on experiences reinforcing this belief. This might lead them to enter and stay in toxic relationships because such relationships align with their internal narrative of unworthiness. In its effort to affirm the existing worldview, the brain may overlook or minimize experiences that could challenge this negative self-perception.

The role of confirmation bias becomes even more pronounced in the context of PTSD. Traumatic experiences can significantly alter an individual's worldview, often skewing it to negative or threatening perceptions. As a result, a person with PTSD might find themselves trapped in repetitive patterns of behavior or thought that reaffirm their altered perceptions of danger, mistrust, or helplessness. For instance, a veteran with PTSD might interpret many situations as potentially threatening, even when they are safe, because their brain is primed to confirm the belief that the world is a dangerous place.

Understanding the role of the brain as a confirmation machine can help address and treat PTSD. It highlights the need for interventions that focus on changing behaviors and reshaping the underlying beliefs and worldviews that drive these behaviors. Therapeutic approaches that challenge and modify these deep-seated beliefs can help break the cycle of confirmation bias, allowing individuals to form a more balanced and realistic perception of themselves and the world around them.

Embracing Cognitive Behavioral Therapy (CBT) in the Context of PTSD

As we initiate our journey in Week 1, we delve into the realm of Cognitive Behavioral Therapy (CBT), an evidenced-based modality for comprehending and managing PTSD. The essence of CBT lies in its focused approach in identifying and transforming patterns of unhelpful thought and behavior that are deeply rooted in the altered perceptions and worldviews shaped by traumatic experiences.

CBT operates on the foundational belief that our thoughts, feelings, and behaviors are interconnected. In the context of PTSD, this therapy helps in recognizing how specific thought patterns, often negative or distorted due to traumatic experiences, can lead to emotional distress and harmful behaviors. These patterns can include persistent thoughts of danger, guilt or shame, or a skewed perception of one's self-worth.

Trauma can significantly alter an individual's worldview, leading to a perpetual state of fear, mistrust, or hopelessness. CBT aims to gently challenge these perceptions, encouraging individuals to question and reevaluate their beliefs and assumptions about the world and themselves. The goal is not to dismiss or invalidate the traumatic experience but to provide a more balanced and realistic perspective that can reduce the intensity of PTSD symptoms.

A key aspect of CBT in the context of PTSD is cognitive restructuring. This involves identifying specific negative or inaccurate thoughts that contribute to emotional distress. Once identified, these thoughts are examined for accuracy and helpfulness and then challenged or replaced with more balanced, realistic thoughts. This process helps break the cycle of negative thinking and reduce the emotional impact of traumatic memories.

Alongside cognitive restructuring, CBT also focuses on modifying behaviors that may be reinforcing PTSD symptoms. This can include addressing avoidance behaviors, where individuals steer clear of situations or memories that remind them of the trauma. By gradually facing these avoided situations in a controlled and safe manner, individuals can reduce fear and anxiety associated with the trauma.

In Week 1 of our self-help program, we lay the groundwork for this transformative journey with CBT. Individuals are empowered to reshape their thoughts and behaviors by engaging in CBT-based exercises and reflections. This proactive involvement is crucial in managing PTSD symptoms and paving the way for recovery and healing.

As we progress through Week 1, remember that the journey with CBT is one of self-discovery and resilience. Through CBT, we aim to equip you with the tools to not only understand the impact of trauma on your thought processes but also to actively engage in reshaping these thoughts toward a more hopeful and balanced future.

Navigating the Landscape of Perception and Reality in PTSD

In Week 1, our journey will focus on exploring the intricate relationship between perception and reality, especially as it pertains to PTSD. Our perceptions, heavily influenced by our personal worldviews and cognitive schemas, play a crucial role in shaping our realities. We'll delve into understanding how our brain functions as a *confirmation machine*, continuously seeking evidence to support our existing beliefs, often leading to a cycle of negative thought patterns that can exacerbate PTSD symptoms.

The cognitive-behavioral framework will guide us in dissecting and reshaping these perceptions. We will examine how trauma-influenced thoughts and beliefs have potentially distorted our view of ourselves and the world. By identifying these thoughts and challenging their validity, we aim to develop a more balanced and realistic perspective, altering our perception of reality.

Our focus will also include understanding the behavioral manifestations that arise from these perceptions. We will explore how certain behaviors, especially those developed as coping mechanisms post-trauma, are directly linked to our thought processes. By gradually facing and modifying these behaviors, we aim to disrupt the cycle of negative thinking and emotional distress associated with PTSD.

The primary goal this week is to enhance self-awareness regarding how our perceptions have been shaped by trauma and to begin the process of cognitive restructuring. Through daily tasks and reflections, we'll engage in a proactive journey of reevaluating and reshaping our thought patterns to foster a healthier interaction with our world.

This week's focus sets the stage for a transformative process in which we not only understand the impact of PTSD on our perception and reality but also actively work toward reclaiming a sense of control and resilience in our lives.

Week 1 Self-Help Guide

These seven days of assignments are structured to provide a comprehensive approach to applying CBT techniques in the context of PTSD. By actively engaging in these exercises, you are taking essential steps toward understanding and reshaping your thought patterns and behaviors, paving the way for recovery and empowerment. The following pages act as a guide with prompts. You are encouraged to create a journal so that you have the necessary space and the freedom to comprehensively expand on your thoughts.

WEEK 1 DAY 1: IDENTIFYING AND CHALLENGING TRAUMA-INFLUENCED THOUGHTS

Objective: The objective of this exercise is to foster self-awareness and critical thinking about how traumatic experiences can shape our thoughts and beliefs about ourselves and the world. By identifying and challenging these thoughts, individuals can begin to shift their perspectives toward a more balanced and less trauma-informed view.

Information: Traumatic experiences often leave us with negative thoughts about ourselves and distorted perceptions of the world. These thoughts can be pervasive and deeply ingrained, affecting our behavior and emotional well-being. By bringing these thoughts to the surface and scrutinizing them, we can start to loosen their hold over us.

Instructions: Take a moment to reflect on your thoughts and beliefs about yourself and the world around you. Identify three thoughts or beliefs in each category that you feel are significantly influenced by your traumatic experience. Write them down clearly. For thoughts about yourself, focus on beliefs that reflect your self-esteem, capabilities, or worthiness. For thoughts about the world, concentrate on beliefs regarding safety, trust, or the nature of relationships.

Processing and Reflection: For each thought or belief you've written down, engage in a reflective process:

- **How Trauma Skews Thoughts:** Consider how your traumatic experience might have contributed to these thoughts or beliefs. Reflect on the connection between what happened and how you perceive yourself and the world now.
- **Evidence Analysis:** Challenge each thought or belief by looking for evidence that supports or contradicts it. Ask yourself:
- What experiences or facts support this belief?
- Are there instances or evidence that challenge or weaken this belief?
- Write down your findings. This step is crucial for introducing nuance into your thinking and opening the door to alternative perspectives.

Reflection:

- After completing the exercise, take some time to reflect on the process and any new insights gained. Did you find evidence that challenged your initial thoughts or beliefs? How does acknowledging this evidence make you feel about these beliefs now?
- Reflect on the possibility of viewing your experiences or yourself in a different light. How might changing these beliefs impact your feelings and behavior moving forward?

Integration: Think of ways you can incorporate these new perspectives into your daily life. This might involve:

- Practicing mindfulness to become more aware of when these thoughts arise and actively reminding yourself of the evidence that challenges them.
- Developing affirmations based on more balanced beliefs about yourself and the world.
- Seeking feedback from trusted individuals about your perceptions and working to adjust them based on this feedback.

Beliefs About Self:

1.

2.

3.

Beliefs about the World:

1.

2.

3.

Reflect on how the trauma might skew these thoughts:

Evidence For:

Evidence Against:

WEEK 1 DAY 2: COGNITIVE RESTRUCTURING PRACTICE

Objective: The aim of today's exercise is to challenge a negative belief formed from a traumatic experience by replacing it with a more balanced and realistic thought. This exercise is designed to help shift your perspective and potentially alter your emotional response to a more positive or neutral one.

Information: Holding onto negative beliefs can significantly impact our emotional well-being and how we interact with the world. Challenging these beliefs allows us to consider alternative viewpoints and reduces the power these negative thoughts have over us.

Instructions:

- **Choose a Negative Belief:** Review the list of negative thoughts or beliefs about yourself and the world you identified on Day 1. Select one belief that stands out to you or feels particularly impactful.
- **Challenge the Belief:** Write down the negative belief clearly at the top of a page.
    - ○ Directly beneath it, challenge this belief by writing a more balanced and realistic thought. Consider the evidence against the negative belief that you identified previously and use it to inform this new thought.

○ Ensure that the new thought acknowledges the complexity of the situation and includes a more compassionate or objective view of yourself or the world.

Example:

- **Negative Belief:** "I am completely incapable of overcoming challenges because of my trauma."
- **Balanced Thought:** "While my trauma has made certain challenges more difficult, I have also developed resilience and coping skills. Overcoming challenges may take time, but I am capable of making progress."

Reflection: Reflect on how adopting this new, balanced thought makes you feel in comparison to the original negative belief. Consider the following questions:

- Does this new thought change your emotional response? If so, how?
- Do you feel more hopeful, calm, or empowered when focusing on the balanced thought?
- How might adopting this balanced thought affect your behavior or attitude in situations that previously triggered the negative belief?

Integration: Think about practical ways to remind yourself of this new balanced thought in your daily life. You might:

- Write it down on a sticky note and place it where you'll see it often.
- Set a daily reminder on your phone to read the balanced thought.
- Practice reciting the balanced thought during meditation or mindfulness exercises.

By consciously challenging and replacing negative beliefs with more balanced thoughts, you're actively working to change your narrative. This process not only helps in reducing the emotional weight of negative beliefs but also encourages a more hopeful and realistic outlook on life.

WEEK 1 DAY 3: UNDERSTANDING BEHAVIORAL RESPONSES

Objective: The focus of today's task is to identify a specific behavior influenced by your trauma and understand what triggers it. By analyzing how this behavior connects to your thoughts and feelings about the trauma, you can begin to consider more realistic perspectives on your responses and the situations that provoke them.

Information: Trauma can lead to various coping mechanisms, some of which may not serve us well in the long term. Understanding the link between our behaviors, the triggers, and our thoughts about the trauma can offer insights into how we might adopt healthier responses.

Instructions:

- **Identify the Behavior:** Reflect on the behaviors you've adopted since experiencing trauma. Choose one behavior that stands out to you as particularly influenced by your trauma (e.g., avoidance, hypervigilance, substance use).

- **What Triggers the Behavior:** Think about the situations or stimuli that typically trigger this behavior. These could be specific events, environments, conversations, or internal feelings. Write these triggers down, aiming to be as specific as possible.

Example:

- **Identify the Behavior:** Avoidance of social situations.
- **What Triggers the Behavior:** Invitations to large gatherings or events where I don't know many people.

Analysis:

- Reflect on how this behavior serves as a response to your thoughts and feelings related to the trauma. Consider what beliefs about yourself or the world might be driving this behavior.
- Analyze the link between the trigger, your immediate thoughts or beliefs (e.g., "I won't be able to handle it," "People will notice I'm anxious"), and how they lead to the behavior.

Example Analysis:

- My avoidance of social situations is driven by the belief that I can't control my anxiety in those settings, and the thought that others will judge me negatively. This belief likely stems from feelings of vulnerability and a lack of confidence post-trauma, reinforcing the idea that avoidance is the only way to protect myself.

Reflection:

- Reflect on a more realistic and balanced way to view the trigger and your capacity to respond to it. Challenge the immediate thoughts or beliefs that lead to the maladaptive behavior by considering alternative outcomes or perspectives.
- Consider how this new perspective might change your response to the trigger in the future. Reflect on the potential benefits of adjusting your behavior.

Example Reflection:

- While it's true that social situations can be anxiety-provoking, my belief that I can't handle them or that others will judge me is based on my worst fears, not the reality of my experiences. Most people are likely too focused on their own social anxieties to critically judge mine. Recognizing that I have previously navigated challenging situations successfully can help me approach social events with more confidence and less avoidance.

Integration: Think about how you can apply this new perspective in real-life situations. Perhaps you could start small by attending shorter or smaller gatherings and practicing coping strategies in advance. The goal is to gradually expose yourself to the triggers in a controlled manner, building resilience and confidence over time.

WEEK 1 DAY 4: BREAKING THE CYCLE OF NEGATIVE THINKING

Objective: This exercise aims to increase your awareness of moments when your thoughts spiral into negativity or fear stemming from your trauma. By identifying these thoughts and their associated emotions, you can begin to practice redirecting them towards interpretations that are more neutral or positive, fostering a more balanced emotional state.

Information: Traumatic experiences can often lead to a pattern of negative thinking, which in turn can amplify feelings of fear, sadness, or anxiety. Learning to recognize and adjust these thought patterns is a crucial step in managing emotional responses and moving towards healing.

Instructions:

1. **Notice and Jot Down:** Throughout your day, pay close attention to instances when you find your thoughts turning negative or becoming fearful, especially those related to your trauma. Write down these thoughts as they occur, noting the specific situations or triggers that led to them

2. **Identify the Emotion(s):** For each thought you've noted, identify the emotions that accompany it. Are you feeling anxious, sad, angry, or perhaps something else? Document these emotions next to the corresponding thoughts.

3. **Analysis:** Reflect on why these particular thoughts might be leading to negative or fearful emotions. Consider the beliefs or assumptions underlying these thoughts and whether they might be exaggerated or distorted in some way.

4. **Develop More Realistic, Objective Thoughts:** For each negative or fearful thought, try to come up with a more realistic and objective counter-thought. This doesn't necessarily mean forcing positivity but rather seeking a more balanced perspective on the situation. Consider what you would tell a friend in a similar situation or try to view the scenario from an outsider's perspective for a more objective outlook.

Reflect on the Impact of More Realistic Thoughts: Contemplate how adopting these more realistic thoughts might change your emotional response. Do you feel less overwhelmed, more hopeful, or perhaps more in control? Reflect on the potential benefits of this shift in perspective, not just in the moment but also for your overall process of healing and recovery.

Integration: Begin incorporating this practice into your daily routine. Whenever you notice negative or fearful thoughts arising, pause to go through this process of analysis and redirection. Over time, this practice can help diminish the intensity of negative emotional reactions and encourage a more resilient mindset.

WEEK 1 DAY 5: EXPLORING EMOTIONAL TRIGGERS

Objective: The goal of today's task is to cultivate mindfulness around your emotional responses, specifically focusing on strong emotions, their triggers, and the thoughts that accompany them. This process aims to help you recognize the connection between these emotions and your trauma, and to identify any distortions in your thinking.

Information: Strong emotions often signal important information about our internal state and how we're interpreting our surroundings. Trauma can influence these interpretations, leading to distorted or exaggerated thoughts that amplify emotional reactions.

Instructions:

1. **Emotion(s):** When you feel a strong emotion, take a moment to pause and identify what you're feeling. Label the emotion as precisely as you can (e.g., anger, fear, sadness).
2. **Trigger(s):** Reflect on what happened right before you felt this strong emotion. Identify any specific event, interaction, or memory that triggered the emotional response. Write this down.
3. **Thoughts:** Note the specific thoughts or mental commentary that was running through your mind at the moment you experienced the strong emotion. These thoughts can often provide clues to why the emotion felt so intense.

4. **How might these thoughts be distorted or exaggerated:** Examine these thoughts critically to identify any potential distortions or exaggerations. Consider whether these thoughts are overgeneralizations, catastrophizing the situation, or applying labels that are not fully accurate. Write down your insights.

5. **What is a more realistic appraisal of the situation:** Try to reframe your initial thoughts into ones that offer a more balanced or realistic appraisal of the situation. This doesn't mean dismissing your feelings but rather adjusting your perspective to align more closely with the facts. Write down this more realistic perspective.

Integration: Practicing this task regularly can help you become more adept at recognizing when your emotional responses might be influenced by distorted thinking related to your trauma. Over time, this awareness can lead to more balanced emotional reactions and a greater sense of control over your responses to triggers. Remember, the aim is not to invalidate your feelings but to understand their origins and assess situations more accurately.

WEEK 1 DAY 6: GRADUAL EXPOSURE TO AVOIDED SITUATIONS

Disclaimer and Caution

Before proceeding, it's crucial to emphasize the importance of safety and self-care. Never put yourself in harm's way. Avoid any situation that could lead to physical harm or confrontation with an aggressor, especially someone connected to your traumatic experience. The goal is to gently challenge comfort zones in a controlled, safe way.

Always be safe.

Objective: The purpose of this exercise is to gently confront aspects of your trauma in a controlled, safe manner. By intentionally choosing a situation or thought you've been avoiding, you'll have the opportunity to observe your emotional and cognitive responses in real time. This task aims to foster resilience and provide insights into your healing process, illustrating that gradual exposure to difficult but non-threatening triggers can be a step towards recovery.

Information: Avoidance is a common coping mechanism in the aftermath of trauma, serving as a short-term strategy to reduce distress. However, long-term avoidance can prevent healing by reinforcing fear. Carefully and safely approaching these avoided situations or thoughts can help diminish their power over you.

Instructions:

1. Choose a Manageable Situation or Thought:

- Select a situation or aspect of your trauma that you've been avoiding, but ensure that engaging with this thought or situation does not compromise your physical or emotional safety. This could be something as simple as driving past a location related to your trauma or allowing yourself to recall a specific memory in a secure setting.
- Plan how you will approach this. If you're revisiting a location, decide when and for how long. If you're allowing yourself to think about a traumatic aspect, choose a quiet, comfortable space where you feel safe.

2. Engage With the Chosen Situation or Thought:

- Proceed to engage with the selected situation or thought as planned. Ensure you have a support mechanism in place, such as a friend you can call or a self-soothing strategy if the experience becomes overwhelming.

3. Reflect and Document Responses:

- **Emotional and Cognitive Responses:** After the exposure, take some time to reflect on your experience. How did you feel during and after the exposure? Were there any surprises in your emotional or cognitive responses?
- **Anxiety Levels:** Assess your anxiety levels before, during, and after the exposure. Were they as high as you anticipated? Did they decrease more quickly than expected? Document any observations.

- **Changes in Perception or Anxiety Levels:** Note any shifts in how you perceive the previously avoided situation or thought. Did the experience become less daunting than it previously seemed?
- **Reflections on the Experience:** Reflect on what this experience teaches you about your ability to face and process aspects of your trauma in a controlled manner. Consider how this might impact your approach to avoidance in the future.

Integration: Integrating the insights gained from this exercise into your broader healing journey can empower you to gradually confront and reduce the impact of avoidance behaviors. Recognize that each small step in facing previously avoided thoughts or situations can contribute significantly to your resilience and recovery.

WEEK 1 DAY 7: REFLECTING ON PERCEPTION AND REALITY

Objective: This day is focused on introspection, offering a chance to review and reflect on the week's assignments, activities, and personal responses. It aims to identify patterns, insights, and shifts in perception, facilitating a deeper understanding of your journey through PTSD management and healing.

Information: Reflection is a powerful tool in the healing process, allowing you to consolidate learning and recognize growth. This exercise encourages you to look back over the past week, evaluate your experiences, and plan how to apply these insights moving forward.

Instructions:

1. **Analyze the Week:**

   - Go through your notes, thoughts, and any documentation from the past six days of assignments and activities. Reflect on your engagement with each task and the emotional or cognitive responses they elicited.
   - Pay attention to any patterns in your thoughts or behaviors that became apparent, changes in your perception, or particular insights that emerged from these exercises.

1. **Key Questions for Reflection:**

- **Views and Beliefs:** How have your perspectives on specific beliefs or thoughts about yourself and the world shifted over the week?
- **Challenging Exercises:** Were there tasks that you found particularly challenging? Reflect on why these stood out to you.
- **Reactions to Trauma:** Have you noticed any changes in your reactions to thoughts or situations related to your trauma? What does this suggest about your healing process?
- **Coping Mechanisms and Thought Processes:** What insights have you gained about your ways of coping and thinking? How do these insights impact your understanding of your responses to trauma?

1. **Processing: Integrating Learnings and Insights:**

- **Document Your Insights:** Summarize the key learnings from each day, noting any progress made and challenges encountered. Acknowledge every insight, recognizing its value in your healing journey.
- **Personal Growth and Change:** Reflect on how the insights from this week might influence your ongoing process of managing and healing from PTSD. Consider the growth you've experienced and how you can build on this foundation in the future.
- **Setting Intentions for Moving Forward:** Based on your reflections, set intentions or goals for the coming week. Identify areas for further exploration or new strategies you'd like to implement, focusing on continuous growth and healing.

Integration: Today's introspection and reflection are vital for acknowledging the progress you've made and for setting the direction of your ongoing journey. Healing from PTSD is a gradual process, and every step forward, no matter how small, is significant. Use today's insights to strengthen your resolve and to refine your approach as you continue to navigate the path to recovery. Remember, each insight gained is a building block in the foundation of your resilience and healing.

| 6 |

Understanding and Transforming Defense Mechanisms and Cognitive Distortions

As we embark on the second week of our therapeutic journey, we delve deeper into self-awareness by exploring defense mechanisms and cognitive distortions. These concepts are fundamental to understanding how we perceive and interact with the world, especially in the context of PTSD and its impact on our mental processes.

Defense Mechanisms

Defense mechanisms are psychological strategies used unconsciously to protect ourselves from anxiety and the awareness of internal or external stressors. They are integral to our psychological makeup, helping us cope with uncomfortable realities and emotional conflicts. However, these mechanisms can hinder our emotional growth and healing when overused or misused. This week, we will explore various defense mechanisms, from pathological and immature to neurotic and mature, each serving a different purpose in our mental and emotional regulation.

In exploring defense mechanisms, it is essential to understand the varying levels and their impact on our psychological health and perception of reality. Defense mechanisms are subconscious ways we cope with reality and maintain our self-image. They range from pathological to mature, each serving a distinct function in our mental and emotional regulation.

Pathological Defenses: Pathological defenses are often employed in response to extreme stress or trauma and are associated with severe psychological distress. They can significantly distort an individual's perception of reality. These mechanisms can be detrimental to mental health, as they often prevent individuals from confronting and processing reality. Key types include:

> *Delusional Projection*: This mechanism involves the external attribution of one's unacceptable feelings, thoughts, or impulses onto someone else. It is not merely shifting blame or responsibility; it involves a complex construct where the individual truly believes these feelings or thoughts belong to others, not themselves. This defense can lead to strained relationships and significant misunderstanding, as the person cannot recognize and own their internal state.

> *Denial*: Denial operates as a refusal to acknowledge reality or facts. Denial could manifest in ignoring a painful event, thought, or feeling. For instance, someone in denial about a traumatic event might act as if it never occurred, refusing to discuss or acknowledge its impact. This mechanism can be a temporary coping strategy to avoid immediate pain. Still, it can lead to long-term psychological difficulties if the underlying issues are not addressed.

Distortion: In this defense, there is a significant reshaping or twisting of external reality to meet internal needs or desires. It's more than just seeing things from a personal perspective; it's actively altering the perception of reality to fit one's emotional or psychological requirements. This can lead to a skewed interpretation of events and interactions, making engaging in healthy, reality-based relationships and decision-making challenging.

Pathological defenses, while offering short-term relief from intense emotional pain, can severely impact mental health and daily functioning. They often inhibit individuals from effectively confronting and processing reality, leading to persistent issues in understanding and interacting with the world around them. Understanding and identifying these defenses in oneself can be the first step towards healing and developing healthier coping mechanisms.

Immature Defenses: Immature defenses are more common in children but not uncommon in adults experiencing significant stress or trauma. They can serve as a psychological retreat from reality. These mechanisms offer temporary emotional relief but can impede effective and mature coping strategies. Key types include:

Acting Out: This defense involves the external expression of an unconscious wish or impulse through actions rather than acknowledging and processing the associated emotions or thoughts. For instance, someone who feels neglected might engage in reckless behavior to attract attention. While this might provide immediate relief or attention, it often leads to inappropriate or harmful behaviors that don't address the underlying emotional needs.

Fantasy: Here, individuals escape to a mental world where their desires and wishes are fulfilled effortlessly, bypassing real-life challenges. This mechanism offers a temporary sanctuary from pain or disappointment but can lead to disengagement from reality. Overreliance on fantasy can result in difficulties facing and dealing with real-life situations, impacting one's ability to form realistic goals and relationships.

Projection: In projection, individuals attribute their unacceptable desires, thoughts, or feelings to others. For example, a hostile person may accuse others of being antagonistic towards them. This mechanism allows individuals to avoid confronting their uncomfortable internal states. It often leads to misunderstandings and conflicts in relationships, as one's own unacknowledged emotions skew the perceived intentions and feelings of others.

Denial: Denial is a defense mechanism where individuals consciously or unconsciously refuse to accept the reality of a situation. It is often used to protect oneself from distressing thoughts or feelings arising from acknowledging the truth. For example, a person diagnosed with a severe illness might deny the diagnosis, believing that it can't be true, as a means of avoiding the fear and anxiety associated with the illness.

Regression: When people use regression as a defense mechanism, they revert to behaviors or responses more characteristic of an earlier stage of development, typically from their childhood. This occurs when individuals feel overwhelmed or anxious and regress to behaviors that once provided comfort or security. For instance, an adult might start thumb-sucking or seeking excessive reassurance when faced with a stressful situation.

Displacement: Displacement involves redirecting one's emotions or impulses away from their source onto a less threatening target. Instead of addressing the actual cause of their frustration or anger, individuals channel these emotions toward something or someone else. For example, someone who had a frustrating day at work might come home and take out their anger on a family member, even if that family member is not the real cause of their frustration.

Undoing is a defense mechanism in which individuals engage in rituals or behaviors to "undo" or make amends for perceived wrongdoings or guilt. It's an attempt to alleviate the discomfort of guilt or anxiety by performing actions that symbolically reverse or counteract the negative thoughts or behaviors. For example, someone who feels guilty about being rude to a friend might go out of their way to be excessively polite and accommodating afterward as a way to undo their perceived mistake.

Minimization: Downplaying the significance of a situation or its emotional impact. This involves trivializing or ignoring the emotional consequences of events.

While these immature defenses can momentarily alleviate distress, their overuse can hinder emotional development and mature coping. They often lead to challenges in effectively navigating life's complexities, as they avoid confrontation and processing of deep-seated emotional issues. Recognizing and addressing these defenses can be crucial for personal growth and developing more adaptive coping mechanisms.

Neurotic Defenses: Neurotic defenses are common and occasionally helpful in managing day-to-day stress. They can become problematic if relied upon excessively. These mechanisms, which include displacement, dissociation, and rationalization, help manage emotional conflicts or internal or external stressors. Overuse can create long-term challenges, particularly in personal and professional relationships.

Displacement: This defense mechanism involves shifting emotional reactions from a primary, threatening target to a secondary, less threatening one. For example, an individual might redirect anger towards a boss onto a family member or pet, as expressing this emotion directly to the boss might be perceived as too risky. While displacement can temporarily alleviate stress, it can also lead to misdirected emotions and unresolved conflicts with the source of distress.

Dissociation: This involves a mental disconnection from reality, ranging from harmless daydreaming to more severe forms of detachment from emotions and physical experiences. In its more extreme forms, it can manifest as a disconnection from one's thoughts, feelings, memories, or sense of identity. While dissociation can offer a temporary escape from immediate stress or trauma, chronic use can lead to difficulties in processing emotions and forming a coherent sense of self.

Rationalization: This defense mechanism involves explaining and justifying one's behavior or feelings with seemingly logical, rational reasons, often avoiding the actual, more distressing motivations or emotions. For example, a person might justify procrastinating on a task by overstating its difficulty or underestimating its importance. While rationalization can protect self-esteem and reduce cognitive dissonance, overuse can lead to a distorted perception of reality and avoidance of accountability for one's actions.

Reaction-Formation: This defense mechanism involves expressing an emotion or behavior that is the direct opposite of one's true feelings, often to conceal unacceptable desires or impulses. It serves as a way to cope with and mask these feelings by adopting a drastically different facade from the internal reality. Reaction-formation is not a conscious decision but a psychological defense that kicks in automatically to protect the individual from confronting emotions or desires that they find threatening or socially unacceptable. Understanding and recognizing this defense mechanism can be crucial in therapy, as it allows for exploring and integrating these hidden aspects of the self, leading to more authentic and harmonious emotional expression.

Intellectualization: Intellectualization is a defense mechanism where individuals excessively focus on facts, data, or logical analysis to distance themselves from their emotions. Instead of confronting their feelings directly, they approach a distressing situation, detached and analytical. This can be a way to cope with emotional turmoil by trying to rationalize or intellectualize it. Doing this often prevents them from fully processing and understanding their emotions.

Repression: Repression is an unconscious defense mechanism in which individuals push distressing thoughts, memories, or emotions out of conscious awareness. It involves forgetting or blocking out painful or traumatic experiences as a way to protect oneself from the emotional distress associated with them. While it may provide temporary relief, repressed emotions can resurface in various ways and impact one's psychological well-being.

Compensation: Compensation occurs when individuals strive for success and achievement in one area of their life to make up for perceived deficiencies or failures in another area. This defense mechanism is driven by a desire to compensate for inadequacy or low self-esteem. For example, someone who feels socially inadequate might excel in their career to gain a sense of worthiness.

Withdrawal: Withdrawal is a defense mechanism characterized by avoiding or retreating from stressful situations or conflicts. When individuals feel overwhelmed or threatened, they may isolate themselves emotionally or physically as a means of self-preservation. This can manifest as withdrawing from social interactions, shutting down emotionally, or physically removing oneself from the source of stress.

Isolation: Isolation involves separating thoughts or feelings from their associated emotions. It's a way of discussing or thinking about distressing events or memories without experiencing the emotions that should naturally accompany them. This defense mechanism allows individuals to talk about painful experiences without becoming emotionally overwhelmed. However, it can hinder emotional processing and prevent a deeper understanding of one's feelings

Over reliance on neurotic defenses can create a cycle where genuine emotions and motives are consistently masked or redirected, leading to unresolved internal conflicts and strain in relationships. Becoming aware of these defense mechanisms and understanding their impact is crucial for emotional growth and developing healthier ways of dealing with stress and conflict.

Mature Defenses: Mature Defenses are recognized as the healthiest and most adaptive ways to manage emotional stress and conflicts. Unlike other defense mechanisms, which may distort reality or avoid dealing with issues, mature defenses help individuals cope with stressors in a way that improves overall well-being and fosters positive relationships with others. Examples of mature defenses include humor, altruism, and sublimation:

Humor: Humor involves finding lightness, irony, or amusement in stressful or difficult situations. It allows an individual to face misfortune or adversity with a lighter perspective, reducing the emotional impact and stress. Humor can create emotional distance from a problem, making it more manageable and less overwhelming. It also fosters social connections and can be a way to share and alleviate stress communally.

Altruism: Altruism is channeling one's difficulties or distress into helping others. This not only aids others in need but also provides the individual with a sense of purpose, accomplishment, and emotional fulfillment. By focusing on the well-being of others, individuals practicing altruism often find their problems seem less overwhelming, and they gain perspective and gratitude.

Sublimation: This defense mechanism redirects negative or socially unacceptable impulses into positive, socially acceptable actions or behaviors. For instance, someone with aggressive tendencies might channel this energy into sports or other competitive activities. Sublimation is considered particularly effective because it allows for expressing instinctual drives or emotions without negative consequences, often resulting in productive and rewarding outcomes.

Mature defenses help effectively manage stress and emotional conflicts and contribute to personal growth and positive social interactions. Unlike less adaptive defense mechanisms, which can hinder emotional development and relationship building, mature defenses enhance an individual's ability to navigate life's challenges with grace and resilience.

Understanding these defense mechanisms helps us identify our subconscious ways of dealing with emotional conflicts and stressors. By recognizing and addressing these mechanisms, especially the less adaptive ones, we can work towards more mature and healthy ways of coping, which is crucial for healing from PTSD and improving overall mental health.

Cognitive Distortions

Cognitive distortions, common in PTSD, are irrational thought patterns influencing one's emotional state and behavior. Understanding and rectifying these can lead to more balanced thinking and emotional well-being. Let's explore these distortions with illustrative examples:

All-or-Nothing Thinking: All-or-Nothing Thinking, also known as black-and-white thinking, represents a cognitive distortion where situations are perceived in extreme, absolute terms, with no acknowledgment of the nuanced middle ground. This thought pattern involves evaluating experiences, oneself, or others in extreme, polarized categories like success or failure, perfect or disastrous, with no room for intermediate or grey areas.

Example: Imagine a scenario at work where you make a minor mistake, perhaps missing a small detail in a report or being a few minutes late to a meeting. Suppose you're engaged in all-or-nothing thinking instead of recognizing this as a minor oversight. In that case, you might catastrophically conclude, "I'm completely incompetent." This exaggerated self-assessment overlooks your numerous successes and instances where you've demonstrated competence and skill. The thought pattern fails to recognize that making occasional mistakes is a normal part of the human experience and does not define your overall abilities or worth.

In this cognitive distortion, your self-evaluation hinges on the most recent or glaring outcome, ignoring a more balanced view of your overall performance and capabilities. It can lead to significant emotional distress, as the pressure to be perfect or to avoid any form of failure becomes overwhelming and unrealistic. Recognizing and challenging this distortion involves acknowledging the spectrum of outcomes and experiences in life and understanding that one mistake does not encompass your entire worth or ability.

Overgeneralization is a cognitive distortion where a single event is seen as a never-ending pattern of defeat or failure. This thought process involves taking one instance or occurrence and generalizing it to an entire category of experiences, often leading to pessimistic conclusions.

Example: Consider a situation where a friend cancels plans with you. If you are overgeneralizing, you might conclude, "No one ever wants to spend time with me," based on this isolated incident. This perspective unfairly extrapolates a single cancellation into a sweeping judgment about your social life, ignoring other instances where friends have happily engaged with you and plans have been successful.

In this example, the cognitive distortion magnifies the significance of one event. It uses it to make an unfounded general rule about all similar events. It negates positive experiences and focuses only on the negative, leading to feelings of rejection and loneliness. To counter overgeneralization, it's important to remind yourself that one event does not dictate a universal pattern. It involves recognizing the uniqueness of each situation and considering a range of experiences rather than allowing one incident to define your overall perspective. This more balanced approach helps develop a more realistic and positive outlook on life events.

Mental Filtering is a cognitive distortion that involves filtering out positive aspects of a situation and focusing exclusively on the negative. This skewed perception can lead to a distorted view of events, situations, or self-image.

Example: Consider a scenario where you receive feedback on a project you've worked hard on. The feedback is mainly positive, with colleagues and supervisors commending your effort, creativity, and attention to detail. However, there is one mild criticism amongst the praise. If you are mentally filtering, your focus will be entirely on this single piece of negative feedback. You might disregard all the positive comments and conclude that the entire project failed because of this one criticism.

This type of cognitive distortion can significantly impact self-esteem and perception of success. By fixating only on the negative and ignoring the positive, you may develop an overly pessimistic view of your abilities and achievements. To combat mental filtering, it's essential to consciously acknowledge positive aspects or feedback. Balancing the negative with the positive helps form a more accurate and fair assessment of situations and personal performance.

Jumping to Conclusions: This cognitive distortion involves making hasty assumptions without sufficient evidence. It usually manifests in two distinct forms: mind reading, where you presume to know others' thoughts or intentions, and fortune telling, where you predict future outcomes, often negatively, without any factual basis.

Example: Imagine you're scheduled to give a presentation at work. Leading up to the event, you feel increasingly anxious. Suppose you're engaging in the 'fortune telling' aspect of jumping to conclusions. In that case, you might think, "This presentation will be a disaster." This conclusion is reached not based on facts or past experiences but purely on your current feelings of anxiety.

Alternatively, if you're engaging in 'mind reading,' you might think, "My colleagues will think I'm boring and unprepared."

Again, this assumption is made without any concrete evidence to support it. You are projecting your fears and insecurities onto others, assuming they share these negative perceptions.

Both forms of jumping to conclusions can be debilitating, as they often lead to increased anxiety and a sense of hopelessness or inadequacy. They can create a self-fulfilling prophecy where you become so convinced of a negative outcome that your behavior unconsciously shifts to make it more likely. To counter this distortion, it's important to challenge these assumptions with rational thinking and seek evidence that either supports or refutes these beliefs.

Magnification or Minimization: This cognitive distortion involves disproportionately blowing things out of proportion (magnification) or inappropriately shrinking something to lesser importance (minimization). It's like viewing the world through a lens that distorts reality, either making things seem much worse or much less significant than they are.

Example: Consider a scenario where you participate in a crucial meeting at work. You've prepared thoroughly, and most of your presentation is well-articulated and well-received. However, at one point, you stumble over your words. If you're engaging in magnification, you might fixate on this moment, thinking, "That was humiliating. Everyone must think I'm incompetent," despite the overall success of your presentation. This exaggerated focus on a minor flaw overshadows your achievements and skews your perception of the entire event.

On the flip side, if you're minimizing, you might downplay positive feedback or achievements. For instance, if colleagues praise your presentation, you might think, "They're just being polite," or "It wasn't that good. I just got lucky." This minimization can prevent you from acknowledging and celebrating your successes, leading to a skewed self-perception and decreased self-esteem.

Both magnification and minimization are harmful because they distort reality, preventing you from seeing things as they are. They can lead to feelings of inadequacy, anxiety, and a skewed self-image. Recognizing when you are magnifying or minimizing can help you reframe your thoughts more realistically, acknowledging your successes and areas for improvement in a balanced way.

Emotional Reasoning: This cognitive distortion involves mistaking your emotions for reality. It's a fallacy when you believe it must be true if you feel something. This thinking can lead to inaccurate conclusions based on your emotional state rather than facts.

Example: Imagine you are about to give a presentation and start feeling extremely anxious. If you're engaging in emotional reasoning, you might interpret these anxious feelings as evidence that something terrible will happen or you're unprepared. You think, "I feel so nervous. This means I'm going to fail," or "My anxiety is a sign that I'm not cut out for this." Feeling anxious before a big event is a typical response and doesn't predict the outcome.

In another scenario, you might feel unloved or unworthy and thus conclude, "I feel unloved, so I must be unlovable," even if there's ample evidence of people caring for you. This distortion makes you view your feelings as facts, ignoring other evidence or perspectives.

Emotional reasoning can trap you in a negative cycle where your emotions dictate your perception of reality, often leading to increased anxiety, depression, and a distorted self-image.

Recognizing when you are engaging in emotional reasoning is vital in challenging and replacing these automatic thoughts with more rational, fact-based assessments. It allows you to differentiate between what you feel and what is true, helping you navigate your emotions more effectively.

Should Statements: This cognitive distortion is characterized by imposing rigid expectations on yourself or others, often leading to disappointment, guilt, or frustration. It manifests in thoughts filled with 'should,' 'ought to,' or 'must,' reflecting a strict set of rules about how one believes things should be.

Example: Consider a situation where you're dealing with a challenging task at work. You might think, "I should always know the answers," or "I must not make any mistakes." This thinking puts unrealistic pressure on yourself, leading to increased stress and feelings of inadequacy when the inevitable human error occurs.

In interpersonal relationships, should statements can be equally harmful. For instance, if you think, "My partner should always understand me without me having to explain," it can lead to frustration and disappointment when your partner doesn't meet these unspoken expectations.

Another common scenario is setting unrealistic emotional standards, such as thinking, "I shouldn't feel sad" or "I should always be happy." Such thoughts invalidate natural emotional responses and can exacerbate negative feelings, as they create a gap between what you're experiencing and what you think you should experience.

Should statements often reflect an idealized or perfectionistic view of the world and can stem from internalized societal or cultural norms. Recognizing and challenging these statements can help reduce guilt and frustration and promote a more flexible, compassionate approach to oneself and others. It involves acknowledging that being human means not always meeting idealized standards and that it's okay to experience a range of emotions and make mistakes.

Labeling and Mislabeling: This cognitive distortion involves assigning a global, negative label to yourself or others based on specific behaviors or incidents. It's an extreme form of over-generalization where a single action or mistake is taken as a definitive statement of one's character or identity.

Example: Imagine you are late to a meeting. Instead of viewing it as a specific incident, you might label yourself "always late" or "unreliable." This label ignores the many instances where you have been punctual and responsible, reducing your identity to a single, isolated event.

Another example is in interpersonal relationships. Suppose a friend or partner makes a mistake or acts in a way you dislike. You might label them as "selfish" or "inconsiderate" rather than seeing the behavior as a one-off or considering the broader context of their actions.

In a work context, you might complete a task less effectively than usual and label yourself "incompetent," overlooking your history of capable and successful work.

Labeling and mislabeling can lead to a distorted self-concept and negatively impact one's self-esteem. It can also harm relationships, reducing complex individuals to simplistic, often negative, caricatures based on limited information.

Challenging labeling and mislabeling involves recognizing that single actions or mistakes do not define people. It requires a more nuanced understanding of human behavior and the acceptance that everyone, including oneself, has a mix of strengths and weaknesses and is capable of change and growth. Focusing on specific behaviors rather than global labels makes it possible to address issues constructively and maintain a balanced view of oneself and others.

Personalization: This cognitive distortion involves taking excessive responsibility for external events or other people's emotions, often assuming that you caused things outside your control. It can lead to unnecessary guilt and a sense of helplessness, blurring the line between one's influence and factors beyond control.

Example: Imagine a scenario where a close friend seems unusually distant or upset. If you're prone to personalization, you might immediately think, "I must have done something to upset them," even if their mood has nothing to do with you. This thought can lead to undue guilt and a compulsion to "fix" things despite not being responsible.

In a work context, if a project you're involved in encounters problems due to external factors like market changes or decisions made by others, you might still feel it's your fault and believe you should have somehow prevented the issues.

Another example is in family dynamics. If there's tension or conflict in the family, someone with a tendency toward personalization might believe it's their responsibility to keep everyone happy and harmonious, internalizing any family issues as personal failures.

To challenge personalization, it's essential to distinguish between being responsible to people and being responsible for them. Understanding that everyone has their agency and that many factors influence events and emotions helps in realizing that not everything revolves around one's actions or presence. By acknowledging and accepting the limits of your control, you can focus on what you can genuinely influence and manage, reducing undue stress and guilt.

By understanding these cognitive distortions, we can identify them in our thoughts and begin challenging and altering them. This leads to more realistic and balanced thinking, reducing the emotional distress associated with PTSD.

As we conclude Week 2 of our journey, reflecting on the transformative insights gained regarding defense mechanisms and cognitive distortions is essential. This week has been a deep dive into the subconscious strategies we use to cope with stress, anxiety, and trauma and the irrational thought patterns that often dictate our emotional responses.

By unpacking these mechanisms and distortions, we've begun the process of not only identifying but also understanding how they shape our interactions with the world and influence our mental health, particularly in the context of PTSD. This understanding is a significant step towards reclaiming control over our cognitive processes and emotional well-being.

The exploration of defense mechanisms from pathological to mature levels has offered a clear view of how these strategies, while initially protective, can become obstacles to our emotional growth and healing if not recognized and appropriately managed. We've seen how pathological defenses like delusional projection and denial can distort reality, how immature defenses such as projection and fantasy can impede effective coping, and how neurotic defenses like displacement and rationalization, though common, can create long-term relational and professional challenges. In contrast, mature defenses like humor and altruism represent healthier ways to manage emotional stress, contributing positively to personal growth and social interactions.

Simultaneously, our journey through the landscape of cognitive distortions has equipped us with the tools to recognize and challenge irrational thought patterns. From all-or-nothing thinking to personalization, we've learned how these distortions contribute to negative emotions and behaviors and how acknowledging and altering these patterns can lead to more balanced and realistic thinking.

As we move forward, we carry a newfound awareness of these psychological aspects. This awareness is empowering; it allows us to discern when we fall into old patterns of defense and distortion and the skills to steer ourselves toward more constructive and adaptive coping methods. This knowledge is not just theoretical but deeply practical, as it directly impacts our journey of healing from PTSD and our overall mental health.

Next week, we will build upon these foundations, further integrating our learning into practical strategies and exercises that promote healing, growth, and resilience. The journey continues, and with each step, we grow stronger, more self-aware, and more capable of navigating the complexities of our inner and outer worlds with grace and understanding.

Week 2 Self-Help Guide

Welcome to a pivotal week dedicated to your healing journey from PTSD. This chapter unfolds through seven meticulously crafted homework assignments, each designed to guide you through the complexities of PTSD with the aim of fostering understanding, resilience, and healing. Our focus will delve into how traumatic experiences have shaped your perception, world views, and schemas, and we will introduce strategies to gently reframe these elements in a way that supports your recovery. Through engaging exercises and reflective tasks, you'll be encouraged to explore and reshape your thoughts and feelings, paving the way for a renewed sense of self. Together, we embark on this healing path, aiming to empower you with the tools and insights needed to reclaim your life from PTSD, one step at a time.

WEEK 2 DAY 1: IDENTIFYING AND REFRAMING DEFENSE MECHANISMS

Objective: The purpose of this exercise is to enhance your self-awareness regarding the use of defense mechanisms and negative thinking patterns in emotionally charged situations. By identifying, challenging, and reframing these patterns, you'll develop healthier coping strategies and responses, fostering personal growth and emotional resilience.

Information: Defense mechanisms are unconscious strategies used to protect ourselves from anxiety and distress. While they can offer short-term relief, they often distort reality, leading to unhelpful thinking patterns and behaviors. Recognizing and addressing these can significantly improve how we respond to stress and emotional challenges.

Task: Reflect on a recent emotionally charged situation. Recall the details, your thoughts, feelings, and reactions. With your understanding of defense mechanisms, identify which ones you might have used. For example, did you resort to denial, projection, rationalization, or humor to cope? Next, identify any negative thinking patterns associated with these defense mechanisms. For instance, if you used denial, were you thinking, "This can't be happening to me"? If you projected, perhaps your thought was, "They're always against me." Similarly, negative behaviors accompanying these thoughts, like avoidance or aggression, should be identified.

Processing: Once you've identified these defense mechanisms and associated negative thoughts and behaviors, engage in the process of reframing them. Begin with a short mindfulness breathing exercise to center yourself. Sit comfortably, breathe deeply, and focus on being present. After this, revisit each identified defense mechanism and negative thought. Challenge these thoughts by asking: Are they factual, or are they distorted perceptions influenced by emotional responses? Try to reframe these thoughts into more balanced and realistic ones. For instance, transform "This can't be happening to me" into "This is challenging, but I can handle it." Discuss better behavioral responses for the future. For example, consider facing the situation with a problem-solving approach instead of avoiding it. Write down these reframed thoughts and alternative behaviors, focusing on how they can lead to more constructive outcomes. This exercise aims to help you recognize and alter unhelpful cognitive and behavioral patterns, fostering healthier coping and responding to emotional situations.

WEEK 2 DAY 2: CHALLENGING COGNITIVE DISTORTIONS

Objective: The aim of this task is to enhance your awareness of cognitive distortions that may color your perception of events and lead to unnecessary emotional distress. By identifying, challenging, and reframing these distortions, you'll learn to adopt more balanced and constructive thinking patterns, fostering emotional well-being.

Information: Cognitive distortions are skewed ways of thinking that can make reality seem worse than it is. Common distortions include all-or-nothing thinking, overgeneralization, and catastrophizing, among others. Recognizing these patterns is the first step toward changing them.

Task: Reflect on a recent situation where you might have experienced cognitive distortions. This could be when you were caught in negative thought patterns like all-or-nothing thinking, overgeneralization, or other common distortions. Try to identify the specific type of distortion that influenced your thinking. For instance, if you thought, "I always fail at everything I try," you might be dealing with overgeneralization.

Processing: Begin with a mindfulness breathing exercise to center yourself and create a calm, focused state of mind. This will help you approach the task with clarity. After the breathing exercise, challenge the cognitive distortions you identified. Write down each distorted thought and provide a more balanced, rational alternative. For example, if your distorted thought was, "I always fail at everything I try," a more reasonable thought could be, "I have had successes and failures, like everyone else, and I can learn from my experiences." This exercise is about recognizing and actively reshaping irrational thoughts into more realistic and positive ones. Reflect on how this process of challenging distortions changes your feelings about the situation.

WEEK 2 DAY 3: EXPLORING EMOTIONAL IMPACT

Objective: The goal of this task is to deepen your understanding of how defense mechanisms and cognitive distortions influence your emotional world, particularly in past interactions or significant life events. By introspectively exploring these psychological patterns, you aim to uncover the ways in which they've shaped your emotional responses—be it through unnecessary guilt, anger, or anxiety. This reflective exercise encourages you to identify specific instances where these patterns played a pivotal role in your emotional experience, offering insights into how they might have contributed to heightened stress or emotional confusion over time.

Information: Defense mechanisms are unconscious psychological strategies used to cope with reality and maintain self-image, while cognitive distortions are biased perspectives we have on ourselves and the world around us. Both play significant roles in influencing our emotional responses to situations, often in ways that we might not be fully aware of. By examining how these mechanisms and distortions have manifested in your reactions to past events, you can begin to understand their impact on your emotional well-being.

Task: Dedicate time to introspectively explore the emotional impact of your defense mechanisms and cognitive distortions in past interactions or significant events. Consider situations where these patterns may have influenced your emotions, such as feeling unnecessarily guilty, angry, or anxious. Describe specific instances and how these psychological patterns might have shaped your emotional responses. For example, if you used a defense mechanism like denial in a stressful situation, reflect on how this may have temporarily alleviated anxiety but possibly led to more stress or confusion later.

Processing: After identifying these instances, engage in a mindfulness technique, such as deep breathing or a body scan meditation, to process the emotions associated with these memories. As you practice mindfulness, pay attention to your emotional responses without judgment or resistance. Consider how recognizing and understanding your defense mechanisms and cognitive distortions can lead to healthier emotional reactions in the future. Reflect on the possibility of responding to similar situations differently, armed with this new awareness. This process is about developing emotional insight and learning to navigate your feelings more consciously and balanced.

WEEK 2 DAY 4: REPLACING DEFENSE MECHANISMS

Objective: This task focuses on identifying and transforming reliance on a specific defense mechanism into healthier, more adaptive strategies. By recognizing a defense mechanism you frequently use, such as denial, projection, or rationalization, the aim is to brainstorm and mentally rehearse alternative, constructive responses for situations where this mechanism typically emerges. This process is designed to foster greater self-awareness and emotional resilience, guiding you towards more authentic and positive interactions.

Information: Defense mechanisms are unconscious processes that protect individuals from anxiety and the awareness of internal or external dangers or stressors. While they can serve short-term adaptive purposes, overreliance on these mechanisms can hinder emotional growth and lead to challenges in coping with reality. This task encourages the exploration of these patterns and the development of more conscious, deliberate coping strategies. Through guided visualization, you'll practice implementing these new strategies, enhancing your ability to respond to challenges with increased control, authenticity, and emotional intelligence.

Task: Select one defense mechanism that you find yourself frequently relying on. This could be anything from denial, projection, or rationalization to more subtle forms like intellectualization. Once identified, brainstorm healthier and more adaptive strategies to use when this defense mechanism typically surfaces. For example, if you often resort to denial in stressful situations, consider ways to acknowledge and confront reality more directly yet compassionately. Think about strategies like open communication, seeking support, or simply allowing yourself to feel and process the emotions involved.

Processing: With these alternative strategies in mind, engage in a mindfulness exercise such as guided visualization. Imagine yourself in a scenario where you would typically employ your defense mechanism. Now, mentally rehearse, implementing the healthier responses you've identified. Visualize how you would feel and act, paying attention to the details of the interaction and your emotional state. This visualization exercise is designed to help you mentally and emotionally prepare to adopt these new responses in real-life situations, reducing your reliance on unhelpful defense mechanisms. Reflect on how these new strategies can lead to more positive outcomes and a greater sense of control and authenticity in your interactions.

WEEK 2 DAY 5: REDEFINING DISTORTED THOUGHTS

Objective: This task is designed to address and reframe a specific cognitive distortion you've recognized in your thought patterns. By selecting a distortion such as catastrophizing, magnification/minimization, or personalization, you'll engage in a reflective process to identify and document real-life evidence that challenges this skewed perspective. The goal is to cultivate a more balanced and realistic viewpoint by highlighting instances that contradict the distortion, fostering an enhanced sense of mental clarity and emotional well-being.

Information: Cognitive distortions are irrational thought patterns that can contribute to negative emotions and behaviors. They often represent an automatic way of thinking that distorts reality, leading to a more pessimistic and skewed perception of oneself and the world. This exercise encourages you to confront these distortions directly by gathering concrete evidence that disputes them, thereby weakening their influence over your emotional state. Following this reflective process with a mindfulness session allows for the internalization of these more accurate, balanced perspectives, potentially leading to significant shifts in your emotional outlook and overall mood.

Task: Choose a specific cognitive distortion you have identified in your thought patterns, such as catastrophizing, magnification/minimization, or personalization. Reflect on this distortion and write down real-life evidence that contradicts or challenges it. For example, if your distortion is catastrophizing (expecting the worst in every situation), list instances where outcomes were positive or not as bad as anticipated. This exercise aims to help you build a more balanced and realistic viewpoint by actively seeking evidence that disproves the distorted thought.

Processing: Once you have your list, engage in a mindfulness session. During this session, focus on internalizing this new, more realistic perspective. Take deep breaths and allow yourself to absorb each piece of contradicting evidence, noticing how it feels to let go of the distortion and embrace a more balanced view. Pay attention to any shifts in your emotional state or attitude. This process reinforces the understanding that your initial thoughts may not always be accurate or helpful and that there are healthier ways to interpret and respond to situations. Reflect on how this exercise impacts your overall mood and outlook, and consider how you can apply this balanced thinking to future situations.

WEEK 2 DAY 6: INTEGRATION AND REFLECTION

Objective: The aim of this task is to consolidate the insights and skills you've developed over the week regarding your defense mechanisms and cognitive distortions. By reflecting on how these patterns have historically influenced your behavior and decisions, you'll devise a comprehensive strategy for applying your newfound understanding and coping strategies to future situations. The goal is to create actionable guidelines for recognizing and altering these patterns, enhancing your emotional well-being and decision-making processes.

Information: Over the course of the week, you've engaged in various exercises designed to increase your awareness of the psychological defenses and distortions that shape your perceptions and reactions. Integrating this knowledge into a coherent strategy requires not only reflection but also planning. This involves identifying triggers, employing mindfulness techniques to stay present, and consciously choosing more adaptive responses or thought patterns. This process is crucial for breaking free from unhelpful cycles and fostering healthier, more constructive ways of handling life's challenges. The concluding extended mindfulness meditation serves as both a practice session for these strategies and a moment to recognize and solidify your commitment to ongoing personal growth and emotional resilience.

Task: Dedicate time to reflect on all the exercises and insights you have gathered throughout the week. This is an opportunity to integrate what you've learned about your defense mechanisms and cognitive distortions into a coherent and comprehensive strategy. Consider how these patterns have influenced your past behaviors and decisions. Then, think about how you can apply your new understanding and coping strategies to similar situations in the future. Write down a step-by-step approach or guidelines you can follow when you notice yourself falling back into old patterns. This could include recognizing the trigger, pausing to identify the defense mechanism or distortion, using mindfulness to ground yourself, and consciously choosing a healthier response or thought pattern.

Processing: Conclude the week with an extended mindfulness meditation session. During this meditation, envision yourself in various situations where you might typically employ defense mechanisms or fall prey to cognitive distortions. Imagine yourself applying your new strategies in these scenarios. Visualize how these changes in approach alter your interactions, decisions, and emotional state. Notice positive changes in your emotional well-being, such as increased calmness, clarity, or confidence. Reflect on how these new strategies make you feel and how they might influence your future behaviors and thoughts. This meditation is about solidifying your commitment to these healthier patterns and acknowledging your progress in understanding and managing your psychological defenses and distortions.

| 7 |

Navigating Trauma Narratives and Internal Landscapes

Building on the prior work, where we focused on perception and reality within the framework of Cognitive Behavioral Therapy (CBT), Week 3 delves into personal trauma narratives. This week is about exploring and articulating the stories we tell ourselves and others about our traumatic experiences. This will propel our journey forward, allowing us to understand and process the impact of trauma more deeply.

Crafting Our Stories from Trauma

Trauma narratives are much more than mere recollections of distressing events; they are the deeply personal stories we construct to give meaning and context to our traumatic experiences. Within these narratives, we weave together the intricate threads of our thoughts, emotions, and memories that are intrinsically linked to the trauma.

The stories we tell ourselves about our trauma are potent forces that shape our perception of the event, ourselves, and our place in the world. They influence how we interpret the past and view our present capabilities and expectations for the future. A trauma narrative can alter our sense of identity, impact our belief systems, and affect our relationships with others and the world at large.

Creating and exploring trauma narratives can help change internal perceptions and associated meaning. This process helps externalize the trauma, moving it from an overwhelming internal burden to an external object that can be examined, understood, and restructured. Through this externalization, we gain a degree of distance and perspective, allowing for a more objective examination of the traumatic event.

Trauma often leaves behind a chaotic imprint on our minds. Developing a narrative is a way of organizing this chaos into a coherent structure. It involves identifying and articulating the emotions and thoughts experienced during and after the traumatic event. This structuring helps recognize patterns, understand triggers, and identify coping strategies that might have been employed.

The act of narrating one's trauma can be empowering. It allows for the reclamation of one's voice and asserting control over the traumatic experience. Through this process, individuals can begin to see themselves not just as victims of their trauma but as survivors and active agents in their healing process.

In essence, trauma narratives are a crucial tool in the journey toward recovery. They provide a means to process and make sense of what has happened and offer a pathway out of the entanglement of trauma. Developing and exploring these narratives can reshape our understanding of the trauma and its impact, paving the way for a more hopeful and resilient future.

TF-CBT for Structured Narrative Development

As we progress into the second week of our journey, Trauma-Focused Cognitive Behavioral Therapy (TF-CBT) becomes a pivotal tool in our arsenal. TF-CBT is uniquely equipped to assist individuals in constructing a coherent and structured narrative of their traumatic experiences. It's a therapeutic approach that combines the principles of cognitive-behavioral therapy with specific sensitivity to the unique aspects of trauma.

One of the core elements of TF-CBT is its encouragement of gradual exposure to the memories, thoughts, and emotions tied to the trauma. This systematic approach allows individuals to confront their trauma in a controlled and safe environment. The idea is not to relive the trauma but to understand and reframe it.

Through TF-CBT, individuals are guided to transform the fragmented and often chaotic memories of trauma into a structured and coherent story. This narrative development is more than just recounting events; it involves identifying the emotions, thoughts, and reactions associated with the trauma. The traumatic experience can be contextualized and understood within the broader narrative of the individual's life.

Creating a trauma narrative in TF-CBT serves multiple therapeutic purposes. It helps demystify the trauma, stripping it of some of its overwhelming power and emotional charge. As individuals narrate their experiences, they gain a new perspective that often leads to a more balanced understanding of the event. Storytelling also provides a sense of closure and completeness, which can be crucial in the healing process.

An integral part of TF-CBT is cognitive restructuring, where individuals learn to identify and challenge distorted thoughts and beliefs related to the trauma. In the context of narrative development, this means looking at how the trauma has influenced one's belief system and actively working to reframe these beliefs into more accurate and adaptive thoughts.

TF-CBT's structured narrative development is a decisive step in the healing journey from trauma. It provides a framework for individuals to understand and process their traumatic experiences in a way that fosters empowerment and resilience. This week, as we delve into creating our trauma narratives, we harness the strengths of TF-CBT to guide us toward a deeper understanding and reconciliation with our past experiences.

Integrating Internal Family Systems Therapy

As we venture into the deeper realms of our psyche in Week 3, Internal Family Systems (IFS) therapy emerges as a vital complement to Trauma-Focused Cognitive Behavioral Therapy (TF-CBT). IFS offers a unique and insightful perspective into the multifaceted nature of our psyche, especially in the context of trauma. It provides a framework for understanding the various parts of ourselves that traumatic experiences have impacted.

Central to IFS is the concept that our psyche comprises multiple parts, each with unique roles, emotions, and viewpoints. Trauma can cause some of these parts to become extreme or assume roles that are ultimately harmful, albeit initially protective. For example, a part might become overly vigilant to protect from future harm, or another might push to suppress painful memories, leading to avoidance behaviors.

This week we will focus on the IFS approach, identifying and exploring these parts. We will seek to understand the roles they have taken on due to trauma. This exploration involves delving into their stories—how they came to be, what they believe, and how they have attempted to protect and preserve the self. This process often reveals that what might initially appear as maladaptive or harmful behaviors are parts attempting to cope with the trauma in the only ways they know how.

A critical aspect of working with IFS is cultivating compassion for these parts. Recognizing the protective intentions of these parts, no matter how extreme they have become, can foster a sense of understanding and compassion. This compassionate perspective is essential for healing, as it allows us to view these parts not as enemies but as integral components of our being that require care and attention.

Through IFS, we aim not only to understand these parts but also to assist them in releasing their extreme roles and integrating them back into the internal system in healthier ways. This reintegration is a journey toward balance and harmony within the self. It involves helping these parts transform from isolated protectors or burden-bearers into valuable internal family members, each contributing positively to the individual's well-being.

IFS therapy in Week 3 is about embracing the complexity of our internal world post-trauma. By understanding and compassionately addressing the parts affected by trauma, we take significant strides toward holistic healing and reintegration, moving beyond mere symptom management to a more profound sense of self-awareness and inner harmony.

Week 3 Goals

- Developing a Trauma Narrative: We will work on articulating our trauma stories, and understanding the facts, emotions, and thoughts surrounding the traumatic event(s).
- Understanding the Impact on Internal Parts: Exploring how different parts of ourselves have been influenced by trauma and how they interact within our internal system.
- Processing and Integration: Reflecting on the narratives and the parts will help in processing the trauma and beginning to integrate these experiences into a coherent whole.

Week 3 marks an essential step in our healing process. By articulating our trauma narratives and understanding the internal parts affected, we begin to take control of our stories and, in turn, our healing. It's a journey that requires courage and compassion, but the insights and growth from this process are invaluable steps toward recovery.

Week 3 Self-Help Guide

These daily assignments aim to blend the structured approach of TF-CBT in developing and refining your trauma narrative with the compassionate understanding of IFS regarding the internal parts affected by trauma. This integrated approach is designed to facilitate a deeper understanding and processing of your traumatic experience, fostering a path toward healing and integration.

WEEK 3 DAY 1: INITIAL TRAUMA NARRATIVE DRAFTING (TF-CBT)

Objective: The objective of this task is to construct a clear narrative of your traumatic event, focusing on the essential facts: what occurred, the setting, and the timing, alongside your immediate thoughts and feelings during the event. This exercise aims to foster a deeper understanding of your experience by articulating it in your own words, which can be a powerful step towards healing.

Guidance: Approach this task gently, with patience and self-compassion. Recognize that recalling a traumatic event can be challenging, and it's important to prioritize your emotional safety. If at any point you feel overwhelmed or distressed, please give yourself permission to take a break. It's crucial to remember that this exercise is intended for your understanding and healing, not for reliving the trauma. Due to the sensitive nature of this task, consider engaging with a trained mental health professional who can provide support and guidance throughout the process. If the thought of beginning this task is overwhelming, it is highly recommended to seek assistance from a professional.

Processing: After completing your narrative, spend some time reflecting on the emotions and thoughts that surfaced during this exercise. Note any surprises or significant revelations about your feelings or reactions. Assess your narrative for any patterns of misaligned or negative thinking that might have influenced your perception of the event. Attempt to reevaluate the situation with a more realistic lens, considering any new insights or perspectives that have emerged. This reflection phase is an integral part of processing your experience, allowing you to challenge and reframe your understanding of the traumatic event.

WEEK 3 DAY 2: IDENTIFYING INTERNAL PARTS (IFS)

Objective: The objective of this exercise is to explore and understand the different 'parts' of your psyche that have been influenced by trauma. By identifying these parts, such as a protective segment that keeps you vigilant or a vulnerable fragment that harbors pain, you aim to gain insight into the multifaceted impact trauma has had on your inner self. Viewing these parts as distinct characters with their own motivations and emotions can facilitate a deeper comprehension of your internal landscape post-trauma.

Guidance: Approach this task with an open mind and empathy towards yourself. Visualize the different parts of your psyche as members of a diverse family, each with unique characteristics, perspectives, and ways of interacting with the world. These parts may not always harmonize, reflecting the complex and sometimes conflicting nature of our responses to trauma. This metaphorical family represents the spectrum of your inner experiences and reactions to traumatic events. Understanding the roles and interactions of these parts can be enlightening, helping you to acknowledge and appreciate the complexity of your psychological responses to trauma.

Processing: After identifying the various parts of your psyche affected by trauma, take some time to reflect on and document the role each part plays. Consider the following for each identified part:

- Describe its primary characteristics and motivations. What emotions does it hold or express?
- Reflect on why this part behaves as it does, especially in response to trauma. What purpose does it serve in your psychological ecosystem?
- Consider how each part interacts with others within your psyche. Are there conflicts or alliances? How do these dynamics affect your overall emotional well-being and response to stress or triggers?

This exercise is about recognizing the presence of these parts and seeking to understand the origins, purposes, and how they contribute to your coping mechanisms. Through this reflective process, you can develop a more compassionate and comprehensive understanding of your inner self, paving the way for integrated healing.

Identified Parts	What They Represent	Analysis & Notes

WEEK 3 DAY 3 THE TRAUMA NARRATIVE

Objective: The purpose of this task is to enrich your narrative by incorporating deeper layers of emotional reactions, thoughts during and after the traumatic event, and any beliefs that formed as a result of the experience. This exercise seeks to provide a more nuanced understanding of how the trauma impacted you not just externally, but emotionally and cognitively as well. By delving into these aspects, you aim to uncover the complex web of feelings, thoughts, and beliefs that were influenced by the trauma.

Guidance: As you revisit your narrative, allow yourself to explore the depths of your emotional responses and the cascade of thoughts that accompanied the trauma. Consider how the event shaped your perception of yourself, others, and the world. Did it lead to any long-standing beliefs or assumptions? Be patient and gentle with yourself as you navigate these deeper waters. Acknowledging the full breadth of your experience can be challenging but is a crucial step in understanding the multifaceted impact of trauma. Approach this task with an open heart, knowing that it's okay to feel a range of emotions.

Processing: After adding these layers to your narrative, take some time to reflect on the enriched understanding you now have of your trauma. Consider:

- How do these added details of emotional reactions and thoughts during and after the event contribute to your overall understanding of the traumatic experience?
- Did incorporating these aspects change your perception of the event or its impact on you? If so, how?
- Reflect on any new insights or connections you've made about how the trauma has influenced your beliefs and assumptions about yourself and the world.

This process of deepening your narrative is not just about recounting what happened but also about integrating these experiences into your larger story. It's about recognizing how the trauma has shaped you and considering how this enhanced narrative can inform your healing journey.

MY TRAUMA

Thought / Beliefs Then

Thought / Beliefs Now

Analysis and Notes on more Realistic, Objective Ways of Thinking

How has your perception changed over time?

Identified Negative Thinking Patterns & Beliefs

WEEK 3 DAY 4: DIALOGUE WITH INTERNAL PARTS (IFS)

Objective: The goal of this exercise is to facilitate a direct dialogue with one of the parts of your psyche that has been significantly influenced by trauma, whether it be a protective part, a vulnerable part, or another aspect of yourself. By engaging in an imaginary conversation with this part, you aim to gain a deeper understanding of its motivations, fears, and needs. This introspective dialogue can help bridge understanding between your conscious self and the underlying aspects of your psyche affected by trauma, fostering a sense of internal harmony and self-compassion.

Task: Engage in an imaginary conversation with one of your identified parts. This could be a protective part, a vulnerable part, or any other aspect of yourself that seems to be significantly influenced by your trauma.

Guidance:

- Setting the Scene: Find a quiet, comfortable space where you won't be disturbed. Take a few deep breaths to center yourself.
- Choosing the Part: Think about the part you want to converse with. It could be a part that's been particularly active or noticeable in your life post-trauma.
- Initiating the Dialogue: Start the conversation by introducing yourself to the part. Acknowledge its presence and express your intention to understand it better.

- Asking Key Questions: Gently ask the part about its role in your life. What fears does it hold? What is its purpose? What does it need from you? Remember, the goal is to understand, not to judge or confront.
- Listening with Empathy: Imagine how this part would respond. Pay attention to the emotions and thoughts that arise. This might feel like an internal monologue or a more vivid imagined conversation.

Processing:

- Reflecting on the Dialogue: After the conversation, take some time to reflect on what you heard and felt. Did the part share any fears or needs that surprised you?
- Understanding the Impact: Consider how this part has influenced your responses to specific situations, especially those related to your trauma.
- Journaling Insights: Write down your reflections. What new understandings have you gained about how this part has been managing or responding to your trauma? How does this part's perspective influence your overall trauma narrative?
- Planning Compassionate Actions: Think about how you can address the needs or fears expressed by this part. What compassionate actions can you take to help this part feel heard and supported?

This exercise is designed to deepen your understanding of the different aspects of yourself affected by trauma. By engaging in this empathetic dialogue, you're taking a significant step towards integrating these parts into a healthier, more harmonious internal system. It's an opportunity for healing and self-compassion, crucial in your journey towards recovery from trauma.

WEEK 3 DAY 5: INTEGRATING TF-CBT AND IFS IN NARRATIVE

Objective: The objective of this task is to enrich your trauma narrative by integrating insights from Internal Family Systems (IFS) dialogues, focusing on the roles and perspectives of the internal parts identified through these conversations. This involves revisiting and revising your existing narrative of the traumatic event to include the motivations, needs, and actions of these parts, thereby creating a more comprehensive and nuanced understanding of your experience. The aim is to foster a deeper connection with these aspects of yourself, recognizing their contributions to your response to trauma and their needs moving forward. This process is designed to facilitate a more empathetic and compassionate view of your internal landscape, enhancing the healing journey by acknowledging the complexity of your trauma response.

Task: Merge the insights from your IFS dialogues with your evolving trauma narrative. This task involves revisiting your trauma narrative and weaving in the perspectives and roles of the internal parts you've identified and conversed with.

Detailed Guidance:

- Review Your Narrative: Begin by re-reading the trauma narrative you have developed so far. Notice any emotions or thoughts that arise as you read through it.
- Adding IFS Insights: Reflect on the dialogues you've had with your internal parts. How do these parts fit into your trauma

story? For instance, if a part of you felt the need to protect you during the traumatic event, how does this influence the narrative of the event?

- Reframing the Narrative: Integrate these insights into your narrative. This might mean adding new sections, altering certain parts, or even reinterpreting events from the perspective of these internal parts.
- Emphasize the Roles and Needs: As you integrate, emphasize the roles and needs of the different parts. Acknowledge their intentions, fears, and contributions to your trauma response.

Processing:

- Reflect on Changes: After integrating these elements, reflect on how your narrative has changed. Does the story feel more complete or complex now? How does it feel to acknowledge these parts in your narrative?
- Emotional Response: Pay attention to your emotional response to the revised narrative. Does acknowledging these parts bring about new feelings or understandings about the trauma?
- Journaling Reflections: Write down your reflections on this integration process. Note how the inclusion of IFS perspectives has influenced your understanding of the trauma and your feelings towards it.
- Identify Any Shifts: Look for any shifts in how you perceive the traumatic event, yourself, and the responses you had. This could be a shift from seeing yourself as a passive victim to recognizing the active roles your internal parts played in coping with the trauma.

Day 5's task is a critical step in synthesizing two powerful therapeutic approaches – TF-CBT and IFS – into your trauma narrative. This integration provides a richer, more nuanced understanding of your trauma experience and fosters a deeper sense of empathy and compassion towards yourself. Acknowledging and integrating the roles of your internal parts is paving the way for a more holistic healing process.

WEEK 3 DAY 6: CHALLENGING DISTORTED BELIEFS (TF-CBT)

Objective: The objective of this task is to critically examine and amend the distorted beliefs or thoughts embedded within your trauma narrative. By identifying these distortions—such as overly negative or absolute thinking—and questioning their validity, you aim to replace them with perspectives that are more balanced and realistic. This process encourages a shift towards a more nuanced understanding of your trauma, moving away from black-and-white thinking towards acknowledging the complexities of your experience. The ultimate goal is to modify how you emotionally engage with your trauma narrative, fostering a more grounded and less distressing connection to your past experiences.

Guidance: As you review your narrative, pay close attention to any statements or beliefs that paint the situation in extremes (e.g., "I always make mistakes" or "Nothing good ever happens to me"). Challenge these thoughts by considering alternative interpretations or outcomes. Ask yourself critical questions like, "Is this thought absolutely true?" or "Can I think of any exceptions to this belief?" This reflective questioning can help illuminate more balanced ways of viewing the situation.

Processing: After identifying and challenging the distorted thoughts within your narrative, take a moment to reflect on the impact of this exercise:

- **How Does Your Narrative Feel Now After Challenging Negativity?** Consider whether the narrative feels less burdensome or more approachable after revising it to include more balanced viewpoints.

- **Objective, Realistic Appraisal:** Summarize the more balanced and realistic perspectives you've introduced into your narrative. How do these changes affect your overall perception of the trauma?

- **Identified Distorted Thought & Beliefs:** List the specific distorted thoughts and beliefs you challenged, alongside the more balanced perspectives you've adopted in their place.

Analysis and Notes

How Does Your Narrative Feel Now After Challenging Negativity?

Objective, Realistic Appraisal

Identified Distorted Thought & Beliefs

WEEK 3 DAY 7: COMPASSIONATE REFLECTION AND INTEGRATION (IFS)

Objective: The objective of this task is to cultivate a deeper sense of compassion and understanding towards the different parts of your psyche that have been affected by trauma. By writing a compassionate message or letter to each of these internal parts, you acknowledge their roles, contributions, and needs within your trauma response. This exercise aims to foster a nurturing internal environment conducive to healing and integration, recognizing each part's efforts to protect and cope with the trauma in its own way.

Guidance: Approach this task with an open heart and a non-judgmental mindset. Address each part individually, acknowledging its intentions, struggles, and the specific ways it has contributed to your overall response to trauma. Express gratitude for its efforts to protect and support you, even if its methods were not always helpful. Offer reassurance, understanding, and a commitment to work together towards a more harmonious and integrated self.

Consider using the following structure for each letter:

- **Address the Part:** "Dear [Protective Part/Vulnerable Part/etc.],"
- **Acknowledge Its Role:** Describe the role and actions of the part during your trauma response, recognizing its intentions.

- **Express Gratitude:** Thank the part for its efforts to help and protect you, acknowledging the challenges it faced.
- **Offer Understanding and Support:** Show empathy for its struggles, and offer your support and cooperation in finding healthier ways to cope and heal.
- **Commit to Healing Together:** Affirm your commitment to work together with this part towards healing, emphasizing collaboration and mutual care.

Processing: After writing your letters, reflect on the impact of this compassionate approach on your relationship with these internal parts and your overall healing journey:

- How does acknowledging and offering compassion to each part change your perception of them and their actions?
- Consider the emotions that arose during this exercise. Did you feel a sense of relief, understanding, or connection?
- Reflect on how this practice of compassion and acknowledgment might influence your ongoing healing process. Do you feel more integrated or at peace with these parts of yourself?

| 8 |

Nurturing Calm Through Mindfulness and Meditation

As we enter Week 4 of our transformative journey, we turn our attention to the serene yet potent practices of Mindfulness and Meditation. In this phase, we delve into how these time-honored traditions, skillfully adapted for contemporary healing, can significantly impact our recovery from PTSD. This week is dedicated to cultivating a state of inner peace, emotional stability, and heightened self-awareness – essential qualities for anyone journeying through the often-stormy seas of PTSD.

Mindfulness is not merely a practice; it is a way of being that allows us to experience life more fully, moment by moment. It teaches us to observe our thoughts and feelings without getting caught up. For individuals coping with PTSD, mindfulness offers a path to gently disengage from the grip of past traumas and the anxiety of future uncertainties. This week, we explore mindfulness as a tool to anchor ourselves in the 'here and now,' enabling a profound sense of connection to our current experiences.

Originating from ancient Buddhist philosophy, mindfulness was introduced to the Western world through the pioneering work of Jon Kabat-Zinn in the late 20th century and other contemporary experts such as Thich Nhat Hanh, Sharon Salzberg, and Jack Kornfield. Kabat-Zinn, who founded the Mindfulness-Based Stress Reduction (MBSR) program at UMass Memorial Medical Center, played an important role in integrating mindfulness meditation practices with contemporary psychological insights. Similarly, Thich Nhat Hanh's teachings emphasize the power of mindfulness in everyday life, while Salzberg and Kornfield have contributed to its widespread practice and understanding through their teachings and writings. Together, these figures have made mindfulness accessible and applicable to a broad audience, extending beyond its religious origins to become a foundational tool in the field of psychology.

Mindfulness, in both its philosophical and psychological contexts, emphasizes the importance of being present and fully engaged with the here and now, with an attitude of openness, curiosity, and non-judgment. This practice encourages an awareness of one's thoughts, emotions, and physical sensations as they occur, fostering a stance of observation rather than reaction. It's this very quality of mindful awareness that has been harnessed in therapeutic settings to aid individuals in recognizing and accepting their internal experiences, promoting healing and integration.

The efficacy of mindfulness has been supported by a growing body of research over the past few decades. Studies have demonstrated its benefits across a spectrum of psychological conditions, including stress, anxiety, depression, and post-traumatic stress disorder (PTSD). Research suggests that mindfulness practices can alter brain regions associated with attention, emotion regulation, and self-awareness, contributing to an overall sense of well-being and resilience. The evidence points to mindfulness not just as a practice but as a foundational tool for psychological healing and well-being, offering a bridge between ancient wisdom and modern science in the journey toward healing from trauma.

Mindfulness and meditation offer a unique opportunity to quiet the mind's relentless chatter and to find a sense of calm amidst the chaos. For those dealing with PTSD, this practice can be a sanctuary, providing much-needed relief from the intrusive memories and hyper-vigilance that characterize the condition.

This week's focus goes beyond temporary relief; it's about laying the foundations for long-term emotional and psychological well-being. Through mindfulness and meditation, we aim to equip you with sustainable skills to manage stress, regulate emotions, and foster a resilient mindset. These practices are about coping with symptoms and transforming your relationship with your mind and body.

In Week 4, we blend the ancient wisdom of mindfulness and meditation with modern therapeutic insights, creating a comprehensive approach to healing from PTSD. We recognize the unique challenges that PTSD presents and tailor these practices to address them effectively. Each day, we will introduce exercises and techniques designed to integrate seamlessly into daily life, offering practical and accessible ways to enhance your journey toward recovery.

As we conclude this introduction, we embark on a week that promises not only relief from the immediate distress of PTSD but also a journey toward lasting inner peace and self-discovery. Week 4 is about embracing each moment, learning to live with awareness and acceptance, and unlocking our potential for profound healing and growth.

Embracing Mindfulness: A Path to Inner Tranquility

Mindfulness offers the chance for tranquility, especially for those battling the tumultuous waves of PTSD. At its heart, mindfulness is the art of being wholly present in the now, a crucial skill for individuals entangled in the lingering shadows of past traumas or ensnared by the anxiety of future uncertainties. This week, we delve into mindfulness, inviting you to experience each moment with acceptance, compassion, and non-judgment.

For many with PTSD, life can feel like an endless replay of painful memories or a constant dread of what lies ahead. Mindfulness offers a way out of this cycle. It teaches us to gently acknowledge our past and fears for the future while firmly rooting ourselves in the present. This practice isn't about forgetting or ignoring our trauma; rather, it's about changing our relationship with our experiences.

Mindfulness encourages us to meet each thought and emotion with gentle curiosity and open-heartedness. This attitude of acceptance and compassion is especially healing in PTSD, where self-criticism and guilt often reign. Through mindfulness, we learn to observe our thoughts and feelings without attaching labels or judgments, allowing us to see ourselves and our experiences in a more compassionate and forgiving light.

Each moment we spend mindfully brings us into a haven free from the grip of past trauma and future worries. In this space, we find clarity and calmness, which can often seem so elusive in the whirlwind of PTSD symptoms. As we practice being in the present, we gradually build our resilience against the intrusive thoughts and emotional upheavals that characterize PTSD.

As we embark on this week's journey, mindfulness is presented as a practice and a way of living. It's about cultivating an ongoing awareness of the present, its richness and complexity, and embracing each moment as it unfolds—with all its challenges and joys. In doing so, we open ourselves to a life that's not defined by our trauma but enriched by our every experience.

Mindfulness, in the context of PTSD, is a powerful tool that offers more than momentary peace; it paves the way for lasting tranquility and a renewed sense of control over our lives. As we progress through this week, we invite you to explore this path to inner tranquility, a journey that promises profound transformation and healing.

Meditation: Reconnecting with Inner Serenity

In the context of PTSD, meditation emerges as a method for relaxation and a profound journey to the deepest realms of the self. It's a practice that transcends the typical boundaries of calming techniques, offering a pathway to inner serenity that is both healing and introspective. This week, we introduce various forms of meditation, each uniquely designed to quieten the constant mental chatter, opening doors to a deeper understanding and connection with the self.

Meditation provides a much-needed respite from the relentless barrage of thoughts and memories that often besiege individuals with PTSD. It's about creating a tranquil space where the mind can rest, free from the usual turmoil and noise. This mental quietude is not just about experiencing silence; it's about nurturing a healing environment where introspection and self-discovery can flourish.

For those grappling with PTSD, intrusive thoughts and a heightened state of arousal can feel like uninvited intruders in the mind. Meditation offers a way to manage these symptoms more effectively. By focusing inward and practicing mindfulness in meditation, you can learn to observe these thoughts without getting swept away. This practice helps in reducing their intensity and frequency, providing a sense of control and calmness.

Meditation comes in many forms, each with its unique benefits and approaches. This week, we'll explore techniques ranging from guided meditations, which help visualize a peaceful and safe space, to mindfulness meditation, focusing on the breath to anchor in the present. We'll also delve into loving-kindness meditation, which fosters compassion and empathy for the self and others.

The beauty of meditation lies in its adaptability and simplicity. Whether it's a few minutes of mindful breathing each morning or a dedicated guided imagery session, these practices can seamlessly integrate into your daily routine. The goal is to make meditation a consistent part of your life, a tool always available to bring you back to balance and peace.

As we conclude this exploration of meditation, we invite you to embrace it as a journey toward reconnecting with your inner serenity. This practice holds the potential not only to alleviate the symptoms of PTSD but to transform your relationship with your thoughts, emotions, and inner experiences. It's a journey that promises a deeper connection with the tranquility within you, a steppingstone to enduring healing and growth.

Week 4 Focus Areas

- Relaxation and Calm: We'll begin with simple relaxation techniques to ease into a state of calm, essential for those with heightened anxiety or stress.
- Mindful Breathing: Breath is our life force, and by focusing on our breathing, we learn to anchor ourselves in the present, an essential step in managing PTSD symptoms.
- Body Awareness: PTSD often disconnects us from our bodies. We'll reconnect with our physical selves through body scan meditations, learning to listen to and honor our body's signals.
- Grounding in the Present: Using simple but effective grounding techniques, we'll practice staying present, especially useful for moments of dissociation or overwhelming emotions.
- Cultivating Positive Mind States: Through guided visualizations and positive affirmations, we'll work on fostering a mindset that supports healing and resilience.

Implementing Mindfulness and Meditation in Daily Life

Each day this week, we will introduce a new practice, building a toolkit of techniques that can be used anytime, anywhere. These practices are designed to be flexible and adaptable, fitting into various lifestyles and needs.

Goals for Week 4

We aim to make mindfulness and meditation a natural part of your daily routine, equipping you with the skills to face PTSD with a renewed sense of calm and control. These practices are intended to empower you, providing a foundation of inner peace that supports your ongoing therapeutic journey.

As Week 4 concludes, you will have gained valuable skills in mindfulness and meditation, creating a solid foundation for emotional and mental stability. This week is about embracing the present, understanding the power of now, and recognizing that even amidst the challenges of PTSD, there can be moments of profound peace and clarity.

Week 4 Self-Help Guide

Welcome to Week four of our journey together. This week, we embark on the path of mindfulness, a practice that invites us to experience life in the present moment, free from judgment and full of acceptance. As you engage with this week's assignments, remember that each task is designed not just as an activity but as a stepping stone towards cultivating a more peaceful and attentive state of being. Mindfulness is our tool to navigate the complexities of our thoughts and emotions, especially beneficial for those working through the symptoms of PTSD.

I encourage you to approach these assignments with openness and curiosity. Mindfulness is about more than just reducing stress; it's about developing a deep, compassionate awareness of your thoughts, feelings, and surroundings. This awareness can be a powerful ally in your journey towards healing and growth.

WEEK 4 DAY 1: INTRODUCTION TO MINDFUL BREATHING

Objective: The goal of this task is to introduce and integrate mindful breathing as a foundational practice in your mindfulness journey, particularly focusing on its application as a relaxation and grounding tool for individuals managing PTSD. Mindful breathing, characterized by a simple yet profoundly effective 5-minute exercise, serves not only as a method for cultivating presence and awareness but also as an essential technique for navigating triggers and intense emotional reactions commonly associated with PTSD. By regularly engaging in this practice, you aim to develop a reliable skill set for regaining emotional and physiological control during moments of heightened stress or anxiety, thereby enhancing your overall capacity for resilience and self-regulation in the face of PTSD symptoms.

Task: Mindful Breathing as a Grounding Tool

Begin your journey into mindfulness with a simple yet profoundly effective 5-minute breathing exercise. This practice is more than just an exercise; it's a vital tool for relaxation and grounding, beneficial when faced with triggers or intense emotional reactions common in PTSD.

How to Practice:

1. Find a Comfortable Spot: Sit or lie in a quiet, comfortable place where you won't be easily disturbed.

2. Observe Your Breath: Close your eyes and shift your attention to your breathing. Notice the natural rhythm of your inhalations and exhalations. Feel the air moving in and out of your nostrils or your chest rising and falling.
3. Stay Present: If your mind starts to wander, gently acknowledge it and bring your focus back to your breath. This is not about controlling your thoughts but about returning to your breathing whenever distractions arise.

The Role of Mindful Breathing in PTSD Management

This breathing exercise is a starting point for mindfulness and a crucial technique for regaining control during heightened stress or anxiety. When PTSD symptoms like flashbacks, hyperarousal, or panic start to surface, this simple practice can be a lifeline. By focusing on your breath, you return to the present, away from the triggering thoughts or memories.

Processing: Reflecting on the Exercise's Impact

- Mind and Body Awareness: Reflect on your body and mind sensations during and after the exercise. Did you notice a change in your heart rate, muscle tension, or overall sense of calm?
- Navigating Distractions: Consider how you handled distractions. Learning to refocus on your breath is a crucial skill in mindfulness, helping you stay grounded in the face of PTSD triggers.
- Evaluating Effectiveness: Consider how effective this technique could be in moments of stress or anxiety. How might you use it in your daily life when faced with PTSD-related challenges?

This mindful breathing exercise is a fundamental relaxation and grounding technique for anyone with PTSD. Its power lies in its simplicity and accessibility. You can practice it anywhere, anytime, making it an invaluable tool for returning to calm and equilibrium. As you progress through this week, remember this practice as your anchor, a constant source of stability amidst the ebbs and flows of your PTSD journey.

WEEK 4 DAY 2: PROGRESSIVE RELAXATION TECHNIQUE

Objective: The objective of this task is to familiarize and engage you with Progressive Muscle Relaxation (PMR), a relaxation technique aimed at reducing physical tension and stress, which are common exacerbators of PTSD symptoms. Through the methodical tensing and then relaxing of different muscle groups, from the toes upwards, you will learn to identify and alleviate tension in the body. This practice is designed not only to diminish the physical manifestations of stress and anxiety associated with PTSD but also to enhance your overall sense of well-being by promoting relaxation and a deeper mind-body connection. By incorporating PMR into your routine, you aim to develop a practical skill that can be utilized to manage and navigate the physiological responses to stress, contributing to a more balanced and calm state of being in the face of PTSD challenges.

Task: Engaging in Progressive Muscle Relaxation

Today's focus is on Progressive Muscle Relaxation (PMR). This method teaches you to relax your muscles through a two-step process of tensing and relaxing different muscle groups. This technique is particularly effective for those with PTSD as it reduces the overall tension and stress levels that exacerbate PTSD symptoms.

How to Practice:

1. Find a Quiet Space: Choose a comfortable and quiet place to sit or lie down without interruptions.
2. Starting from the Toes: Begin with your toes. Inhale and squeeze these muscles as tightly as possible for about 5 seconds, then exhale and release the tension, letting your toes completely relax.
3. Progress Up the Body: Gradually move up through your body – feet, calves, knees, thighs, buttocks, abdomen, chest, hands, arms, shoulders, neck, and finally, face. Repeat the tense-and-relax process with each muscle group.
4. Take Your Time: Spend 5 seconds tensing each muscle group and up to 30 seconds relaxing. Notice the difference between the sensations of tension and relaxation.

The Role of PMR in PTSD Symptom Management

PMR can be particularly useful in managing the physical symptoms of PTSD, such as muscle tension, restlessness, and difficulty sleeping. By learning to relax your muscles, you can significantly reduce physical discomfort and anxiety, leading to an overall sense of calm.

Processing: Reflecting on the Experience

- Noting Tension Areas: After completing the exercise, reflect on areas with more pronounced tension. Were certain muscle groups harder to relax? Recognizing these areas can provide insights into where you carry your stress.
- Body Awareness: How did your body feel before and after the exercise? Did you notice a decrease in overall tension? Did the exercise bring a sense of relaxation or ease to your body?
- Mind-Body Connection: Consider how this exercise made you feel mentally. Often, relaxing the body can also lead to a calming of the mind, which is crucial for managing PTSD symptoms.

Progressive Muscle Relaxation is a valuable tool in your PTSD healing toolkit. It not only helps in reducing physical tension but also promotes a better mind-body connection, an essential aspect of PTSD recovery. As you continue to practice PMR, you may find it easier to navigate moments of stress and anxiety, using this technique as a method to restore balance and tranquility.

WEEK 4 DAY 3 BODY SCAN

Objective: The aim of this task is to engage in Body Scan Meditation, a mindfulness practice designed to enhance awareness of physical sensations throughout the body. This technique is particularly beneficial for individuals with PTSD, as it facilitates a deeper connection with the body, helping to identify and acknowledge sensations that may be ignored or suppressed due to trauma. Through focused attention from the toes to the top of the head, this exercise encourages a non-judgmental observation of bodily sensations, promoting a reconnection with the physical self that trauma often disrupts. By integrating Body Scan Meditation into your healing process, you aim to cultivate a mindful presence that supports emotional and physical awareness, offering insights into how trauma manifests in the body and paving the way for greater healing and integration.

Task: Deepening Awareness with Body Scan Meditation

Today, we immerse ourselves in Body Scan Meditation, a mindfulness technique that helps develop a deeper awareness of the physical body. This exercise is particularly beneficial for individuals with PTSD, as it aids in reconnecting with and recognizing bodily sensations that might often be ignored or suppressed due to trauma.

How to Practice:

1. Prepare Your Space: Find a quiet, comfortable place to lie undisturbed. You might use a mat or a bed, whichever feels most comfortable.

2. Start the Scan: Close your eyes and take a few deep breaths to center yourself. Begin your body scan at the toes, focusing on any sensations you feel in this area – warmth, tingling, tightness, or maybe nothing.
3. Move Through the Body: Gradually move your focus up from your toes, to your feet, ankles, calves, knees, thighs, and so on, up to the top of your head. Spend a moment in each area, simply observing any sensations.
4. Embrace Non-Judgment: Approach this exercise with an attitude of curiosity and non-judgment. The goal is not to change anything but to simply become aware of the different sensations in each part of your body.

The Role of Body Scan in PTSD Healing

Body Scan Meditation is more than just a relaxation technique; it's a practice of mindful awareness. For those experiencing PTSD, this practice is critical in developing a deeper understanding of how trauma is held in the body and how it affects physical and emotional responses. By noticing and acknowledging bodily sensations, you can break the pattern of disconnection often caused by trauma.

Processing: Reflecting on the Body Scan Experience

- Noticing Body Sensations: Reflect on any surprising or new sensations after completing the meditation. Were there areas of tension, relaxation, discomfort, or perhaps areas where you felt little to no sensation?
- Connecting with the Body: How did spending these moments connecting with your body feel? Many with PTSD find this connection challenging yet ultimately healing.
- Emotional Responses: Did this exercise evoke any emotions? It's not uncommon for body awareness practices to release emotions stored in the body.

This Body Scan Meditation is a step towards embracing a fuller awareness of your body. It encourages a harmonious connection between mind and body, which is essential in the journey of healing from PTSD. As you continue with this practice, you may find it becomes a powerful tool for understanding and managing your responses to stress and trauma.

WEEK 4 DAY 4: MINDFULNESS IN DAILY ACTIVITIES

Objective: The objective for Day 4 is to seamlessly weave mindfulness into the fabric of everyday activities, transforming ordinary, routine tasks into exercises of deep awareness and presence. By consciously engaging in a daily activity with full mindfulness—be it eating, showering, or walking—the aim is to cultivate an enhanced sense of engagement with the present moment, utilizing all senses to fully experience the task at hand. This practice not only serves to enrich mundane aspects of daily life but also acts as a grounding technique for individuals navigating the challenges of PTSD. Through mindful observation and sensory engagement, this exercise promotes a shift from automatic, mindless actions to a state of mindful awareness, offering a counterbalance to the tendencies toward dissociation or hyper-focus on traumatic memories that often accompany PTSD.

Task: Bringing Mindfulness to Routine Activities

On Day 4, we focus on integrating mindfulness into everyday activities. This exercise involves selecting an ordinary daily task – eating, showering, or even walking – and performing it with complete mindfulness. The aim is to immerse yourself entirely in the experience, engaging all your senses and observing every detail.

How to Practice:

1. Choose Your Activity: Select a routine activity you do every day. It could be as simple as brushing teeth, drinking tea, or commuting.
2. Engage Your Senses: As you begin the activity, focus on engaging all your senses. Notice the textures, smells, sounds, tastes, and visual elements.
3. Mindful Observation: Pay attention to every aspect of the activity. For example, if you're eating, notice the colors of your food, the sensation of chewing, the flavors, and even the sounds of utensils.
4. Present Moment Awareness: Keep your attention anchored in the present moment throughout the activity. If your mind wanders, gently bring it back to the task.

The Role of Mindfulness in Everyday Life

Integrating mindfulness into daily activities can transform mundane routines into moments of awareness and appreciation. For those dealing with PTSD, this practice offers a way to stay grounded and present, counteracting tendencies toward dissociation or rumination on traumatic memories.

Processing: Reflecting on the Mindful Experience

- Changed Perspectives: Reflect on how engaging mindfully changed your experience of the activity. Did you find more enjoyment or appreciation in the task?
- New Observations: What details did you notice that you usually overlook? This could be anything from the sensation of water on your skin during a shower to the sound of birds during a walk.
- Emotional and Mental Effects: How did this mindfulness exercise affect your emotional state and thought patterns? Did you feel calmer, more connected, or perhaps even surprised by the experience?

Practicing mindfulness in daily activities trains your mind to stay present and engaged, turning ordinary moments into opportunities for awareness and connection. This practice is especially beneficial in managing PTSD symptoms, offering a sense of calm and grounding in the here and now. As you continue to apply mindfulness to everyday tasks, you may find it becomes a natural and rewarding part of your daily routine.

WEEK 4 DAY 5: GROUNDING EXERCISE

Objective: The goal for Day 5 is to master and apply the 5-4-3-2-1 Grounding Technique, a simple yet profoundly effective method designed to alleviate symptoms of distress commonly experienced by individuals with PTSD. This technique focuses on harnessing the power of sensory awareness to anchor oneself in the present moment, offering a practical strategy to counteract episodes of heightened stress, anxiety, or flashbacks. By methodically shifting attention from distressing thoughts or feelings to the immediate sensory environment, the 5-4-3-2-1 method aims to foster a sense of safety, stability, and groundedness. Practicing this technique encourages a reconnection with the external world, diminishing the intensity of internal distress and promoting a calming, centered state of being.

Task: Engaging in the 5-4-3-2-1 Grounding Technique

How to Practice:

1. Find a Comfortable Space: Sit or stand where you feel safe and can observe your surroundings.
2. Engage Your Senses:
    - 5 Things You Can See: Look around and identify five items you can see. Name each one either out loud or in your mind.
    - 4 Things You Can Touch: Notice and touch four objects around you. Feel their texture, temperature, and shape.

- 3 Things You Can Hear: Close your eyes and identify three sounds in your environment. They can be near or far.
- 2 Things You Can Smell: Acknowledge two things you can smell. If you can't immediately smell anything, think of your favorite scents.
- 1 Thing You Can Taste: Focus on one thing you can taste at the moment or recall a taste you enjoy.
3. Take Your Time: Move through each sense at your own pace, fully experiencing each step.

Grounding techniques like the 5-4-3-2-1 method are particularly beneficial for managing symptoms of PTSD. They provide a practical way to shift attention away from traumatic memories or overwhelming emotions and bring you back to the safety of the present moment.

Processing: Reflecting on the Grounding Experience

- Sense of Presence: After completing the exercise, reflect on how it affected your sense of presence. Did you feel more grounded and connected to the here and now?
- Awareness Shift: Notice any changes in your awareness. Did the exercise help in redirecting your focus from distressing thoughts or sensations?
- Emotional Response: How did you feel during and after the exercise? Grounding techniques can often bring a sense of calm and security, which is vital for those with PTSD.

Grounding exercises like the 5-4-3-2-1 technique are simple yet powerful tools in your PTSD coping toolkit. They can be practiced anywhere, anytime, providing a quick and effective way to manage moments of distress. Incorporating grounding exercises into your daily routine can become a reliable resource for maintaining presence and stability in your journey toward healing.

WEEK 4 DAY 6 LOVING KINDNESS

Objective: On Day 6, the focus is on embracing Loving-Kindness Meditation (LKM) to cultivate feelings of compassion, empathy, and unconditional positive regard towards oneself and others. This meditation technique is invaluable for individuals with PTSD, offering a path to mitigate the often accompanying feelings of isolation, anger, or guilt. By actively directing thoughts of love and kindness first towards oneself and gradually expanding to include loved ones, acquaintances, and eventually all beings, participants aim to foster a sense of interconnectedness and warmth. This practice not only aims to enhance personal well-being and self-acceptance but also encourages a broader perspective of universal compassion, essential for emotional healing and resilience.

Task: Practicing Loving-Kindness Meditation

How to Practice:

1. Find a Quiet Place: Choose a comfortable and peaceful spot to sit undisturbed.
2. Begin with Yourself: Close your eyes and focus on your breath briefly. Then, start directing feelings of love, kindness, and compassion towards yourself. You might use phrases like "May I be happy, may I be healthy, may I be safe, may I live with ease."
3. Expand to Others:
   ○ Loved Ones: Next, visualize people close to you – family, friends – and extend the same sentiments towards them.

- Acquaintances: Think of acquaintances or neutral people in your life and send them loving-kindness.
- All Beings: Finally, extend these feelings to encompass all beings, wishing them happiness, health, safety, and ease.
4. Maintain an Open Heart: As you move through each stage, maintain an open, non-judgmental heart. Allow yourself to genuinely feel the warmth and compassion in your words.

Loving-Kindness Meditation helps to break down barriers of negativity, resentment, or self-criticism that are common in PTSD. By generating positive emotions toward yourself and others, you foster a more compassionate and empathetic outlook, essential for healing and personal growth.

Processing: Reflecting on the Loving-Kindness Experience

- Emotional Shifts: After the meditation, take some time to reflect on how your emotional state changed throughout the exercise. Did you feel a sense of warmth, peace, or connection?
- Responses to Different Groups: Observe the feelings that arose when directing kindness towards different groups. Was it easier to feel compassion for some than for others? How did it feel to extend kindness beyond your immediate circle?
- Impact on Self-Perception: Consider how practicing loving-kindness towards yourself influenced your self-perception. Did it challenge any negative beliefs or feelings you hold about yourself?

Loving-Kindness Meditation is a journey towards cultivating a compassionate heart. As you continue to practice LKM, you may find a growing sense of connection to yourself and the world around you, a vital element in the recovery from PTSD. This practice not only soothes the mind but also heals the heart, paving the way for a more empathetic and connected existence.

WEEK 4 DAY 7: REFLECTION AND PLANNING

Objective: The goal for Day 7 is to engage in a reflective process, taking stock of the mindfulness practices introduced throughout the week and contemplating their integration into daily life for enduring benefits. This day is dedicated to assessing the impact of each technique on managing PTSD symptoms, understanding their applicability in various life situations, and devising a plan for their continued use. Through this reflective exercise, you aim to consolidate your learning, recognize the value of mindfulness in your healing journey, and commit to incorporating these practices into your routine as a sustainable component of your overall strategy for managing PTSD. This step back offers a broader view of how mindfulness can support emotional regulation, enhance well-being, and foster resilience, ensuring that the insights and skills developed this week are not just momentary gains but foundational elements of a long-term approach to healing and growth.

Task: Reflecting on the Week's Mindfulness Practices

How to Reflect and Plan:

1. Review the Week: Revisit each mindfulness practice from the week. Recall how each exercise made you feel and the insights you gained from them.

2. Assess the Fit: Consider how each practice could fit into your daily routine. Can mindful breathing be a morning ritual? Could progressive relaxation help unwind before bed?
3. Set Intentions: Decide how to incorporate these practices into your life. It might involve scheduling specific times for meditation or using grounding techniques during moments of stress.

The Importance of Mindfulness in PTSD Recovery

Mindfulness practices offer a profound way to manage the symptoms of PTSD. They help cultivate presence, reduce stress, and enhance emotional regulation. By integrating these practices into your daily life, you're equipping yourself with tools to combat the challenges of PTSD.

Processing: Reflecting on Personal Resonance and Long-Term Benefits

- Personal Resonance: Consider which practices resonated most with you. Was there a particular exercise that felt especially soothing or enlightening? Identify the practices that felt most natural and beneficial to you.
- Long-Term Benefits: Reflect on how these mindfulness practices can benefit your PTSD journey in the long run. How can they help manage triggers, reduce anxiety, or improve your overall well-being?
- Commitment to Practice: Think about your commitment to continuing these practices. How can you ensure that they become a consistent part of your life? Are there any adjustments needed to make them more accessible or enjoyable?

As we draw this week to a close, it's important to recognize that the essence of mindfulness transcends beyond mere exercises; it represents a profound shift in how we engage with our inner and outer worlds. The mindfulness practices introduced this week aren't just tools for managing PTSD symptoms; they are gateways to a deeper understanding of ourselves and our experiences.

The journey through mindfulness that you've embarked upon this week has the potential to bring about transformative changes in your life. These practices are designed not only to alleviate the immediate symptoms of PTSD but also to foster long-term resilience and emotional balance. They help cultivate a heightened awareness, allowing you to approach your experiences with greater clarity and equanimity.

As you move forward, consider how mindfulness can be woven into the fabric of your daily routine. It's about creating moments of presence amidst the chaos of everyday life. Whether through a few minutes of focused breathing, a mindful walk, or a reflective pause during the day, these practices can become your anchor, helping you stay grounded in distress.

Incorporating mindfulness into your life is more than just a coping mechanism for PTSD; it is a pathway to holistic healing and personal growth. It encourages a compassionate and non-judgmental relationship with your thoughts and emotions, fostering a deeper sense of self-acceptance. This compassionate stance can be a powerful catalyst for healing, transforming how you relate to your trauma and yourself.

As we conclude this week, let's reflect on the journey ahead. Mindfulness is a lifelong companion, offering guidance and solace as you navigate the complexities of PTSD and recovery. Its benefits extend far beyond the confines of this program, providing you with a sustainable approach to managing stress, enhancing emotional regulation, and ultimately leading you toward a path of healing, resilience, and inner peace.

Embrace this journey with an open heart and mind, knowing that each mindful step is a step towards a more balanced, peaceful, and fulfilling life.

| 9 |

Emotional Processing

Navigating the Emotional Terrain of PTSD

As we enter Week 5 of our PTSD free journey, we address emotional processing and awareness. This stage is fundamental on the path to PTSD recovery, as it involves delving into the intricate and often challenging world of our emotions. Trauma can profoundly affect our emotional landscape, leading to feelings that are either intensely overwhelming or, conversely, numbingly distant. This week, we commit to unraveling these complex emotional threads to build a deeper, more nuanced understanding of how our traumatic experiences have shaped our emotional responses.

Embracing a Multifaceted Approach to Emotional Healing

To guide us through this journey, we will be embracing a blend of therapeutic modalities, each offering unique insights and tools for emotional healing:

- Internal Family Systems (IFS): IFS provides a robust framework for exploring the diverse emotional parts within us. It helps us identify and interact with various aspects of ourselves, each carrying distinct emotions related to our trauma. Through IFS, we will learn to approach these parts with empathy and understanding, creating a harmonious internal environment conducive to healing.

- Cognitive Processing Therapy (CPT): CPT offers a structured approach to challenge and modify the unhelpful beliefs and emotions stemming from trauma. It encourages us to dissect and reconstruct our traumatic narratives, allowing us to reshape our emotional responses more adaptively and healthily.
- Transpersonal Psychology: This modality expands our exploration of the spiritual and existential dimensions of our emotions. Transpersonal Psychology encourages us to delve into the deeper meanings and existential questions that arise from our emotional experiences, offering a broader perspective that transcends conventional psychological boundaries.

Week 5 is an emotional exploration to clarity and connection. Engaging with these diverse modalities aims to foster a more profound awareness of our emotions, understand their origins and impacts, and learn how to process them healthily and constructively. This week is about transforming our relationship with our emotions, moving from fear or avoidance to acceptance and growth. As we progress, we will discover how to navigate our emotional world with greater confidence, resilience, and self-compassion, paving the way for a more holistic and empowering recovery from PTSD.

The Importance of Emotional Processing in PTSD

Trauma, by its very nature, can disrupt our standard emotional processing. It often leaves individuals either disengaged from their emotions or overwhelmed by a torrent of feelings. This disconnection or over-saturation can become a significant barrier in the path to recovery from PTSD. Emotions, when not processed or understood, can manifest in various forms—from physical symptoms to behavioral changes, impacting quality of life.

The importance of emotional processing in the context of PTSD cannot be overstated. It involves more than just acknowledging these feelings; it's about understanding their origins, recognizing their impact, and learning healthy ways to express and manage them. This week, we aim to create a nurturing environment for you to safely reconnect with your emotions, especially those suppressed or misinterpreted due to traumatic experiences.

In this process, it's essential to establish a safe space, both internally and externally, where you can explore these complex emotional landscapes without judgment or fear. This safe space is where you can begin to untangle the intricate web of feelings and make sense of them. Whether fear, anger, guilt, or sadness, each emotion carries valuable information about our experiences and ourselves.

Engaging in emotional processing helps gain valuable understanding and compassion for ourselves. This understanding is crucial for healing, allowing us to transform our relationship with our emotions. Instead of viewing them as overwhelming or threatening, we can begin to see them as guides that help us navigate our healing journey. Processing these emotions gives us the power to rewrite our internal narratives, moving from a state of victimhood to one of empowerment and resilience.

As we move through this week, remember that emotional processing is a journey, not a destination. It's about developing the tools and skills to continuously engage with our emotional world in a way that supports our healing and growth. This journey is an integral part of recovering from PTSD, leading us toward a more balanced, peaceful, and fulfilling life.

Internal Family Systems (IFS) therapy introduces a transformative approach to understanding and managing our emotional responses, especially in the context of PTSD. IFS posits that our psyche is not a singular entity but a complex system of various parts, each with unique feelings, memories, and perspectives. These parts, often formed in response to life experiences, especially traumatic ones, play distinct roles in our internal world.

Week 5 Objectives with IFS:

1. Identifying Emotional Parts Impacted by Trauma:
    ○ This week, we embark on a journey to identify the different parts of us affected by trauma. These parts may present as fearful, angry, ashamed, or numb entities within our psyche.
    ○ Through guided introspection, you will learn to recognize these parts, acknowledge their presence, and understand their origins.
2. Understanding the Roles and Intentions of These Parts:
    ○ Each part, no matter how painful or challenging it may seem, originated with a purpose – often to protect or cope with difficult experiences. This week, you'll explore the roles these parts have assumed in your life.
    ○ By unraveling their intentions, you can see these parts not as adversaries but as aspects of yourself that once helped you survive and cope.
3. Approaching Parts with Compassion and Curiosity:
    ○ A critical aspect of IFS therapy is approaching these parts with compassion and curiosity rather than judgment or fear. This approach fosters a nurturing internal environment conducive to healing.
    ○ You will engage in exercises designed to help you communicate with these parts, offering them understanding and care, and in doing so, begin the process of healing and integration.

By exploring these emotional parts through the lens of IFS, you gain deep insight of how your emotional responses to trauma have been shaped. As you learn to engage with these parts empathetically, you enable a reintegration of your internal system. This reintegration fosters a more harmonious internal dialogue, reduces internal conflicts, and helps you achieve emotional balance and wholeness.

Week 5 with IFS is about building a bridge of understanding and compassion to the various parts of ourselves. This process not only aids in the immediate alleviation of PTSD symptoms but also paves the way for long-term emotional resilience and integration. It's a journey toward recognizing and embracing the entirety of our emotional experience, leading to a more cohesive and empowered sense of self.

Transpersonal Psychology: A Deeper Emotional Understanding

Transpersonal Psychology offers a distinct and expansive perspective that enriches our understanding of the human emotional landscape, especially in navigating the aftermath of trauma. This approach transcends traditional psychological boundaries by incorporating spiritual and transcendent dimensions into the exploration of human experience. It extends psychology's reach beyond the personal to include broader aspects of existence, providing a holistic framework for understanding how we relate to the transcendent and the interconnectedness of all life. By acknowledging these dimensions, transpersonal psychology fosters a comprehensive appreciation of human emotions, connecting them with our deeper sense of self and our relationship to the broader universe.

Historically rooted in the works of pioneers like William James, Carl Jung, and Abraham Maslow, transpersonal psychology emerged in the late 1960s as a response to the limitations of conventional psychological theories. These founders sought to address aspects of the human experience that were ignored by mainstream psychology, such as spirituality, peak experiences, and the potential for human transformation.

Philosophically, transpersonal psychology draws on ancient wisdom traditions, integrating insights from Buddhism, Taoism, Sufism, and other spiritual practices with contemporary psychological understanding. This synthesis offers a more inclusive view of the mind, one that considers our capacities for transcendence, spiritual awakening, and unity with the larger web of existence.

Research in transpersonal psychology has explored various practices for fostering spiritual awareness and psychological growth, such as meditation, mindfulness, and altered states of consciousness. Evidence suggests these practices can lead to significant improvements in psychological well-being, resilience against stress, and a greater sense of meaning and purpose in life. Studies have highlighted the benefits of transpersonal approaches in treating PTSD, depression, and anxiety, showing how these practices can help individuals reconnect with their inner selves, cultivate emotional healing, and foster a sense of connectedness with others and the world.

Transpersonal psychology enriches our understanding of the human psyche by integrating the spiritual and transcendent with the psychological. It offers valuable insights and practices for healing and growth, especially for those recovering from trauma, by emphasizing the importance of our connection to something greater than ourselves. This approach not only aids in healing but also in the pursuit of a more fulfilling, connected, and spiritually informed life.

Week 5 Objectives with Transpersonal Psychology:

1. Exploring the Deeper Meanings Behind Emotional Responses:
   ○ This week, we delve into the profound meanings and lessons embedded in our emotional responses to trauma. We will explore how these emotions are psychological reactions and can be gateways to deeper self-understanding and spiritual growth.
   ○ Exercises will guide you to uncover your emotions' hidden messages and insights, revealing how they are integral to your personal and spiritual journey.
2. Engaging in Practices to Connect with Inner Wisdom and Resilience:

- Transpersonal Psychology emphasizes the importance of connecting with our inner wisdom and resilience. This connection is vital for healing from PTSD, as it taps into our innate strength and ability to overcome adversity.
- Practices such as guided meditations, reflective journaling, and mindfulness exercises will be introduced to help you forge this connection, enhancing your ability to listen to and trust your inner voice.

3. Developing a Holistic Understanding of Our Emotions:
  - This week's journey is about transcending traditional psychological perspectives and embracing a holistic view of our emotions. We'll explore how our feelings are interwoven with our spiritual beliefs, life's purpose, and our broader existential narratives.
  - Through various activities and reflections, you'll learn to see your emotions as reactions to trauma and as integral components of your entire being—mind, body, and spirit.

Transpersonal Psychology is an invitation to explore the depths of your emotions in the context of a broader human experience. This exploration is about understanding and processing emotions and finding meaning, connection, and a sense of wholeness. As we integrate these insights into our healing process, we open ourselves to a more enriched and fulfilling journey toward recovery from PTSD.

Week 5 is about building a bridge between our emotional experiences and our conscious understanding. By exploring the depths of our emotional parts through IFS and gaining a broader perspective through Transpersonal Psychology, we aim to achieve a more profound emotional awareness. This process is about managing symptoms and empowering ourselves with the tools and insights necessary for a deeper, more meaningful healing journey.

Week 5 Self-Help Guide

Week 5 is about deepening your understanding of your emotional world and its connections to a more expansive human experience. Through IFS and Transpersonal Psychology, you're encouraged to embrace a holistic view of your emotions, seeing them as integral to your healing journey. As you progress through these exercises, you are laying the groundwork for a more profound and compassionate relationship with yourself.

WEEK 5 DAY 1: IDENTIFYING EMOTIONAL PARTS (IFS)

Objective: The goal for today is to engage in deep introspection to identify and understand the diverse emotional responses that have been influenced or shaped by your traumatic experiences. This task encourages you to dedicate time to quiet reflection, allowing you to explore the full spectrum of emotions—ranging from fear and anger to sadness, guilt, and perhaps other feelings that have yet to be fully recognized. By examining how these emotions have served as reactions to your trauma, you aim to gain a clearer understanding of your internal emotional landscape post-trauma, facilitating a pathway towards acknowledging, accepting, and eventually integrating these emotional parts for healing and personal growth.

Task: Reflecting on Emotional Parts Shaped by Trauma

Processing: Journaling Emotional Expressions

- Journaling Activity: Once you have identified these emotional parts, your task is to journal about them. Write down each emotional part you have identified and describe them. How do they feel? What characterizes them?
- Daily Life Reflection: Reflect on how these emotional parts manifest in your everyday life. Do they influence your reactions to certain situations? Do they affect your interactions with others? How do they impact your decision-making or your mood throughout the day?

- Emotional Patterns: Identify any patterns or triggers that bring these emotional parts to the forefront. Are there specific times, places, or people that tend to evoke these feelings more strongly?

Goal for Today

The goal for today is to begin acknowledging and understanding the different emotional facets of your experience with trauma. By identifying and articulating these emotions, you're taking the first step toward processing them more healthily and constructively. Remember, this exercise is about observation and recognition, not judgment. Be kind and compassionate to yourself as you explore these emotional parts.

WEEK 5 DAY 2: DIALOGUE WITH EMOTIONAL PARTS (IFS)

Objective: Leveraging the insights gained from Day 1, today's task is centered on engaging in a deeper, more introspective conversation with one of the emotional parts you previously identified. The aim is to select an emotion that holds significant resonance or impact on your daily life, such as fear, anger, sadness, guilt, or shame. By initiating a dialogue with this emotional part, you intend to explore its origins, understand its purpose, and recognize how it influences your thoughts, behaviors, and interactions. This process is designed to foster a greater understanding and acceptance of this aspect of your emotional landscape, facilitating a path toward healing and personal growth by integrating this knowledge into your broader sense of self.

Task: Set aside a quiet time and space where you can focus without interruption. Close your eyes and imagine this emotional part as a distinct entity within you. Start an internal dialogue with this part:

- Ask about its fears: What is it afraid of? What worst-case scenarios does it imagine?
- Inquire about its needs: What does this part need from you or others to feel safe or heard?
- Understand its role: Why does it think it's present in your life? What purpose does it serve? How does it believe it's helping you?

Processing: Reflective Journaling

- Journaling Activity: After completing your dialogue, take time to journal about the experience. Write down the questions you asked and the responses you felt or imagined from this emotional part.
- Insights and Understanding: Reflect on what you learned from this dialogue. What insights did you gain about how this emotional part has been coping with your trauma? Did you discover any surprising aspects or perspectives of this part of yourself?
- Emotional Response: Also, note how engaging in this dialogue made you feel. Did it bring up any new emotions? Did you feel a sense of understanding, compassion, or perhaps discomfort in confronting this part?

Goal for Today

Today's objective is to deepen your understanding of your emotional landscape by actively engaging with it. This exercise aims to foster empathy and insight into how different parts of you have been managing the effects of your trauma. By doing so, you're acknowledging these parts and beginning to integrate them more healthily into your overall sense of self.

WEEK 5 DAY 3: EXPLORING DEEPER MEANINGS (TRANSPERSONAL PSYCHOLOGY)

Objective: The aim for today is to delve into the deeper meanings and potential lessons contained within your emotional responses to trauma, through the lens of Transpersonal Psychology. This exploration is not just about understanding your immediate emotional reactions, but also about uncovering insights into your deeper self, life path, and spiritual journey that these emotions may signify. By examining your feelings in the context of Transpersonal Psychology, you seek to transcend the surface-level experiences and tap into a more profound understanding of how these emotional responses connect with and inform your broader existential and spiritual existence. This process is intended to foster personal growth, enhance self-awareness, and contribute to a more integrated and holistic perspective on healing from trauma.

- Select one powerful emotional response you have experienced in relation to your trauma. This could be a persistent feeling that has been challenging to understand or manage.
- Spend some quiet time reflecting on this emotion. Ask yourself, "What might this feeling be trying to teach or reveal to me?" Consider its role or purpose beyond just being a reaction to a traumatic event.

Processing: Connecting Emotions with Broader Life Experiences

- Journaling Activity: After your reflection, write about your insights. Write down your thoughts on what this emotion might symbolize or indicate in the context of your broader life journey.
- Life Experiences and Beliefs: Explore how this emotion is interconnected with your other life experiences or spiritual beliefs. Does it reflect a recurring theme or challenge in your life? How does it align with or challenge your spiritual or existential views?
- Patterns and Growth: Reflect on any patterns or growth opportunities this emotion might point to. Is it highlighting areas where you may need to focus more attention, change your perspective, or embrace personal growth?

Goal for Today

Today aims to deepen your understanding of your emotional responses by exploring their significance. This exercise is not just about managing or reducing the intensity of the emotion but rather about gaining a broader, more insightful perspective on what these feelings signify in the grand scheme of your personal and spiritual development. It's about finding meaning in the midst of emotional challenges and using that understanding as a tool for healing and personal growth.

WEEK 5 DAY 4: CONNECTING WITH INNER WISDOM (TRANSPERSONAL PSYCHOLOGY)

Objective: Day 4 is dedicated to immersing yourself in the tranquil depths of your inner being through a practice of guided meditation, inspired by the principles of Transpersonal Psychology. This meditation aims to forge a deeper connection with your inner wisdom, tapping into the wellspring of guidance, clarity, and insight that resides within. By engaging in this meditative journey, you seek to access and harmonize with this profound source of internal knowledge, facilitating a greater understanding of yourself and your path to healing. The goal is to cultivate a sense of peace, self-awareness, and alignment with your core essence, empowering you to navigate life's challenges with a grounded and enlightened perspective.

- Find a quiet, comfortable space where you won't be disturbed. You may sit or lie down in a relaxed yet alert position.
- Select a guided meditation focused on connecting with inner wisdom. Various online resources, including audio recordings and written scripts, can guide you through this process.
- As you meditate, allow yourself to be open to whatever arises. There's no right or wrong here; it's about being present and receptive to your inner experience.

Processing: Reflective Journaling Post-Meditation

- Journaling Activity: After completing your meditation, take some time to journal about the experience. Write down any messages, feelings, or insights that came up during the meditation.
- Emerging Insights: Reflect on what these insights might mean for you in the context of your healing journey. Did you receive any intuitive guidance or clarity about your emotions or trauma?
- Emotional and Spiritual Resonance: Note how connecting with your inner wisdom made you feel. Did it bring a sense of peace, empowerment, or perhaps raised more questions? How does this connection impact your perspective on your emotional healing process?

Goal for Today

Today's goal is to foster a deeper connection with your inner self, tapping into the reservoir of wisdom that lies within. This practice is essential in the context of PTSD, as it can provide you with unique insights and guidance tailored to your healing process. By regularly engaging with your inner wisdom, you can better understand your emotions, trauma, and the path forward toward healing and wholeness.

WEEK 5 DAY 5: INTEGRATING EMOTIONAL PARTS (IFS)

Objective: On Day 5, the focus shifts towards an Internal Family Systems (IFS) inspired exercise designed to cultivate harmony and understanding among the diverse emotional parts identified in previous sessions. Through a guided visualization process, this task aims to promote a sense of unity and compassion within your internal ecosystem, encouraging dialogue and reconciliation between conflicting parts. The ultimate goal is to create a more integrated sense of self, where all emotional aspects can coexist with mutual respect and empathy, contributing to a healthier, more cohesive internal landscape conducive to healing and personal development.

- Find a quiet and comfortable space to relax and focus without interruptions.
- Close your eyes and visualize a safe, peaceful space where all your emotional parts can gather. Imagine each part – fear, anger, sadness, guilt, etc., arriving and taking a place in this space.
- Begin the process of encouraging a dialogue among these parts. Visualize them sharing their experiences, fears, and needs with each other.
- Act as a compassionate mediator in this meeting. Encourage understanding and empathy among your emotional parts. Help them see how they are all integral parts of you and how each has played a role in your response to trauma.

Processing: Reflecting on Internal Integration

- Reflective Journaling: After completing the visualization, take some time to write about the experience. Write down how the interaction between your emotional parts unfolded. Did they find common ground? Were there moments of conflict or resolution?
- Emotional Resonance: Reflect on how this exercise made you feel. Did it bring peace, clarity, or perhaps an understanding of the complexities within you? Note any emotions or sensations that arose during the process.
- Sense of Resolution: Consider whether this exercise brought a sense of resolution or peace to any internal conflicts. How does this harmonious meeting impact your view of your emotional parts and your overall healing journey?

Goal for Today

Today's exercise aims to create a sense of unity and compassion within your internal system. Visualizing a harmonious meeting of your emotional parts will facilitate an environment of understanding and empathy within yourself. This process is key to integrating these parts into a more cohesive and healthy self-concept, essential for ongoing healing and growth from PTSD.

WEEK 5 DAY 6: HOLISTIC EMOTIONAL REFLECTION (TRANSPERSONAL PSYCHOLOGY)

Objective: Day 6 is dedicated to adopting the holistic view of Transpersonal Psychology to examine the intricate interconnections between our emotions, physical sensations, thoughts, and spiritual beliefs. This exploration is aimed at crafting a comprehensive understanding of how these diverse elements of our being intertwine and mutually influence one another, especially in the realms of trauma and healing. By engaging in this exercise, you aspire to gain insights into the complex dynamics of your inner life, recognizing how each aspect contributes to your overall experience of trauma and your journey towards recovery. The goal is to foster a deeper sense of self-awareness and integration, empowering you to navigate your healing process with a more informed and holistic perspective.

- Set aside time for quiet reflection. Begin by focusing on a particular emotion prominent in your PTSD experience.
- As you concentrate on this emotion, pay attention to any physical sensations in your body. Note where these sensations occur and their nature (e.g., tension, warmth, restlessness).
- Then, reflect on the thoughts or thought patterns that accompany this emotion. Are there recurring themes, memories, or beliefs linked to it?

- Finally, consider how this emotion connects with your broader spiritual beliefs or existential views. Does it challenge, affirm, or inform these beliefs?

Processing: Creating a Holistic Emotional Map

- Mind Map or Journaling: Create a mind map or write a detailed journal entry that visually or descriptively illustrates your identified connections. Show how your emotional experience is linked to physical sensations, thoughts, and spiritual beliefs.
- Analyzing the Impact: Reflect on how these interconnected aspects of your emotions affect your overall well-being. Do specific thoughts intensify your emotional response? Do physical sensations bring certain emotions to the forefront? How do your spiritual beliefs provide context or understanding for these emotions?
- Holistic Insights: Consider what new insights or understandings emerge from viewing your emotions in this interconnected way. How does this holistic perspective influence your approach to managing or healing from your trauma?

Goal for Today

Today's exercise aims to foster a deeper understanding of the multifaceted nature of your emotions. By recognizing the complex interplay between your emotions, physical body, thoughts, and spiritual beliefs, you can gain a more nuanced and comprehensive view of your emotional landscape. This holistic awareness is key to navigating the healing process more effectively, allowing for a more integrated and balanced approach to recovering from PTSD.

| 10 |

Building Coping Skills and Resilience

Welcome to Week 6 of our transformative journey. This week the focus will be on fortifying your coping skills and resilience. Healing from PTSD is not just about understanding or processing your trauma; it's equally about learning how to effectively manage the day-to-day challenges that arise because of your experiences.

This week aims to equip you with practical, effective strategies to help you navigate these challenges more easily and confidently. To achieve this, we'll be tapping into the potent techniques of Trauma-Focused Cognitive Behavioral Therapy (TF-CBT) and integrating the empowering principles of Positive Psychology.

TF-CBT: This modality offers a treasure trove of coping mechanisms specifically designed for trauma survivors. You'll learn to identify and modify unhelpful thought patterns and behaviors, utilize stress management techniques, and adopt problem-solving skills tailored to your unique experiences and needs.

Positive Psychology: Here, we'll shift our lens to focus on your inherent strengths and virtues. By emphasizing the positive aspects of your life and personality, we can foster resilience – the ability to bounce back and maintain mental health amidst life's challenges. You'll learn to recognize and harness your strengths through engaging exercises, practice gratitude, and build a resilient mindset.

This week is about learning effective techniques and integrating skills into your daily life to create a stronger, more resilient version of yourself. By the end of this week, you'll have a deeper appreciation of your inner strength and a robust set of tools to help you manage the ongoing journey of healing from PTSD.

Delving into Adaptive Coping through TF-CBT

In the initial part of Week 6, our goal is to master adaptive coping strategies utilizing the Trauma-Focused Cognitive Behavioral Therapy (TF-CBT) framework. These coping strategies are methods to manage stress and lifelines that enable us to navigate through the stormy seas of difficult emotions with more grace and efficacy. TF-CBT provides a diverse array of practical tools, each designed to meet the unique challenges faced by trauma survivors, ultimately aiming to diminish the severity of PTSD symptoms and enhance daily functioning.

Diverse Coping Techniques

In our exploration of the diverse coping techniques in Week 6, we initiate a journey with a primary focus on a process known as cognitive restructuring. This transformative process is carefully crafted to assist you in identifying and altering negative thought patterns that can often linger due to traumatic experiences.

Understanding Cognitive Patterns: Our first task is understanding the specific thought patterns contributing to stress and anxiety. These thought patterns may encompass beliefs about yourself, others, or the world at large, and they often bear the marks of your past traumatic experiences. We lay the foundation for positive change by delving into these cognitive patterns.

Techniques for Reframing Thoughts: The heart of cognitive restructuring lies in the methods for reframing your thoughts. You will acquire the tools and skills to challenge and transform these negative beliefs into more positive and realistic thoughts. This process involves engaging in activities like journaling, keeping thought records, and guided reflections, all of which encourage the development of a new perspective on the challenges you face.

Long-term Impact on Healing: The significance of altering these deep-seated thought patterns cannot be overstated. Through cognitive restructuring, you can significantly reduce feelings of distress and cultivate a more positive outlook on life. This cognitive shift is not just a momentary change but a fundamental step in your journey toward recovery and healing.

Week 6 offers you the chance to explore diverse coping techniques, with a central focus on cognitive restructuring. This process of thought transformation holds the power to reshape your perception of yourself, others, and the world around you. As you engage with these techniques and integrate them into your daily life, you take a significant stride toward a more positive and empowered existence on your path to recovery.

Stress Management and Problem-Solving Skills

As we progress, our journey of exploration and growth takes a deeper dive into stress management and problem-solving skills. These skills are instrumental in your path toward effectively managing stressors related to PTSD and enhancing your overall well-being.

Stress Management Techniques: This week, you will embark on a journey to discover various stress management techniques. These methods help you maintain calm and grounding when confronting triggers or challenging situations. You'll explore relaxation techniques that soothe the mind and body, engage in mindfulness exercises that promote present-moment awareness, and learn how to identify and proactively prepare for potential stressors that may arise in your life.

Building Problem-Solving Abilities: Besides stress management, we significantly focus on developing your problem-solving abilities. Confronting and navigating the challenges posed by PTSD requires a strategic approach. This week, you'll delve into the art of breaking down complex problems into manageable parts. You'll learn to set realistic goals and explore a repertoire of different strategies for effectively tackling the issues that come your way. These problem-solving skills are not only valuable in managing PTSD but also in various aspects of your life.

Real-life Application: The essence of these skills lies in their real-life application. They serve as tools for reducing the impact of PTSD on your daily life. By becoming proficient in stress management and problem-solving, you can regain control and confidence in the face of adversity. These skills empower you to navigate challenges more effectively and to address stressors, ultimately enhancing your overall well-being proactively.

In Week 6, we invite you to embrace the opportunity to acquire and refine stress management and problem-solving skills. When integrated into your daily life, these skills contribute to a more peaceful existence and signify a crucial step toward healing and personal growth.

Personalized Coping Toolkit

In Week 6 of our self-help guide, we place significant emphasis on the creation of a personalized coping toolkit, which plays a crucial role for managing PTSD effectively and improving your overall well-being.

Customization to Individual Needs: We invite you to explore various coping techniques this week. This exploration lets you discern which strategies resonate most with you and align best with your unique circumstances. This customization process ensures your toolkit is finely tailored to address your needs and challenges.

Hands-on Practice and Application: The process of assembling your personalized coping toolkit is experiential and practical. We strongly emphasize actively practicing these coping skills in real-life situations. This hands-on approach ensures that the techniques you learn are not merely theoretical concepts but are genuinely effective when applied to the real challenges you encounter.

Resource for Ongoing Management: Your personalized coping toolkit is a valuable and enduring resource in your ongoing healing journey. Within this toolkit, you will find an array of strategies designed to help you manage stress, reframe negative thoughts, and solve problems— essential components in effectively managing PTSD. This toolkit remains at your disposal, providing guidance and support as you navigate the complexities of PTSD beyond this program.

By the conclusion of Week 6, you will have amassed a robust set of tools and skills. These tools empower you to confront the challenges of PTSD with resilience and inner strength. This week transcends mere learning of techniques; it's about seamlessly integrating these skills into your daily life. This integration paves the way for long-term healing and personal growth, marking a significant step toward a healthier and more fulfilling life.

Tailoring Strategies to Your Needs

Week 6 of our program emphasizes the customization and personalization of coping strategies derived from TF-CBT (Trauma-Focused Cognitive-Behavioral Therapy). The effectiveness of these techniques hinges on their relevance and applicability to your unique situation. This week is dedicated to ensuring that the coping strategies you learn are broadly effective and finely tuned to resonate with your individual experiences, preferences, and lifestyle.

We recognize that everyone's journey with trauma is unique. As such, the coping strategies we explore during this week are designed to be as diverse as the individuals who use them. You will be guided to reflect on your personal history, unique challenges, and how trauma has impacted your life. This introspection will help identify which techniques align best with your specific needs and preferences.

Furthermore, it's essential that the coping strategies we introduce integrate seamlessly into your everyday life. We encourage you to consider your daily routine, responsibilities, and lifestyle when selecting and adapting these techniques. Whether it's a quick breathing exercise that can be done at your desk during a busy workday or a nightly journaling practice before bed, the goal is to make these strategies a natural and manageable part of your day.

This week's focus goes beyond just learning these strategies; we also emphasize their sustainable application. You will be supported in developing a plan to incorporate these techniques into your daily routine in a manageable and realistic way. This might include setting aside specific times for practice, creating reminders, or finding creative ways to integrate these strategies into your existing habits and routines.

As you implement these strategies, there will be an ongoing emphasis on adaptation and evaluation. We encourage you to continuously assess the effectiveness of each technique and adjust as needed. This trial, evaluation, and adjustment process is crucial to developing a set of coping skills tailored to your needs.

Week 6 is designed to provide you with various coping strategies while equipping you with the skills to adapt and integrate them into your life in an effective and sustainable way. This personalized approach ensures that the coping skills you develop are more than just techniques; they become integral tools for managing PTSD and enhancing your overall well-being.

Building a Strong Foundation

In the process of managing PTSD, coping strategies play a pivotal role. They are more than just a collection of skills; they form the solid groundwork upon which your ongoing healing and personal development will flourish.

This foundation, akin to the cornerstone of a sturdy structure, is integral to your journey toward recovery. These coping skills are the building blocks of a deeper, long-term healing process. By mastering these techniques, you gain the strength to navigate the complexities of PTSD with increased confidence and control.

Perhaps one of the most profound aspects of this foundation lies in its ability to change your perspective on the challenges posed by PTSD. Rather than perceiving these challenges as insurmountable obstacles, you'll begin to see them as opportunities for growth and empowerment. This shift in mindset is crucial in cultivating resilience and taking a proactive approach to your recovery.

The skills you acquire through this process are empowering in themselves. They equip you with practical and effective methods to address the symptoms of PTSD, reducing feelings of helplessness and vulnerability. This empowerment marks a significant step toward regaining agency in your life, enabling you to make decisions and take actions that promote your well-being.

These coping strategies are not confined to a therapeutic context; they are designed to seamlessly integrate into your daily life. This integration ensures that the benefits of what you've learned extend into every facet of your everyday experience. It enhances your ability to cope with stress, regulate emotions, and maintain a balanced state of mind.

Moreover, this foundation serves as a platform for future learning and growth. As you progress on your healing journey, the skills and insights acquired during this phase will serve as a solid base. They will be expanded upon and deepened, providing a springboard to explore more advanced coping strategies and therapeutic techniques.

Week 6 of this program will assist you in developing a comprehensive toolkit of coping strategies. These strategies not only address the symptoms of PTSD but also elevate your overall quality of life.

This strong foundation sets the stage for ongoing healing, growth, and personal empowerment.

Positive Psychology

The latter part of Week 6 embraces the enriching principles of Positive Psychology. This approach goes beyond traditional methods, focusing on cultivating well-being and resilience, which are essential for overcoming adversities associated with PTSD.

Positive Psychology operates on a unique premise: emphasizing strengths, virtues, and the positive aspect of life is as crucial as addressing weaknesses or problems. Throughout this week, there's a deep exploration into how leveraging your unique strengths can profoundly influence your journey toward healing from PTSD. Recognizing and appreciating your inherent qualities is more than an exercise; it's a journey to rediscover a sense of empowerment and self-efficacy deeply embedded within you.

A significant component of this week is dedicated to exercises that aid in identifying your strengths. You will delve into a process of self-reflection, assessment activities, and discussions, all designed to bring these strengths into sharp focus. The objective is to recognize these strengths and how they can be applied in your daily life to bolster resilience. This involves a transformative process where you learn to view yourself through a lens of capability and potential.

Gratitude journaling emerges as a critical exercise during this week. This simple yet powerful practice involves taking time each day to reflect on and write down aspects of life you're grateful for. It's a practice that has been shown to shift focus from trauma and negativity to appreciation and positivity. This shift is significant, aiding in emotional balance and offering a new perspective on life.

Alongside gratitude, journaling is a strength-based reflection. This involves taking a moment to acknowledge and appreciate your abilities and achievements, no matter how small. This practice is about recognizing the victories in your journey, reinforcing a positive self-image, and building confidence in your capability to handle life's challenges.

Moreover, this week includes engaging in various resilience-building practices. These exercises and transformative practices are designed to strengthen your capacity to withstand and recover from stressful situations. These include mindfulness techniques, visualization exercises, and setting achievable goals. Each of these practices aims to enhance your resilience, providing you with tools to face challenges with renewed strength and a positive outlook.

As we wrap up Week 6, you stand at a pivotal point in your journey of healing from PTSD. This week has been about much more than learning new skills; it's been about a transformation in how you approach the challenges posed by PTSD and life itself. You've embarked on a path that leads to effective coping and a profound understanding of your inner resilience.

Throughout this week, you've engaged with various coping strategies tailored to your unique experiences and needs. You've learned to challenge and reframe negative thought patterns, developed techniques for stress management, and honed your problem-solving skills. These tools are theoretical concepts and practical, real-world strategies you can call upon in times of need.

Moreover, the latter part of the week opened your eyes to the principles of Positive Psychology, emphasizing the importance of focusing on strengths and virtues. This perspective shift—from a focus on trauma and weaknesses to one of appreciation and potential—is a critical step in your healing journey. You've learned to recognize and celebrate your strengths, practice gratitude, and engage in resilience-building exercises that enhance your ability to bounce back from adversities.

The culmination of these experiences provides you with a more comprehensive understanding of how to navigate the often-turbulent waters of PTSD. But beyond this, it enriches your life in broader, more profound ways. The skills and insights you've gained this week significantly enhance your overall life satisfaction and well-being. They offer a lens through which you can view your trauma and your entire life experience with greater clarity, positivity, and hope.

Integrating these coping strategies and resilience-building practices into your daily routine is key as you move forward. Each day presents an opportunity to apply what you've learned, strengthen your coping mechanisms, and build resilience. This ongoing practice empowers you to face life's challenges with a renewed sense of confidence, stability, and optimism.

Week 6 has set the stage for continuous growth and empowerment. You are now equipped with a toolkit that not only aids in your recovery from PTSD but also serves as a foundation for a more fulfilled and resilient life. As you progress through this journey, remember that the skills you've developed are a testament to your strength and capacity for healing and growth.

Week 6 Self-Help Guide

Welcome to Week Six, a critical phase in your healing journey from PTSD, where we focus on honing your coping skills and problem-solving abilities. This week, we introduce seven carefully designed homework assignments aimed at strengthening your resilience and equipping you with practical tools for managing the challenges associated with PTSD. Each exercise will guide you through processes that encourage not just understanding and coping with your symptoms, but actively engaging in solving the problems they present. This hands-on approach will empower you to take control of your healing process, using coping strategies that are both effective and tailored to your personal experience. As we journey through this week, remember that developing these skills is a pivotal step towards rebuilding your sense of self and navigating the path to recovery with confidence. Let's embark on this week with an open mind and a commitment to growth, as we explore the power of coping skills and problem-solving in healing from PTSD.

WEEK 6 DAY 1 COGNITIVE REFRAMING PRACTICE

Objective: The task for today centers on identifying and transforming a recurring negative thought related to your trauma into a more positive and realistic perspective. This process involves recognizing a limiting or distressing belief about yourself, others, or the world, documenting it, and then actively reframing it to reflect a more balanced and truthful viewpoint. The aim is to challenge the original thought's validity, encouraging a shift in emotional response and self-perception towards a more hopeful and compassionate stance. This exercise is designed to enhance your resilience against negative thought patterns, boosting self-efficacy and self-compassion, and empowering you with strategies to manage similar thoughts more effectively in the future.

Re-framed Thought: After identifying and writing down the recurring negative thought, transform it into a re-framed thought that offers a more balanced and compassionate viewpoint. For example, if the original thought is "I will never be able to overcome my trauma," a re-framed thought could be, "Recovering from trauma is a gradual process, and it's okay to seek support and take it one step at a time."

Processing:

- **Reflecting on Emotional Changes:** Reflect on the emotional shift that occurs after reframing the thought. Do you notice a reduction in distress or an increase in hopefulness? How does changing the narrative around the trauma influence your feelings towards it and yourself?

- **Noting Changes in Self-Perception:** Observe any changes in how you view yourself or the situation after engaging in this reframing exercise. Do you feel a greater sense of strength or resilience? Has there been an increase in self-compassion or understanding?
- **Journaling the Experience:** Document the entire process, including the original negative thought, the re-framed thought, and your reflections on the emotional and perceptual changes experienced. This journaling serves not only as a tool for personal insight but also as a reminder of your ability to alter your thought patterns and emotional responses in a positive direction.

RE-FRAMED THOUGHT

PROCESSING

THOUGHTS

WEEK 6 DAY 2:
EMOTION-FOCUSED COPING
EXERCISE

Objective: Today's task is centered around selecting a specific emotion that frequently arises as a result of your trauma, such as anxiety, anger, or fear, and engaging in mindful journaling about this emotion. This exercise aims to deepen your understanding of how this emotion manifests in your thoughts and behavior, its triggers, and the sensations it brings. By carefully documenting and reflecting on this emotion, you're enhancing emotional awareness and developing more effective regulation strategies.

Mindful Journaling:

- **Select an Emotion:** Identify an emotion that is prominently linked to your trauma.
- **Describe the Emotion:** In your journal, detail the chosen emotion. Explore what typically triggers this feeling and how it influences your thoughts and actions. Aim to capture the physical sensations, associated thoughts, and any observable patterns.

Processing: Reflecting on Emotional Awareness and Regulation:

- **Analyzing Emotional Patterns:** Post-journaling, analyze any discovered patterns or specific triggers. Identify circumstances or thought processes that amplify this emotion.

- **Evaluating Coping Mechanisms:** Assess your current methods of coping with this emotion. Determine the effectiveness of these strategies and whether they alleviate or intensify PTSD symptoms.
- **Developing New Strategies:** Reflect on alternative, healthier strategies for managing this emotion. Consider techniques such as reframing negative thoughts or exploring new expression outlets.
- **Journaling Insights:** Document the insights gained from this reflection and list any new coping mechanisms you plan to implement. This entry will serve as a valuable tool for navigating future occurrences of the emotion.

EMOTION(s): [Identify and describe the specific emotion you're focusing on.]

DESCRIBE THE EMOTION: [Provide a detailed account of the emotion, its triggers, and its impact on your thoughts and behavior.]

PROCESS THE EMOTION: [Summarize the patterns observed, evaluate current coping mechanisms, and outline new strategies for emotional regulation.]

WEEK 6 DAY 3:
PROBLEM-SOLVING EXERCISE

Objective: Systematically address a specific problem you encounter as a result of your PTSD symptoms by breaking it down into smaller, more manageable components and brainstorming potential solutions. This structured approach aims to empower you with a methodical strategy for identifying and evaluating possible solutions, facilitating the selection and implementation of the most feasible ones. By dissecting the problem and considering it from multiple angles, you enhance your ability to manage PTSD-related challenges more effectively, reducing the overwhelm and facilitating a sense of control and progress in your healing journey. This task encourages critical thinking, problem-solving, and proactive planning, contributing to a more empowered and resilient approach to managing PTSD symptoms.

Task: Identify a problem related to your PTSD symptoms. Break it down into smaller parts and brainstorm possible solutions.

Processing: Evaluate the potential solutions and plan how to implement the most feasible one. Reflect on how breaking the problem down helps in managing it more effectively.

Instructions for Use:

- Problem Aspect: Break down the main problem related to your PTSD symptoms into smaller, more manageable parts. Each row represents a different aspect of the problem.

- Possible Solutions: For each aspect, brainstorm several potential solutions.
- Evaluation of Solutions: Assess each solution's feasibility, advantages, and drawbacks.
- Implementation Plan: Choose the most practical solution for each aspect and outline a plan for implementing it.

Problem-Solving Exercise Grid

Problem	Possible Solutions	Evaluation of Solutions	Implementation Plan
Specific aspect of problem	List possible solutions	Evaluate pros and cons	How to implement solution

WEEK 6 DAY 4: GRATITUDE JOURNALING

Objective: The aim of this task is to embark on a journey of gratitude by establishing a gratitude journaling practice. Each day, you will dedicate time to document three specific things for which you are grateful, ranging from the simplicity of daily pleasures to significant life events or relationships. This exercise is designed to cultivate an attitude of gratitude, enhancing your awareness of life's positive aspects and fostering a deeper sense of appreciation and contentment. By being specific and genuine in your entries, you encourage a mindful acknowledgment of gratitude in both grand and mundane moments, contributing to emotional resilience and a more positive outlook, particularly in navigating the complexities of PTSD.

Task: Begin a journey of gratitude by starting a gratitude journal. Each day, dedicate some time to write down three things you are grateful for. These can range from simple pleasures like a sunny day to significant events or people. The key is to be specific and genuine about your gratitude.

Detailed Directions:

1. Choose a Quiet Time: Find a quiet moment in your day, preferably in the morning or before bedtime, to focus on gratitude.
2. Be Specific: Instead of general statements, be specific about what you're grateful for. For example, instead of writing, "I'm grateful

for my family," you might say, "I'm grateful for my sister's supportive phone call today."

3. Include Small Joys: Remember that gratitude can also be found in small, everyday moments. It might be the taste of your favorite coffee, a kind gesture from a stranger, or the comfort of your favorite chair.

Processing:

- Reflect on Your Feelings: After writing in your journal, take a few moments to reflect on how acknowledging these things makes you feel. Do you notice a shift in your mood or a sense of calmness?
- Observe Changes: Over time, observe any changes in your perception of your daily life. You might find that you notice more positive aspects throughout your day or feel a deeper appreciation for things you previously took for granted.
- Long-term Impact: Consider how this practice of gratitude can impact your life in the long term, especially concerning your PTSD symptoms. Does it help in reducing feelings of anxiety or negativity? Does it bring a sense of balance to your emotional state?
- Journal Reflections: Review your entries at the end of each week to see the many things you've been grateful for. Reflect on the themes and patterns that emerge and how they relate to your journey of healing from PTSD.

By incorporating gratitude journaling into your routine, you create a positive space in your day that can counterbalance the challenges posed by PTSD, leading to an enhanced sense of well-being and emotional resilience.

WEEK 6 DAY 5: STRENGTH-BASED REFLECTION JOURNAL

Objective: The objective of today's exercise is to engage in a strength-based reflection, focusing on identifying and deeply exploring personal strengths or recent achievements. This involves contemplating a character trait you value within yourself or a specific instance of accomplishment, regardless of its magnitude. Through detailed reflective writing, you're encouraged to delve into the scenario, actions taken, and their significance, with a particular emphasis on the emotional experience associated with this strength or achievement. The goal is to enhance self-awareness, bolster self-esteem, and reinforce resilience by acknowledging and appreciating your inner resources and how they contribute to navigating and managing PTSD symptoms. This reflective practice aims to shift self-perception positively, highlight personal growth areas, and underscore the role of individual strengths in the broader context of healing and daily life challenges.

Task: Today's exercise involves identifying and reflecting on personal strengths or achievements. This can be something you've recently accomplished, a character trait you're proud of, or a challenge you've overcome, no matter how small or seemingly insignificant. Write about this strength or achievement in detail, focusing on your feelings, actions, and the impact it had.

Detailed Directions:

1. Personal Strength Identification: Think about a quality in yourself that you value or a recent moment where you felt proud of yourself. It could be related to your kindness, creativity, determination, or even a small task you completed.
2. Reflective Writing: Write a detailed account of this strength or achievement. Describe the scenario, your actions, and why they are significant. For instance, if your strength is empathy, you might write about a time you provided emotional support to a friend.
3. Emphasis on Emotions: While writing, pay attention to the emotions you experienced during this time. How did it feel to exhibit this strength or achieve this goal?

Processing:

- Impact on Self-Image: Reflect on how recognizing and focusing on this strength or achievement makes you feel about yourself. Does it shift your self-perception in a more positive direction?
- Resilience Building: Consider how this strength or achievement has helped you cope with or manage your PTSD symptoms. How can this quality or experience be used as a tool for resilience in challenging times?
- Long-term Perspective: Think about how you can continue to develop and utilize this strength in your daily life. How can it support your long-term healing journey from PTSD?
- Journal Reflections: Make a note of any insights or emotions that arise from this exercise. Over time, look for patterns or recurring strengths that emerge in your journal, and think about how they contribute to your overall growth and healing process.

This exercise is designed to help you recognize and appreciate your strengths and achievements, fostering a positive self-image and contributing to your resilience against PTSD symptoms. By focusing on your capabilities and successes, you build a foundation of self-confidence and empowerment that supports your healing journey.

Strength-Based Reflection:

WEEK 6 DAY 5.2: STRENGTH-BASED REFLECTION JOURNAL

Objective: To engage in a self-reflective exercise that identifies personal strengths through the recognition of qualities or moments of pride, explores the significance of specific actions within scenarios, emphasizes the emotions experienced, and assesses their impact on self-image, resilience, and long-term perspective.

Guidance: For the **Personal Strength Identification**, think of moments or qualities that genuinely reflect your character and accomplishments. For the **Reflective Writing**, select a scenario that clearly demonstrates the identified strength and articulate not just what happened, but how it showcases your personal growth or values. When focusing on **Emotions**, be honest and detailed about what you felt, exploring both positive and negative emotions to gain a full understanding of the experience.

Task:

- *Personal Strength Identification:* Identify a quality or a moment in your life you are particularly proud of. Describe this moment or quality in detail.
- *Reflective Writing:* Choose a scenario where this quality or moment was evident. Outline the actions you took and explain why this scenario is significant to you.

- *Emphasis on Emotions*: Reflect on the emotions you experienced during this scenario. Describe these emotions and their intensity.

Processing:

- *Impact on Self-Image*: Consider how identifying this strength and reflecting on the related scenario and emotions affects your perception of yourself. Does it enhance your self-esteem or change how you view your capabilities?
- *Resilience Building*: Reflect on how this exercise might contribute to your resilience. Do these reflections inspire confidence in your ability to handle future challenges?
- *Long-term Perspective*: Think about how this strength and your ability to recognize and learn from it can influence your long-term goals and vision for your life.

Journal Reflections: Write detailed entries based on each section. Start with the strength or proud moment, followed by the scenario and actions, and then delve into the emotions experienced. Conclude with reflections on how this exercise impacts your self-image, resilience, and long-term outlook. This comprehensive reflection process aims to deepen your self-awareness and appreciation of your personal growth journey.

Personal Strength Identification:
- Quality or Proud Moment:

- Description:

Reflective Writing:
- Scenario:

- Actions:

- Why it's significant to you:

Emphasis on Emotions:
- Emotions Experienced:

Processing:
- Impact on Self-Image:

- Resilience Building:

- Long-term Perspective:

Journal Reflections:

WEEK 6 DAY 6: RESILIENCE-BUILDING PRACTICES

Task: Create a Personal Resilience Journal

1. Journal Setup:
   - Find a notebook or create a digital document for your resilience journal.
   - Date the first page.
2. Mindful Breathing Exercise:
   - Begin with a 5-minute mindful breathing exercise to center yourself. Breathe deeply and focus on the present moment.
3. Journal Prompts:
   - Prompt 1: Reflections on Resilience: Write about a time when you displayed resilience. Describe the situation, your actions, and the outcome.
   - Prompt 2: Qualities of Resilience: List the qualities you believe contribute to your resilience (e.g., determination, flexibility, optimism).
   - Prompt 3: Current Challenges: Identify a current challenge in your life. How can you apply your resilience to this situation?
4. Set a Small, Achievable Goal:
   - Identify a small goal you can achieve in the next week, contributing to building your resilience. For example, this

could be practicing mindfulness daily, reaching out to a supportive friend, or dedicating time to a hobby.

- ○ Write this goal in your journal and outline the steps you plan to take to achieve it.

5. Emotional Response and Anticipation:
    - ○ Reflect on how you feel about this goal. Are you anxious, hopeful, determined?
    - ○ Anticipate how accomplishing this goal will enhance your resilience.

6. Plan for Integration:
    - ○ Decide on a specific time each day to revisit your journal.
    - ○ Set a reminder to ensure you follow through.

7. End-of-Day Reflection:
    - ○ At the end of Day 6, write a brief reflection on your experiences of the day, particularly when you felt resilient or recognized a need for resilience

JOURNAL

Date:

Mindful Breathing Exercise:

- Duration: 5 minutes
- Notes on Experience:

1. Reflections on Resilience:
    - ○ Describe a past situation where you showed resilience:
    - ○ Your actions:

- Outcome:

2. Qualities of Resilience:
   - List qualities you believe contribute to your resilience:

3. Current Challenges:
   - Current challenge you're facing:

   - How can your resilience help in this situation:

Set a Small, Achievable Goal:

- Goal:

Steps to achieve it:

1.

2.

3.

Emotional Response and Anticipation:

- Feelings about this goal:

- Anticipated outcome:

End-of-Day Reflection:

- Reflections on today's experiences:

WEEK 6 CONCLUSION

As you conclude Week 6 of your therapeutic journey, it's remarkable to see how far you've come, embarking on a transformative path that has led you through the intricate maze of coping strategies and resilience-building practices. This week has been a significant chapter in your journey, marked by an in-depth exploration and integration of diverse and potent skills.

You've delved into the nuances of cognitive reframing, learning to shift your perspective and reframe challenging thoughts in a more positive and empowering light. This skill is crucial in altering the narrative of your experiences, allowing you to see situations from a perspective that fosters healing and growth.

Stress management techniques have become a cornerstone of your daily routine, equipping you with the tools to navigate stressors with grace and composure. Whether through mindful breathing, progressive relaxation, or other methods, you've learned to maintain calm and balance in the face of life's inevitable pressures.

Problem-solving exercises have sharpened your ability to tackle issues head-on, fostering a solution-focused mindset that empowers you to address challenges constructively. This skill enhances your agency and effectiveness in handling personal and professional hurdles.

Gratitude journaling has opened a world of positivity, helping you recognize and appreciate the good in your life, even amidst trials. This practice can shift your focus from what's lacking to the abundance surrounding you, cultivating a sense of contentment and joy.

Strength-based reflection has encouraged you to identify and celebrate your inner strengths, acknowledging your achievements and the qualities that make you unique and resilient. This self-recognition is vital in building self-esteem and a positive self-image.

Resilience practices have fortified your ability to bounce back from adversity. By embracing these practices, you've built a robust framework supporting your ability to adapt and thrive in life's challenges.

By weaving these skills into the fabric of your daily life, you've laid a foundation for a more fulfilled, resilient existence. These practices are not just about managing symptoms of PTSD; they are about redefining and enriching your life experience. As you continue incorporating these techniques into your daily routine, you empower yourself to face life's challenges with confidence, optimism, and a sense of control. This empowerment paves the way for continuous personal growth and self-improvement.

Remember, the progress you've made and the skills you've acquired are a testament to your strength, resilience, and capacity for healing and growth. As you move forward, carry these skills with pride and confidence, knowing they are transformative tools that enable you to navigate life's journey with resilience and hope.

| 11 |

The Inner Self

Week 7 of our journey through healing from PTSD marks a significant transition into a deeper, more introspective phase of self-discovery and self-healing. This week is dedicated to nurturing self-compassion, bolstering self-esteem, and recognizing our inherent self-worth. In the aftermath of trauma, our perception of self can be significantly altered – often leading to feelings of inadequacy, guilt, or shame. Week 7 is a pivotal moment in the healing process as we learn to reframe these perceptions and cultivate a relationship with ourselves rooted in kindness, understanding, and acceptance.

The importance of this week cannot be overstated, as how we relate to ourselves sets the tone for our overall recovery and well-being. A damaged self-relationship can perpetuate the cycle of PTSD symptoms, while a nurturing and compassionate self-relationship can be the foundation upon which we rebuild our lives post-trauma. This week, we embark on a journey to mend the fractures within our self-concept and to reconcile with parts of ourselves that we may have neglected or misunderstood in the wake of our traumatic experiences.

The journey of Week 7 involves delving into the layers of our self-perception, dissecting the narratives we've constructed about who we are, and challenging the negative beliefs that have taken root in our minds. It's about relearning who we are at our core, beyond the trauma and the scars it has left behind. Through various therapeutic exercises and reflections, we aim to transform our internal dialogue into one that is more empowering and true to our authentic selves.

This week is not just about healing; it's about flourishing. It's about moving beyond mere survival of trauma and stepping into a space where we can thrive. We explore the art of self-compassion as a tool for healing and a way of living – a skill that enhances every aspect of our lives, from how we handle stress and adversity to how we interact with others and pursue our goals and dreams.

As we progress through Week 7, we are invited to embrace ourselves entirely, with all our complexities and contradictions. We learn to extend to ourselves the compassion, patience, and kindness we would offer a dear friend. By the end of this transformative week, we aim to emerge with a renewed sense of self – one that is more resilient, confident, and grounded in the unwavering belief in our worth and capabilities.

This week, we again explore the intricate terrains of our inner landscape using the lens of Internal Family Systems (IFS). To review, IFS helps us identify and understand the fragmented parts within ourselves, each shaped by our experiences and influencing our self-concept. We recognize these parts not as flaws but as aspects of our being that have their own stories and purposes.

Alongside IFS, we will continue to integrate the principles of Cognitive Therapy by addressing the negative thought patterns that often entangle our minds following trauma. By constantly analyzing and reframing these thoughts, we will see ourselves and our experiences in a new light that fosters growth and self-compassion.

In Week 7, we emphasize cultivating self-compassion through the lens of Compassion Focused Therapy (CFT). This approach is particularly resonant for individuals recovering from PTSD, as it addresses the critical need for self-kindness in the aftermath of trauma. CFT, rooted in the understanding that compassion is a skill that can be learned and strengthened, offers us a path to treat ourselves with the same level of kindness, understanding, and empathy that we would naturally extend to others. This week is about learning to turn that compassionate lens inward, to heal and nurture ourselves.

CFT is based on the premise that our brains are wired for both threat and safety responses and that trauma can significantly skew this balance toward constant threat perception. This skewed perception often manifests in self-criticism, shame, and an inability to feel safe within our minds. CFT aims to rectify this imbalance by activating our brain's capacity for compassion and self-soothing. By doing so, we not only alleviate the symptoms of PTSD but also cultivate a sense of inner safety and well-being.

During this week, we engage in various CFT practices designed to deepen our sense of self-love and acceptance. These practices include compassionate self talk, where we learn to identify and alter our harsh inner critic, replacing it with a more supportive and understanding voice. We also explore compassion-focused imagery, where we visualize ourselves in complete safety and comfort, thus training our brains to more readily access feelings of calmness and self-compassion.

Another critical aspect of CFT we explore is mindfulness in the context of compassion. We practice being present with our feelings, particularly those that are uncomfortable or painful, with a compassionate and non-judgmental attitude. This practice helps us to understand and accept our emotions without being overwhelmed by them, an essential skill in the journey of healing from trauma.

We also engage in exercises that encourage us to connect with the common humanity aspect of compassion. This involves recognizing that suffering and imperfection are part of the shared human experience. Doing this makes us feel more connected to others and less isolated in our struggles.

The objective of this week's focus on CFT is not only to alleviate the suffering associated with PTSD but also to create a nurturing inner space where growth and healing can occur. By the end of the week, we aim to have developed a more compassionate relationship with ourselves, marked by increased self-acceptance, decreased self-criticism, and a greater capacity for self-soothing and resilience. This compassionate foundation paves the way for continued healing and personal growth beyond the scope of this program.

Reflective activities and mindful practices mark the journey through Week 7. We begin by exploring our inner selves, identifying the parts that make up our whole, and understanding their roles and origins. We then address the negative thought patterns linked to these parts, using cognitive techniques to challenge and transform them.

In our path to self-compassion, we engage in meditative practices that enhance our emotional connection with ourselves. This process is enriched by outdoor activities that provide a physical and symbolic space for introspection and growth. These activities offer solitude and reflection, allowing us to revisit and mentally transform our internal terrains.

As we nurture our inner world, we extend this growth outward, strengthening our relationships with others. Social interactions become opportunities to apply the insights and techniques we've learned, enhancing our self-concept and how we connect with people around us.

Concluding Week 7, we find ourselves in a space where our relationship with ourselves has transformed. The combined insights from IFS, Cognitive Therapy, and CFT have carved out a path of self-discovery and compassion. We emerge with a strengthened sense of self, equipped with tools and understanding to continue our healing journey with resilience and empathy.

Week 7 Self-Help Guide

Welcome to Week Seven, a transformative period in your healing journey from PTSD, dedicated to the principles of Internal Family Systems (IFS) and the exploration of your inner self. This week, you will be introduced to seven carefully structured homework assignments designed to guide you through the process of understanding and harmonizing the various parts of your internal family. Each assignment aims to provide you with the insights and tools necessary to foster a healthier relationship with yourself and your emotions. Through engaging exercises, you will learn to identify and interact with different aspects of your psyche, bringing about a sense of balance and peace within. This journey into the IFS framework is not just about healing from PTSD; it's about unlocking a deeper level of self-awareness and self-compassion. As we explore the dynamic landscape of your inner world, remember that every step forward is a step towards a more integrated and empowered self. Let's embark on this week with courage and curiosity, ready to embrace the healing power of understanding our internal family systems.

WEEK 7 DAY 1 EXPLORING INNER LANDSCAPE (FOUNDATION)

Objective: The aim of this exercise is to engage in a process of self-discovery and internal exploration to identify and understand the fragmented "parts" within yourself that may require attention or healing. By acknowledging these aspects of your self-concept, you aim to gain insight into the origins, purposes, and impacts of these internal "parts" on your emotions, thoughts, and behaviors. This reflective practice encourages a deeper connection with your inner self, facilitating a pathway toward integrated healing and self-awareness.

Guidance: Approach this exercise with openness and compassion towards yourself. Recognize that each "part" has played a role in your life's journey, often emerging as a response to experiences or needs. As you proceed, maintain a non-judgmental stance, allowing for a safe space to explore these aspects of your identity.

Task:

1. **Finding a Quiet Space:** Choose a serene location where you can reflect without interruptions.
2. **Centering Yourself:** Close your eyes and take several deep, mindful breaths to ground yourself in the present moment.
3. **Identifying Fragmented Parts:** Reflect on the different "parts" of your internal family. These may manifest as distinct emotions, thought patterns, behaviors, or beliefs that seem to operate independently within you.

4. **Naming the Parts:** Once you have identified these "parts," assign names to them. Naming these aspects can help in acknowledging their presence and understanding their roles.
5. **Understanding Origins:** Contemplate deeply to determine when and how each part was formed. Consider what experiences or needs led to the emergence of these "parts."
6. **Exploring Purposes:** Identify the purpose or role of each "part" in your life. Reflect on how they have influenced your reactions and decision-making processes.
7. **Journaling:** Process your experience through journaling. Document the "parts" you've identified, their origins, purposes, and any reflections or insights that arise during this exercise.

Processing:

- **Reflecting on Integration:** After completing the journaling process, take some time to reflect on how these "parts" interact within your internal system and how acknowledging them affects your sense of self.
- **Contemplating Healing Pathways:** Consider how this awareness of your internal "parts" can inform your healing journey. Think about steps you might take to address the needs or heal the wounds of these "parts."
- **Assessing Emotional Impact:** Reflect on the emotional impact of this exercise. How does recognizing and naming these "parts" make you feel? Do you notice a shift in how you relate to yourself?

Part/Name	Where did it form	Purpose

Journaling/Processing

WEEK 7 DAY 2 - UNDERSTANDING NEGATIVE THOUGHT PATTERNS (BUILDING ON DAY 1)

Objective: To deepen self-understanding and transform negative thought patterns related to fragmented "parts" of self into more positive and empowering beliefs.

Guidance: This process is based on Cognitive Behavioral Therapy (CBT) principles, which emphasize the identification, challenge, and reframing of negative thoughts.

Task:

1. **Revisit Your List**: Start with revisiting the list of fragmented "parts" you identified previously. Reflect on these parts and the roles they play in your life.

2. **Analyze and Challenge**: For each part, identify any negative thought patterns. Ask yourself, "Is this thought accurate? Is it helpful?"

3. **Reframe Thoughts**: Challenge these negative thoughts by reframing them into positive, empowering beliefs. For instance, if a part of you feels unworthy, reframe it to, "I have inherent worth and value."

4. **Record and Reflect**: Write down your revised thoughts. Reflect on how changing these thoughts makes you feel and what impact it may have on your self-perception.

Reflection: After completing this exercise, spend some time reflecting on the process. How did it feel to challenge and change these thoughts? What emotions or insights emerged during this practice?

Integration: Incorporate this practice of challenging and reframing negative thoughts into your daily routine. Regularly acknowledging and adjusting your thought patterns can significantly impact your mood and outlook. Remember, the goal is not to eliminate negative thoughts entirely but to develop a more balanced and compassionate perspective towards yourself.

Part/Name	Negative Thought Patterns	Reframe Negative Thinking

Journaling/Processing

WEEK 7 DAY 3 - CULTIVATING SELF-COMPASSION (BUILDING ON DAY 2)

Objective: To cultivate self-compassion through meditation, fostering a nurturing and accepting relationship with all parts of yourself.

Guidance: Self-compassion is the practice of offering the same kindness and care to ourselves that we would offer to a good friend. This meditation aims to deepen your connection with yourself, especially with the parts you've identified as needing attention and care. By visualizing yourself as a loving and nurturing presence, you can begin to heal and integrate these fragmented parts with kindness.

Task:

1. **Prepare Your Space**: Choose a quiet, comfortable spot where you won't be disturbed. This could be a cozy corner of your room, a garden, or any place that feels peaceful to you.
2. **Begin the Meditation**: Sit or lie down in a comfortable position. Close your eyes, take a few deep breaths, and allow your body to relax.
3. **Visualize Compassion**: Imagine yourself surrounded by a warm, loving light. Visualize this light as a manifestation of your compassion and kindness.
4. **Offer Support to Your Parts**: One by one, bring to mind the different "parts" of yourself you've identified. Imagine offering

each of these parts your love, understanding, and support. Visualize yourself as a compassionate friend to these parts, embracing them with kindness.

5. **Extend Kindness and Love**: Focus on the feeling of extending unconditional kindness and love to these parts of yourself. Notice any emotions that arise, allowing them to be present without judgment.

6. **Conclude the Session**: Gently bring the meditation to a close when you're ready. Take a moment to thank yourself for this act of self-compassion before opening your eyes.

Reflection: After your meditation session, reflect on the experience. Write about any emotions or insights that surfaced during the meditation. How did it feel to offer kindness and support to yourself? How has this practice affected your relationship with the parts you've identified and your overall self-concept?

Integration: Incorporate self-compassion meditation into your regular self-care routine. Even a few minutes a day can significantly impact your wellbeing. Over time, this practice can help you develop a more compassionate, supportive, and integrated sense of self.

Part/Name	Journaling/Processing on Emotions / Impact

Notes

WEEK 7 DAY 4 - MAPPING INTERNAL GROWTH (INTEGRATING IFS AND COGNITIVE THERAPY)

Objective: To engage in an outdoor activity that fosters a connection with nature and introspection, utilizing this environment to metaphorically explore and transform the "parts" of yourself through cognitive therapy techniques.

Guidance: Nature offers a unique backdrop for reflection and self-discovery. By choosing an activity that immerses you in the outdoors, you create an opportunity to physically and mentally navigate through the various aspects of your self-concept. This task is designed to help you visualize and confront the fragmented "parts" of yourself in a supportive, natural setting, using the landscapes around you as metaphors for internal growth and transformation.

Task:

1. **Select Your Activity**: Choose an outdoor activity that resonates with you and allows for contemplation. Whether it's a hike, a leisurely walk, or a bike ride, ensure it's something that brings you joy and peace.
2. **Consciously Engage with Your "Parts"**: As you begin your activity, bring to mind the "parts" of yourself you've identified. Allow yourself to reflect on these aspects without judgment.

3. **Visualize Parts as Terrains**: Imagine each "part" as a specific type of terrain you encounter on your journey. Visualize the transformations you wish to see in these terrains as you apply cognitive therapy techniques to challenge and reframe negative thoughts.

4. **Apply Cognitive Therapy Techniques**: Confront each "terrain" with the cognitive therapy skills you've learned. Challenge negative thoughts and beliefs, reframing them into more positive and empowering ones.

5. **Mentally Map Your Progress**: Create a mental map of your journey, visualizing how the terrain changes with your cognitive efforts. See the rough paths become smooth, the gardens bloom, and the streams clear, symbolizing your internal growth.

6. **Mark Your Progress**: Acknowledge the transformed terrains as milestones of personal growth. Celebrate these areas as achievements in your journey towards a healthier self-concept.

7. **Reflect and Journal**: After your activity, find a quiet spot to reflect on your experience. Journal about the terrains you encountered, the challenges you faced, and the transformations you achieved. Recognize your growth and the potential for continued self-improvement.

Reflection: Reflect on how connecting with nature and visualizing your internal landscape as varied terrains helped you understand and transform aspects of yourself. How did challenging and reframing your thoughts in this context feel? What insights did you gain about your potential for growth and change?

Integration: Incorporate regular outdoor activities into your routine as a practice for reflection and self-discovery. Use these moments to continually engage with and transform the "parts" of yourself, leveraging the healing power of nature and cognitive therapy techniques for ongoing personal development.

WEEK 7 DAY 5 - EMBRACING SELF-LOVE (INTEGRATING IFS AND COMPASSION FOCUSED THERAPY)

Objective: To cultivate self-compassion and gratitude towards the different aspects of yourself, recognizing their value and transformation through your journey in cognitive therapy.

Guidance: Reflection and self-compassion are pivotal in the journey of self-improvement and healing. This task is designed to help you acknowledge and appreciate the diverse "parts" of your personality, especially those you've been working on through cognitive therapy. By envisioning these aspects as cherished companions, you emphasize their importance in your personal growth and healing process.

Task:

1. **Choose Your Reflection Space**: Find a peaceful and comfortable spot that feels conducive to deep reflection. This could be a quiet room in your home, a garden, or any place where you feel at ease and undisturbed.
2. **Reflect on Your Journey**: Take a moment to think about the "parts" you've identified and the progress you've made through cognitive therapy. Recognize the challenges you've faced and the growth you've achieved.

3. **Practice Self-Compassion**: Visualize each of these "parts" as if they were dear friends or companions on your life's journey. Understand that, like friends, they have roles in your experiences and growth.

4. **Express Gratitude and Love**: Feel gratitude for each part, appreciating the lessons and strength they've brought into your life. Acknowledge their presence as crucial to your journey, offering love and acceptance.

5. **Write a Letter**: Compose a letter to each "part," treating them as individual entities. In your letters, express your gratitude, acknowledge their transformation, and celebrate the journey you've embarked on together. Reflect on how each has contributed to your current sense of self and your path towards healing.

Reflection: After writing your letters, reflect on the process. How did it feel to express gratitude and love towards these parts of yourself? What emotions arose during this exercise? Did you discover any new perspectives on your journey of healing and self-improvement?

Integration: Keep these letters in a personal space where you can revisit them. They serve as reminders of your resilience, growth, and the compassion you're capable of offering yourself. Let this practice of writing and reflection be a tool you can return to whenever you need to reconnect with self-compassion and gratitude on your healing journey.

Part/Name	Letter

Notes

WEEK 7 DAY 6 - STRENGTHENING RELATIONSHIPS

Objective: To apply cognitive therapy techniques and practice self-compassion in a social setting, aiming to enhance your self-concept and the quality of your relationships.

Guidance: Engaging in social activities can sometimes bring to the surface insecurities and negative thought patterns. This task encourages you to actively use the cognitive therapy techniques you've learned to address these thoughts in real-time. Additionally, by practicing self-compassion and extending kindness to yourself and others, you can create a more positive social experience, contributing to improved self-concept and strengthened relationships.

Task:

1. **Choose a Positive Social Activity**: Select an activity that involves interaction with others and that you consider safe and enjoyable. This could range from a coffee meet-up with a friend to a group hike.

2. **Apply Cognitive Therapy Techniques**: As you interact with others, stay mindful of your thoughts. If you notice negative or self-critical thoughts emerging, gently challenge them. Ask yourself if these thoughts are based on facts or if they are distortions of reality.

3. **Practice Self-Compassion**: Remind yourself that it's okay to be imperfect and that everyone has moments of insecurity. Treat

yourself with the same kindness and understanding you would offer a good friend.

4. **Extend Kindness to Others**: Make an effort to be kind and understanding towards the people you are interacting with. Notice how this positive outward behavior impacts your internal state.

5. **Reflect on Your Experience**: After the social activity, take some time to reflect on your experience. How did applying cognitive therapy techniques affect your thoughts and feelings during the interaction? How did practicing self-compassion and kindness influence your behavior and the quality of the social interaction?

Reflection: Consider the impact of combining cognitive and compassion-focused therapy techniques on your self-concept and your interactions with others. Did you notice any changes in how you perceive yourself or in the dynamics of your relationships? Write about any insights or revelations that emerged from this experience.

Integration: Integrate the use of cognitive therapy techniques and the practice of self-compassion into your daily interactions. By making this a regular practice, you can continue to improve your self-concept and foster more meaningful and positive relationships with others.

Describe the Situation

Identify your Negative Thoughts

Identify Any Negative or Unwanted Behaviors

Reframed Compassionate Based Thoughts

Redirected Behaviors Based on Compassion Thinking

Reflection

| 12 |

Integrating the
Fragmented Self

As we embark on Week 8, we stand at the cusp of a transformative threshold in our journey toward healing from PTSD. This week represents a time when the varied elements of our previous work unite, forging a pathway to profound self-integration. It's a moment where the fragmented aspects of our psyche, once dissonant and scattered, begin to harmonize, converging into a symphony of self-understanding and renewal. This phase is a step in recovery and a transformative pathway toward a rejuvenated self.

In this critical week, we engage deeply with the principles of Internal Family Systems (IFS) and Transpersonal Psychology. These powerful modalities emerge as the twin pillars supporting our quest for wholeness. With IFS, we embark on an introspective voyage, navigating the intricate landscape of our inner selves. We venture into the depths of our psyche, seeking dialogue and reconciliation between the disparate parts shaped by our trauma. This journey is akin to an internal alchemy, where understanding, empathy, and acceptance transmute inner conflict into inner peace.

Simultaneously, Transpersonal Psychology invites us to transcend beyond the boundaries of conventional therapy. This week, we explore the realms of our being that intersect with the spiritual and the transcendent. We engage in practices that elevate our perspective, allowing us to view our trauma and healing journey through a lens of holistic interconnectedness. This exploration invites a profound awakening - realizing our place in a larger tapestry of existence and appreciating our journey as an integral component of a universal narrative.

Week 8 is a portal to a new phase of existence. As you immerse yourself in the activities and reflections of this week you are engaging in a soul-deep process of transformation. This week challenges you to confront and embrace the entirety of your being—the pain, the growth, the resilience, and the potential for transcendence.

By the end of this transformative week, expect to encounter a more integrated, aware, and empowered self. The insights and experiences of this week are intended to resonate intensely, provoking profound introspection and catalyzing lasting change. This is an evolution into a deeper, insightful, and resilient version of yourself. Welcome to Week 8—a journey into the heart of your being, a journey of integration and awakening.

Integrating with IFS

As we continue exploring Week 8, the Internal Family Systems (IFS) model becomes a pivotal tool in our self-integration journey. This powerful approach allows us to delve into the multifaceted nature of our psyche, recognizing that the many parts within us, shaped by our experiences of trauma, often function in silos, sometimes in disharmony and conflict. This week is dedicated to significantly deepening our engagement with these parts, fostering a profound understanding and reconciliation among them. Our goal is to transform this internal discord into cohesive self-support and cooperation.

This transformative process with IFS begins with an intricate exploration of the various roles our internal parts play:

Protectors. Protectors play a crucial role, especially in the context of trauma and PTSD. These parts, emerging in response to life's adversities, function as the guardians of our innermost selves, standing as vigilant sentinels to shield us from further harm.

Protectors are born out of necessity. They develop in the wake of traumatic experiences, stepping forward to prevent us from re-living pain or falling into vulnerability again. Their emergence is evidence of the mind's incredible capacity for self-preservation and adaptation. These protectors assert themselves in moments of danger or distress, taking control to steer us away from perceived threats.

The manifestations of these protector parts are diverse and multi-faceted. They may appear as anger, a fiery shield that keeps others at a distance, preventing them from getting close enough to potentially cause harm. This anger, often seen as a negative emotion, is a protector's way of asserting boundaries and exerting control over a situation that feels threatening.

Some protectors manifest as cynicism or skepticism. Having witnessed the fallibility of people and the world, these parts adopt a stance of doubt and mistrust to guard against future disappointments or betrayals. By expecting the worst, they believe they can prevent being caught off guard or hurt again.

Humor, too, can be a guise for a protector. It acts as a buffer, a way to diffuse tension, distract from pain, or lighten the heaviness of our emotional burdens. Humor can create distance from the intensity of our experiences, offering a respite, however brief, from the weight of trauma.

Despite their seemingly tough exterior, protectors are fundamentally rooted in vulnerability. They are not the embodiment of resilience but rather a response to a lack of it. They step in when our vulnerabilities are too raw, too exposed. Their toughness is a facade, a necessary armor constructed to shield the softer, more vulnerable parts of us— the parts that have been hurt, the parts that fear further hurt.

Understanding and appreciating our protector parts involves acknowledging their purpose and origin. It's about seeing beyond their surface expressions to the fears and vulnerabilities they are guarding. This week, we will engage with these protector parts, seeking to understand their intentions and learning to work with them rather than against them. We will explore ways to assure them they are valued and that their protective measures, while necessary, can be modulated in the present where safety exists. This understanding paves the way for a more harmonious internal environment, where protectors can ease their vigilance and allow for a greater sense of peace and integration within us.

Exiles. The exiles play a poignant and profound role when navigating the aftermath of trauma. Often shrouded in the shadows of our psyche, these parts carry the burdens of our deepest hurts, unprocessed traumas, and unresolved emotional experiences. They are repositories of raw, unfiltered emotions—pain, grief, fear, and despair—feelings so intense and overwhelming that they are often relegated to the farthest corners of our consciousness.

The exiles are akin to wounded inner children, holding onto the scars of past experiences. These parts often encapsulate the moments of our deepest vulnerabilities when we feel helpless, afraid, or utterly alone. They are the bearers of memories we might rather forget experiences that were too painful to face head-on. In our attempt to protect ourselves from re-living these agonizing emotions, we often unconsciously exile these parts, pushing them away from the forefront of our conscious minds.

However, exiling these parts, while initially a protective measure, can have profound implications on our overall well-being and mental health. These exiled parts, though hidden, continue to influence our behaviors, emotional responses, and even our perceptions of the world around us. They are the undercurrents that can unexpectedly surge to the surface, manifesting in various ways – perhaps as inexplicable anxiety, sudden bouts of sadness, or unexplained fears.

The journey of Week 8 involves turning our compassionate attention to these exiled parts. It's about bravely venturing into the depths of our inner world to acknowledge and engage with these wounded fragments of ourselves. This process is about recognizing and validating the experiences of these exiled parts. It's a journey of bringing light to the shadows and offering understanding and compassion to the parts of us that have long been neglected or misunderstood.

As we engage with our exiles, we create a space for healing and reconciliation. We learn to listen to their stories, understand their pain, and recognize their needs. This engagement is a delicate balance. It's about offering comfort without becoming engulfed by the intensity of their emotions. We approach these parts with the gentleness and care that one would provide to a hurt child, recognizing that within these exiled parts lies the key to deep emotional healing and integration.

Through this thoughtful and empathetic engagement, we begin re-integrating these exiled parts into our overall sense of self. We acknowledge that while they carry painful memories, they are also reservoirs of strength, resilience, and survival. By embracing our exiles, we move toward a more whole, integrated self—one where every part, no matter how hurt or hidden, is recognized, valued, and has a place in the narrative of our healing journey.

Managers. In the aftermath of trauma, managers take on a pivotal role. These parts function as the overseers of our internal landscape, diligently working to impose order, control, and stability. They are the strategists, constantly on the alert, striving to steer us away from situations or emotions that might awaken the pain of the exiles.

Managers often manifest in socially lauded or personally valued ways. Such as a drive for achievement, the pursuit of perfection, or a need to please and care for others. They are the parts that prompt us to excel in our careers, maintain harmonious relationships, and uphold societal norms. In their most effective state, managers help us navigate life's challenges with competence and assurance.

However, beneath this façade of control and efficiency, managers are motivated by a deep-seated need to protect. Their primary aim is to prevent the resurgence of trauma to keep the exiles' pain securely locked away. While seemingly beneficial, this vigilant oversight can sometimes lead to rigid patterns and inflexible behaviors. Managers may resist change or new experiences, preferring the safety of the known and the predictable. They can be critical, perfectionistic, and overly controlling, driven by an underlying fear of chaos or emotional upheaval.

In Week 8, we delve into understanding and harmonizing with these managerial parts. We will learn to recognize their protective intentions and appreciate their efforts to maintain balance and order. However, it's also about gently challenging their often-rigid methods. We learn to communicate with these parts, acknowledging their concerns while encouraging more adaptive and flexible approaches.

The process involves exploring the roots of these managerial behaviors and understanding why they need such control and what fears or beliefs drive these actions. We engage in reflective practices that help us see beyond the immediate utility of these behaviors, understanding how they might be limiting our growth or exacerbating our trauma responses.

As we foster a dialogue with our managers, we encourage them to loosen their grip and trust our ability to face and process pain. We reassure them that acknowledging and integrating the exiles can lead to healing rather than harm. This dialogue helps soften the managers' approach, allowing for a more balanced and holistic self-governance. The aim is to reach a state where our managerial parts are no longer the controllers and strict overseers but compassionate caretakers, contributing to a more flexible, adaptive, and integrated self. This transformation is critical to our journey toward healing from PTSD, as it enables us to embrace change, growth, and emotional depth with greater confidence and resilience.

Firefighters. Firefighters emerge as critical yet often misunderstood parts. These parts are the emergency responders of our psyche, springing into action when our exiles—the parts harboring deep emotional pain—are activated or threatened. Unlike the protectors, who work consistently to keep us safe, and managers, who strive to maintain order, firefighters are the ones who react in times of acute distress or perceived danger to our well-being.

Firefighters typically take immediate, often drastic, measures to extinguish or numb intense emotional pain. Their tactics might include impulsive behaviors, substance use, or other forms of escapism. Their sole aim is to quell the overwhelming emotions erupting from the exiles—the fear, grief, or shame that threaten to engulf us. It's a role born out of urgency, a response to what is perceived as an emotional conflagration.

However, the actions of firefighters, while offering temporary relief, can often lead to further complications or detrimental consequences. Their methods, though effective in the short term, can become problematic coping mechanisms, creating cycles of behavior that distance us even further from addressing our core emotional wounds.

To be integrated, we must understand and harmonize these firefighter parts. This involves acknowledging their essential role in our survival and resilience, particularly in the immediate aftermath of trauma. However, it also involves recognizing the long-term impact of their strategies and finding more constructive ways to manage emotional distress.

The process entails engaging in an empathetic dialogue with our firefighter parts. We explore the triggers that spur them into action, delving into the underlying fears and vulnerabilities they strive to protect. By understanding these triggers, we can anticipate and prepare for their activation, finding healthier ways to address the emotional upheaval they are responding to.

We also work on developing alternative strategies for emotional regulation that honor the firefighters' intent but do so in less disruptive or harmful ways. This might include mindfulness practices, engaging in creative outlets, or seeking supportive relationships—avenues that allow for the safe and constructive expression and processing of emotions.

The goal is to transform our relationship with our firefighter parts. Rather than viewing them as disruptive forces, we start to see them as integral players in our emotional ecosystem whose energy and quick response can be channeled into positive and healing actions. This shift enables us to face and process our emotional pain with greater awareness, resilience, and self-compassion.

As we journey through this week, we aim to appreciate and understand each part's unique contributions and burdens. We create a space for dialogue among these parts through a series of reflective exercises. These exercises encourage an open conversation within ourselves, where each part is heard, acknowledged, and understood. This internal dialogue is akin to a peace negotiation, where conflicting interests are harmoniously resolved, and common ground is established. We learn to view these parts not as adversaries but as essential components of our whole self, each with a vital role in our life story.

As we engage in these activities, we foster new internal dynamics where cooperation and mutual support replace conflict and isolation. We practice techniques that help these parts work together, understanding their interconnectedness and collective contribution to our well-being. This is a process of internal diplomacy, where the goal is not just coexistence but active collaboration and unity.

As we integrate the fragmented self, it's essential to understand and embrace the core concepts of the 8 Cs and the 5 Ps. These principles guide us toward that final integrated, harmonious self.

The IFS 8 Cs:

1. *Confidence*: Cultivating an inner sense of assurance and self-reliance is crucial for navigating our internal world's complexities.
2. *Calmness*: Fostering a sense of inner peace is essential for soothing and managing parts that are in distress.
3. *Creativity*: Encouraging a spirit of innovation and imaginative thinking in approaching internal conflicts and healing.
4. *Clarity*: Striving for clear understanding and insight into the roles and needs of our various parts.
5. *Curiosity*: Maintaining an open, non-judgmental, and inquisitive stance toward all internal parts, facilitating deeper exploration and understanding.

6. *Courage*: Building the bravery required to confront and engage with challenging parts, including those holding pain and trauma.
7. *Compassion*: Developing a deep empathy and kindness toward all parts of the self, especially those suffering.
8. *Connectedness*: Nurturing a sense of belonging and interconnectedness among all parts, promoting unity and harmony within the self.

The IFS 5 Ps:

1. *Presence*: Being fully in the moment and attentively engaged with each part, allowing for a more profound connection and understanding.
2. *Patience*: Allowing time and space for each part to express itself and for the healing process to unfold naturally.
3. *Perspective*: Maintaining an overarching view that appreciates the complexity and interrelation of all parts within the self.
4. *Persistence*: Demonstrating a steady commitment to self-integration, even when facing challenges or setbacks.
5. *Playfulness*: Embracing a light-hearted and playful approach when engaging with internal parts, easing the process and inviting creativity and spontaneity.

Keep these principles in mind as you engage in the exercises and reflective practices throughout this week. They are concepts and practical tools to guide your interaction with your internal parts. As you deepen your dialogue with your parts, try to embody these qualities and observe how they influence your process of self-integration.

The *8 Cs* and *5 Ps* offer a framework that encourages a holistic and compassionate approach to dealing with the fragmented aspects of the self. By embracing these principles, you'll be well-equipped to navigate the complexities of your inner world and cultivating a state of greater peace, understanding, and unity.

By the end of this week, expect to feel a sense of increased internal harmony and balance. This newfound peace brings with it the presence of a cohesive, supportive internal environment. This week's work sets the stage for a more integrated self, where the various parts of our psyche are not just aware of each other but actively engaged in a supportive, cooperative relationship. This internal harmony is a crucial foundation for continued healing and growth as we progress on our journey to overcome PTSD.

Holistic Self-Integration with Transpersonal Psychology

As we immerse ourselves in the depths of Transpersonal Psychology, we are introduced to a realm where the journey of self-integration transcends the individualistic focus of conventional therapy. This expansive approach encourages us to look beyond the immediate scope of our personal experiences and to perceive our existence as just a tiny aspect of the more significant universal existence.

Self-Transcendence: At the heart of this week's exploration is the concept of self-transcendence, which involves going beyond the self-focused boundaries of our identity and experiences. This journey of transcendence allows us to connect with aspects of existence that are larger than ourselves—be it nature, the universe, humanity, or the divine. In the context of healing from PTSD, self-transcendence offers a powerful pathway to finding meaning and purpose beyond our pain and struggles. It opens the door to a profound understanding that our experiences, including traumas, are part of a greater narrative of personal evolution and growth.

Spiritual Interconnectedness: Another key facet of this week is the exploration of our spiritual interconnectedness. This concept encourages us to recognize that we are not isolated entities but are deeply connected to the world and people around us. By understanding and embracing this interconnectedness, we gain a sense of belonging and find comfort in the shared human experience. This realization can be particularly healing for those with PTSD, as it counters feelings of isolation and alienation that often accompany traumatic experiences. It nurtures a sense of empathy for us and others, fostering a compassionate understanding that we are all part of a collective journey.

Exploring Deeper Meanings: This week encourages us to probe deeper meanings behind our life experiences. This involves a superficial understanding of events and a deeper contemplation of their significance in the grand scheme of our life's journey. We are prompted to ask ourselves: What lessons can be learned from our traumas? How have these experiences shaped our understanding of ourselves and the world? This exploration is not about finding justification for the pain we have endured but about discovering how our experiences contribute to our growth, wisdom, and resilience.

Activities and reflections this week are designed to facilitate these profound explorations. Through meditations, reflective journaling, and guided discussions, we embark on a journey to uncover the deeper layers of our being. We are encouraged to let go of our limited self-perceptions and embrace a more expansive, interconnected view of ourselves. This holistic perspective fosters a sense of wholeness and peace, crucial for the healing and integration we seek in overcoming PTSD and opening us to a world of deeper understanding, connection, and purpose.

This week's journey is guided by practices and reflections that encourage us to consider our place within the universe, recognizing our small yet significant role in the grand scheme of life. We engage in meditative practices that open us to spiritual exploration, helping us connect with a sense of purpose beyond the confines of our individual experiences. These practices elevate our perspective, enabling us to see our life, including our traumas, as part of a larger narrative of growth and evolution.

We also delve into exercises that connect us with a sense of universal interconnectedness. These activities aim to foster a deep appreciation for the intricate web of life, of which we are an integral part. By acknowledging our connection to something greater than ourselves, we gain a sense of belonging and significance that can be profoundly healing.

Furthermore, this week is also about cultivating a deep sense of gratitude. Through reflective practices, we learn to appreciate life's myriad experiences, understanding them as opportunities for learning and growth. This gratitude attitude helps us embrace our life's journey, including the challenges and traumas, with a renewed sense of purpose and acceptance.

As we find ourselves at this transformative juncture, the integration achieved through the IFS model and the holistic insights provided by Transpersonal Psychology brings us to profound self-awareness and harmony. This integrated approach to self-understanding and healing empowers us to view our journey through PTSD as an opportunity for deep, transformative growth and self-discovery. This week's work lays the foundation for a more integrated, aware, and empowered self—one in harmony with its internal dynamics and place in the larger universe.

A Threshold of Transformation

As we step into this transformative workspace, we stand at a threshold, poised for a profound metamorphosis. This week is a culmination of our journey thus far, a deep dive into the heart of our healing process. Embrace this transformative path, leading to a more integrated and evolved self.

Throughout this week, the exercises and reflections are meticulously crafted to be potent and provocative, guiding us through a labyrinth of self-exploration and introspection. We're encouraged to weave together the fragmented parts of our psyche, creating self-awareness, acceptance, and compassion. This integration process is a delicate yet powerful endeavor that promises to reshape our understanding of ourselves and our experiences.

As we immerse ourselves in this transformative work, we're redefining our relationship to the past. The traumas that once seemed insurmountable obstacles now become landmarks on our journey of self-discovery. We learn to view our experiences through a lens of growth and transformation, recognizing the strength and resilience that have emerged from our struggles.

By the end of Week 8, we aim to cross a pivotal threshold in our healing journey. This week is a significant milestone in a much larger narrative of growth and evolution. We emerge from this week with a newfound sense of wholeness, a deeper appreciation for our journey, and a rejuvenated spirit. Our experiences, once fragmented and dissonant, now harmonize into a symphony of self-awareness and empowerment. This week marks a momentous leap forward, not just in our journey of healing from PTSD but in our ongoing odyssey of self-discovery and transformation.

Week 8 Self-Help Guide

Welcome to Week Eight, a continuation of our journey through the Internal Family Systems (IFS) model, with a focused intent on the integration of the fragmented self. Building on the insights and experiences of the previous week, this phase introduces seven new assignments crafted to deepen your engagement with IFS principles and facilitate the healing process. This week, we'll explore more advanced techniques for identifying, acknowledging, and harmonizing the various parts of your psyche, guiding you towards a more unified and coherent sense of self. Each task is designed not only to enhance your understanding of the IFS framework but also to apply it in a way that promotes the integration of your inner parts. This step is crucial for moving beyond mere awareness to achieving a state of balance and inner peace, essential for healing from PTSD. As we proceed, remember that integration is a gentle process of acceptance and transformation, paving the way for a stronger, more resilient self. Let's embrace this week with an open heart and a commitment to the ongoing journey of self-discovery and integration.

WEEK 8 WEEK 8, DAY 1: DEEPENING IFS DIALOGUE

Objective: Engage in a reflective and transformative dialogue with the identified parts of your Internal Family Systems (IFS) framework—Protectors, Exiles, Managers, and Firefighters—to understand their evolution and roles, fostering a future of internal harmony and cohesion.

Task: Today's task involves revisiting and deepening the dialogue with the essential parts you've identified in your previous IFS work. This exercise is designed to be reflective, insightful, and transformative, encapsulating your journey over the past six weeks. You'll connect these parts to the specific roles within the IFS framework—Protectors, Exiles, Managers, and Firefighters—understanding their evolution and envisioning a future of cohesive harmony.

Guidance:

1. Review Past IFS Work: Start by revisiting the work you have done in previous weeks. Look back at your journal entries, notes, or any other records of your IFS journey. Pay attention to the parts you identified and your dialogues with them. Notice any patterns, emotions, or thoughts that stand out.

2. Categorize Your Parts: Reflect on each part you've worked with and categorize them as Protectors, Exiles, Managers, or Firefighters. This categorization helps in understanding their roles and contributions to your psyche. Ask yourself how these parts have tried to protect, manage, or extinguish emotional pain.

3. Engage in a Deep Dialogue: Engage in a deep, mindful dialogue with these parts. Acknowledge their presence and express gratitude for their roles, however challenging they may have been. Ask them how they have evolved over the past weeks and what they need now to work in harmony with the other parts.

4. Envision a Harmonious Future: Imagine a future where these parts work together cohesively. How would that look and feel? What changes might be necessary for this harmony to be achieved? Visualize a scenario where all parts are acknowledged, respected, and integrated.

5. Reflect and Journal: After your dialogue, take some time to reflect on this integrative experience. How does reconnecting and deepening your understanding of these parts change your inner narrative? How do you feel about the potential for harmony within your psyche? Journal these reflections, focusing on insights, emotions, and visions for the future.

Processing: This exercise is about recognizing the journey of each part and acknowledging their growth and potential for integration. It's a time for you to see the beauty in the complexity of your internal system and appreciate how each part contributes to your whole being. This process is not just about healing from trauma; it's about evolving into a more integrated, aware, and empowered individual.

As you journal, consider how this deepened understanding and envisioning of harmony can influence your daily life. How might these insights help you respond to challenges or triggers in the future? What steps can you take to continue fostering this internal harmony? This reflective process is a significant step in your journey toward a more cohesive and peaceful internal existence.

Transpersonal Vision Quest: Embark on a meditative journey to connect with your higher self or a transcendent perspective. Use guided visualization or meditation to tap into deeper meanings and spiritual connections of your life story, including your trauma. Reflect on insights or shifts in perspective.

WEEK 8 WEEK 8, DAY 2: MEDITATIVE VISUALIZATION AND REFLECTION - ENVISIONING THE ULTIMATE SELF

Objective: To engage in a meditative visualization exercise that embodies the 8 Cs (Confidence, Calmness, Creativity, Clarity, Curiosity, Courage, Compassion, Connectedness) and the 5 Ps (Presence, Patience, Perspective, Persistence, Playfulness) of the Internal Family Systems (IFS) model, crafting a vivid vision of one's ultimate self and reflecting on the journey towards healing and self-integration.

Task: Engage in a meditative visualization exercise focused on envisioning your ultimate self, guided by the principles of the 8 Cs and the 5 Ps of IFS.

1. Preparation: Find a quiet, comfortable space where you won't be disturbed. Sit or lie down in a relaxed posture.
2. Beginning the Meditation: Start by focusing on your breath, allowing yourself to settle into a calm and centered state.
3. Invoking the 8 Cs:
    ○ Confidence: Visualize a scenario where you embody complete self-assurance. Imagine yourself handling a challenging situation effortlessly.
    ○ Calmness: Picture a serene setting where you feel utterly at peace. Feel this tranquility permeating every part of your being.

- Creativity: Imagine engaging in an activity where your creativity flows unbounded, showcasing your innovative spirit.
- Clarity: Envision a moment of profound understanding and insight where the complexities of your life make complete sense.
- Curiosity: Picture yourself exploring something new with an open, inquisitive mind, free from judgment or preconceptions.
- Courage: Visualize confronting a fear or a difficult part of yourself with bravery and determination.
- Compassion: Imagine a scene where you extend deep empathy and kindness to yourself, especially to the hurt parts.
- Connectedness: Feel a sense of unity and harmony within, where all parts of you work together synchronously.

4. Embracing the 5 Ps:
   - Presence: Bring your attention to this moment, feeling fully alive and engaged in the visualization.
   - Patience: Allow the images and sensations to unfold at their own pace, without rush or force.
   - Perspective: Maintain an overarching view of yourself, appreciating the journey you've embarked on.
   - Persistence: Commit to this vision, understanding that it's a guiding star on your journey to healing and wholeness.
   - Playfulness: Approach this exercise with a light-heartedness, allowing joy and ease to permeate your visualization.

5. Deepening the Visualization: Spend several minutes immersing yourself in this visualization, exploring the sensations, emotions, and thoughts that arise as you embody these qualities.

Processing: After completing the meditation, take some time to write about the experience. Reflect on the following:

- How did embodying each of the 8 Cs and the 5 Ps feel?

- Which qualities felt most natural to you and which ones did you find more challenging to connect with?
- How does this vision of your ultimate self differ from your current state?
- What insights or inspirations emerged from this exercise about your journey toward healing and self-integration?

This exercise is designed to help you create a vivid, compelling vision of who you can become as you integrate the fragmented parts of yourself. It sets a powerful intention for your journey toward a more harmonious and fulfilling life.

WEEK 8, DAY 3: PERSONAL CEREMONY OF GRATITUDE AND FUTURE VISION

Objective: To conduct a personal ceremony incorporating gratitude and visualization, aimed at acknowledging personal growth, enhancing self-compassion, and shaping a vision of a future unburdened by PTSD, where one's strengths and positive attributes are fully realized and celebrated.

Task: Create a personal ceremony that blends gratitude and visualization, celebrating your journey and affirming your strengths and positive attributes. This ceremony is a powerful way to acknowledge your growth, foster self-compassion, and envision a future where you are fully integrated and free from the grip of PTSD.

1. Preparation: Choose a quiet, comfortable space where you feel safe and undisturbed. You might want to create a serene ambiance with soft music, candles, or anything else that adds a sense of sacredness to your space.
2. Listing Attributes and Strengths: Reflect on and write down your positive attributes and strengths. Think about the qualities you've discovered or strengthened through your journey— resilience, courage, empathy, patience, etc. Acknowledge each attribute and understand how they have contributed to your growth.

3. Envisioning the Future: Now, with these attributes in mind, close your eyes and start visualizing your future in different domains of your life: Health, Spirituality, Family, Career, and Friends.
   - Health: Visualize yourself leading a healthy, vibrant life full of energy and well-being.
   - Spiritual: Imagine being deeply connected with your spiritual self or the universe and experiencing a profound sense of peace and purpose.
   - Family: Picture harmonious relationships with family members filled with love, understanding, and support.
   - Career: Envision success and fulfillment in your professional endeavors, using your skills and passions.
   - Friends: See yourself surrounded by a supportive and loving circle of friends, sharing joy and companionship.
4. Stepping Through the Threshold: As you hold these visions, imagine yourself stepping through a symbolic threshold, moving from this future vision into the present moment, where you embody all these characteristics. Feel this transition as a powerful affirmation of your transformation.
5. Embracing the Moment: Breathe deeply, absorbing this moment's essence. Notice how it feels to be this version of yourself—your thoughts, emotions, and sensations. Allow yourself to inhabit this space of transformation fully.
6. Gratitude and Loving-Kindness: Express gratitude toward yourself for undertaking this journey. Embrace yourself with loving-kindness, acknowledging the courage it took to embark on this path. Feel the excitement and curiosity as you open yourself to new possibilities.

Processing: After the ceremony, take some time to write about the experience. Reflect on:

- The feelings and thoughts that emerged as you listed your attributes and strengths.

- How did it feel to visualize your future self in different life domains?
- What emotions did you experience as you stepped through the threshold?
- How does embracing this new version of yourself change your outlook on life and your future?
- What are you most thankful for about this journey?

This ceremony celebrates you—of all you have overcome and are becoming. It's a moment to honor your resilience, embrace your future, and step confidently into a life of newfound possibilities.

WEEK 8 DAY 4: SYMBOLIC THRESHOLD CROSSING

Objective: To engage in a symbolic act that embodies the transition from fragmentation to wholeness, serving as a tangible representation of inner growth and the journey towards an integrated, empowered self, and to reflect on this transformative experience.

Task: Engage in a symbolic act representing your transition from fragmentation to a newfound sense of wholeness and integration. This exercise is a physical manifestation of the inner work you have been doing, signifying your move toward a unified, empowered self. Choose an act that resonates with your journey and holds deep meaning.

1. Planning the Act: Reflect on what kind of symbolic act represents your journey. It could be:
    - A walk in a nature setting that holds special significance to you, symbolizing your journey through different terrains of life.
    - Crossing a literal bridge representing the transition from one phase of life to another.
    - Planting a tree or a flower, denoting growth, grounding, and new beginnings.
    - Any other personal act that symbolizes crossing a threshold for you.
2. Preparing for the Act: Set your intentions as you prepare for this act. Acknowledge the significance of this moment and what it

represents in your journey. This is a physical act and a profound statement of your evolution.

3. Enacting the Symbolic Act: Carry out your chosen act with mindfulness and presence. As you perform this act:
   - Notice your surroundings, the sensations in your body, and the emotions that arise.
   - Reflect on the journey that has brought you to this point— the challenges, the growth, the insights.
   - Feel the symbolic significance of each step or action you take during this act.

4. Crossing the Threshold: As you complete your act, take a moment to acknowledge this as your point of crossing into a new phase of being. Feel the shift within you as you embrace this transition.

Processing: After completing your symbolic act, spend some time journaling about the experience. Reflect on:

- The emotions and thoughts that surfaced during the act.
- How the act represented your journey from fragmentation to wholeness.
- Any insights or revelations that came to you during this process.
- How you felt before, during, and after completing the act.
- What this threshold crossing signifies for your future journey.

Reflection: This act is a powerful externalization of your internal transformation. It's a ritual that marks your progress and celebrates your resilience and strength. As you move forward, carry the significance of this act with you, letting it remind you of your capacity for growth, healing, and renewal.

WEEK 8 DAY 5: CRAFTING YOUR NEW NARRATIVE

Objective: To write a detailed life narrative that encapsulates the integration of lessons, strengths, and insights gained, serving as a declaration of the transformed self post-healing and transformation, and to reflect on this narrative as a blueprint for future growth and identity.

Task: Write a detailed life narrative from the perspective of fully integrating all the lessons, strengths, and insights you've gained throughout this journey. This new narrative reflects not just where you've been but a powerful declaration of who you are now, embodying the healing and transformation you've achieved.

1. Setting the Stage: Choose a quiet, comfortable space where you can reflect and write without interruption.
2. Envisioning the New Self: Close your eyes and imagine your life as someone transcending past traumas. Envision how you interact with the world, handle challenges, and relate to others.
3. Writing the Narrative: Begin writing your story, starting from this present moment and projecting into the future. Include:
   - How you've overcome the challenges of PTSD.
   - How your relationships have evolved.
   - Achievements and successes you've attained, both personal and professional.
   - How you handle stress and challenges differently now.
   - The new hobbies, interests, or passions you've embraced.

- The sense of peace and fulfillment you experience in daily life.

Processing: Reflect on the narrative you've created. Notice how it feels to see yourself in this new light. Observe any emotional responses or thoughts as you read through your story. How does this narrative align with your self-perception, and what steps can you take to make this vision a reality?

Reflection: This narrative is your blueprint for the future. It's a living document you can return to and revise as you grow and evolve. Let it inspire and motivate you as you embark on the next chapter of your life.

WEEK 8 DAY 6: LIVING YOUR TRANSFORMATION

Objective: To embody and live out the qualities and behaviors of the transformed self described in your new narrative for a day, engaging in reflective practices to assess alignment with this envisioned identity and to glean insights into personal growth and potential.

Task: Today, live as if you are already the person you described in your new narrative. Embrace each moment with the confidence, resilience, and wisdom you've cultivated. Engage in activities that align with this new version of yourself.

1. Morning Reflection: Start your day with a meditation or quiet reflection, envisioning yourself embodying the qualities you've developed.
2. Acting it Out: Throughout the day, consciously adopt the behaviors, attitudes, and responses of your transformed self. This might include:
   ◦ Approaching challenges with calmness and clarity.
   ◦ Interacting with others from a place of compassion and understanding.
   ◦ Pursuing activities that align with your new interests and passions.
   ◦ Practicing gratitude and mindfulness in everyday moments.
3. Evening Reflection: End your day by reflecting on your experiences. What felt different? How did people respond to the new

you? What insights did you gain about yourself and your potential for change?

Processing: Journal about your experience of living as your transformed self. Note any challenges you faced and how you overcame them. Reflect on the aspects of this experience that felt most natural and fulfilling.

Reflection: This exercise is a powerful enactment of your capacity for change and growth. By physically embodying your transformed self, you make the abstract tangible. This experience provides a glimpse into the life that awaits you as you continue to apply the lessons and skills you've learned. Embrace this new version of yourself with confidence and openness to your future's endless possibilities.

| 13 |

Visualization and Future Planning

As we continue our transformative journey, we find ourselves at a pivotal juncture. This week celebrates our progress and a forward-looking exploration of what lies ahead. It's a time to harness the insights, tools, and therapeutic strategies we've acquired, weaving them into a vision for our future that genuinely resonates with our deepest aspirations and the growth we've experienced.

Throughout this journey, we've navigated the complex landscapes of trauma, self-awareness, and healing. We've unearthed deep-seated emotions, challenged long-held beliefs, and discovered inner strengths we may not have known existed. Now, we stand at a point where we can project these discoveries into a future that acknowledges our past and embraces the potential of what we can become.

Entering into Week 9, we do so with a sense of empowerment and clarity. The work we've done thus far has not only been about healing from PTSD but also about discovering who we are and who we want to be. This week, we take all that we have learned, all that we have felt and experienced, and use it to craft a vision for our future—a vision that is as boundless and hopeful as the journey we've embarked upon.

We all envision an ideal version of ourselves, characterized by desired virtues, traits, and behaviors. However, realizing this vision can be frustrating and challenging due to uncertainties about how to achieve it. The progress we've made thus far serves as a foundation, enabling us to move closer to becoming that better version of ourselves. It's now up to us to persist in our journey towards actualizing this ideal self.

We begin by harnessing the clarity and intentionality fostered through Cognitive Behavioral Therapy (CBT). We will continue to identify, challenge, and reframe lingering negative thought patterns. We will focus on recognizing behaviors that no longer serve us and actively redirecting our actions to align with our future goals. This continual cognitive and behavioral adjustment process is crucial for maintaining our progress and moving confidently into the future.

Incorporating Internal Family Systems (IFS) into our future planning, we maintain an ongoing dialogue with our internal parts, ensuring they remain cohesive and harmonious. This ongoing interaction with our parts ensures that every aspect of ourselves is acknowledged and integrated into our vision for the future. By doing so, we ensure that our plans reflect our conscious desires and deeper emotional and psychological needs.

Mindfulness remains a cornerstone of our practice, providing a foundation of relaxation, calmness, and present-moment awareness. As we envision our future, mindfulness keeps us grounded and centered, enabling us to approach our goals with a clear and focused mind. It allows us to plan with intention and purpose without being overwhelmed by anxiety or fear about what lies ahead.

Solution-focused therapy offers a structured approach to envisioning a positive future. We build on our strengths and past successes, using them as a springboard to imagine and create a future that excites and motivates us. This modality encourages us to set clear, attainable goals and to visualize the steps needed to achieve them.

Finally, Transpersonal Psychology invites us to explore the spiritual and existential dimensions of our life's path. We are encouraged to look beyond our individual experiences and to see ourselves as part of a larger, interconnected whole. This perspective fosters a sense of purpose that transcends personal achievement, aligning our future goals with our deeper values and place in the world.

As Week 9 unfolds, we engage in a dynamic interplay of these modalities, each enriching our visualization and future planning process. This week is about more than setting goals; it's about creating a future deeply aligned with who we have become through this journey. It's a future that holds healing, growth, and a profound sense of purpose and fulfillment.

Week 9 Self-Help Guide

Welcome to Week Nine, where we turn our focus toward envisioning a PTSD FREE future, using visualization, reflection, and goal-setting as our guiding lights. This week, we introduce seven engaging homework assignments designed to propel you forward on your healing journey. Each task is carefully crafted to help you harness the power of visualization to see beyond your current circumstances, encouraging deep reflection on your desires, strengths, and potential. Through goal-setting exercises, you will begin to outline actionable steps towards creating the life you envision, one where PTSD no longer dictates your possibilities. This week is about looking ahead with hope and determination, grounding yourself in the present while actively shaping a future where you thrive. Let's embark on this week with optimism and a clear vision, ready to set the foundation for a life filled with meaning, joy, and fulfillment beyond PTSD.

WEEK 9 DAY 1: VISION BOARD CREATION

Objective: To create a vision board that visually represents your aspirations and goals across various life areas, including health, career, relationships, personal growth, and spiritual development, incorporating symbols of healing, growth, and transformation, and then reflect on how these elements align with your experiences, emotions, and therapeutic progress, particularly in overcoming or managing PTSD.

Task: Your task today is to create a vision board, a powerful visual representation of your aspirations and goals. Begin by gathering materials like magazines, printouts, markers, and a large piece of paper or a corkboard. Look for images, words, and symbols that resonate with your future aspirations. Consider all key areas of your life, such as health, career, relationships, personal growth, and spiritual development. Place these elements on your board in a way that visually appeals to and inspires you. This board should reflect your goals and the essence of the journey you aspire to embark upon. Include elements that symbolize healing, growth, and transformation.

Processing: Once your vision board is complete, take some time to reflect on each element you've included. Ask yourself:

- How do these images and words connect with my experiences so far?
- What emotions or thoughts do they evoke regarding my future?

- How do these goals align with the changes and growth I've experienced throughout this therapeutic journey?
- In what ways do these aspirations reflect a future where I have overcome or effectively managed my PTSD symptoms?
- Are there any elements on this board that surprise me or challenge my current perceptions?

Reflection: Write down your reflections in a journal. This process is about visualizing a future and recognizing and appreciating how far you've come in your healing journey. Your vision board is a living document; as you grow and evolve, feel free to add or adjust elements to reflect your changing aspirations and insights.

WEEK 9 DAY 2: POSITIVE FUTURE VISUALIZATION

Objective: To perform a guided visualization exercise focusing on a future where personal goals are achieved, reflecting on the emotions, relationships, accomplishments, and the role of overcoming PTSD in shaping this future. Following the visualization, journal about the experience, detailing the emotions felt, achievements visualized, the influence of the therapeutic journey on these future outcomes, and insights gained, culminating in the creation of a roadmap for realizing this envisioned future.

Task:

1. **Find a Quiet Space**: Choose a serene location that ensures privacy. Consider playing soft instrumental music to enhance focus.
2. **Center Yourself**: Close your eyes and take deep breaths to achieve a state of calmness.
3. **Visualize Your Future**: Imagine achieving your key goals. Detail this future:
   - **Relationships**: Envision interactions with others; assess if they are more fulfilling.
   - **Emotions**: Identify the feelings this future brings; peace, joy, confidence?
   - **Accomplishments**: Reflect on your successes and the sensation of achieving them.

- **Impact of Overcoming PTSD**: Contemplate how managing PTSD has shaped this positive future.

Processing:

1. **Ground Yourself**: After the visualization, reconnect with the present moment.
2. **Journal Your Experience**:
   - Describe the emotions experienced during the visualization.
   - Detail the envisioned achievements and notable changes.
   - Reflect on how your journey has contributed to these future successes.
   - Note any insights or revelations.
3. **Plan Future Steps**: Draft a roadmap to actualize this vision. Prepare to set concrete goals next week.

This task aims to strengthen the link between your current efforts and the aspirational future, underscoring that ongoing steps are laying the foundation for a rewarding and emotionally healthy future.

WEEK 9 DAY 3: GOAL-SETTING

Objective: Utilize Cognitive Behavioral Therapy (CBT) techniques to establish SMART goals (Specific, Measurable, Achievable, Relevant, Time-bound) in areas of personal growth, career, health, relationships, or spirituality, reflecting on future visions. Challenge and reframe any limiting beliefs encountered during this process to reinforce a positive mindset and enhance the belief in achieving these goals.

Task:

- For today's exercise, you will use Cognitive Behavioral Therapy (CBT) techniques to set clear and achievable goals based on your reflection from last week. The focus here is on creating SMART goals – Specific, Measurable, Achievable, Relevant, and Time-bound goals.
- Consider last week's vision for your future, as explored in the previous exercises. Consider the areas of life you want to focus on, such as personal growth, career, health, relationships, or spirituality.
- Write down specific goals in these areas. For instance, if you're focusing on health, a SMART goal might be: "To increase my physical activity by walking 30 minutes, three times a week for the next two months."
- Make sure each goal is:
  - Specific: Clearly define what you want to achieve.
  - Measurable: Determine how you will measure progress and success.

- Achievable: Ensure the goal is attainable with your resources and time.
- Relevant: The goal should align with your broader aspirations and be meaningful to you.
- Time-bound: Set a reasonable deadline for achieving the goal.

Processing:

- After setting your goals, take some time to reflect on the process:
    - Were there any limiting beliefs or negative thoughts that emerged while you were setting these goals? These might include doubts about your abilities or fears of failure.
    - Use CBT techniques to challenge and reframe these limiting beliefs. For example, if a belief is "I always fail at sticking to routines," reframe it to "In the past, I've had challenges with routines, but I'm learning new strategies and can improve."
    - Write down these reframed beliefs alongside your goals. This practice helps in reinforcing a positive mindset and belief in your ability to achieve what you've set out to do.
    - Consider how these reframed beliefs can be integrated into your daily life. They can serve as affirmations or reminders to keep you motivated and focused on your goals.

This exercise empowers you by setting clear, attainable goals and transforming negative thought patterns that might impede your progress. It's about taking control of your future, one step at a time, with a positive and realistic approach.

WEEK 9 DAY 4: MINDFUL MEDITATION FOR PRESENT AND FUTURE SELF

Objective: To engage in a mindfulness meditation that connects your present self with your envisioned future self, focusing on accepting current experiences without judgment and visualizing future aspirations. Reflect on the qualities needed for this transition, the influence of present mindfulness on future realization, and any emotions or insights that emerge, fostering a deeper understanding of personal growth and the journey toward achieving your goals.

Task:

- Today's exercise involves a mindfulness meditation that creates a bridge between your present and future self. This practice is about acknowledging where you are now and envisioning your aspirations.
- Start by finding a quiet, comfortable space to sit or lie down without distractions. Begin with a few deep breaths to center yourself.
- Spend the first part of the meditation focusing on your present self. Notice your current thoughts, feelings, and bodily sensations. Acknowledge them without judgment, simply observing them as they are.
- After you feel grounded in the present moment, gently transition your focus to your future self. Envision yourself having achieved

your goals and living the life you desire. Picture how you look, feel, and act in this coming state.

- Imagine the positive changes and growth you have experienced. Think about the qualities and achievements of your future self – how does this version of you navigate life? What wisdom or qualities have you developed?

Processing:

- After the meditation, take some time to journal or reflect on the experience:
  - Write about the differences and similarities you noticed between your present and future self. What qualities do you currently possess that will aid in becoming your envisioned future self? What aspects do you hope to develop or change?
  - Reflect on how being mindful of your present state can influence your perception and realization of your future. How does acknowledging and accepting your current experiences shape your journey toward your goals?
  - Consider the emotions or insights that arose during the meditation. Did you feel a sense of continuity between your present and future self, or were there distinct differences? How does this inform your understanding of your personal growth and evolution?

This meditative practice fosters a deeper connection with your current and future self, creating a sense of continuity and purpose. Mindfully acknowledging your present state and envisaging a hopeful and realistic future, you can navigate your path with greater clarity and intention.

WEEK 9 DAY 5: ENGAGING WITH INNER PARTS (IFS)

Objective: To conduct an internal dialogue with various IFS parts, exploring their roles, concerns, and contributions towards future aspirations. This involves engaging protectors, managers, and exiles in conversation, addressing any hesitations, and understanding how each part can support achieving your goals. Reflect on this dialogue through journaling, focusing on reactions, support, concerns of different parts, and insights on integrating all parts in the pursuit of your aspirations, aiming for a cohesive approach to your future goals.

Task:

- Today, you will internally dialogue with your various IFS parts to discuss your future aspirations and plans. This exercise is about understanding how each part of you can play a role in achieving your goals and dreams.
- Find a quiet, comfortable space where you can relax and focus inwardly. Close your eyes and take a few deep breaths to center yourself.
- One by one, invite each of your IFS parts to participate in a conversation about your future. You might start with your protectors, move to your managers, and finally, address your exiles.
- Ask each part how they see themselves contributing to or being affected by your plans. Discuss any roles they might play, any concerns they have, or any support they can offer.

- Pay special attention to any parts that express hesitation or concern. Engage them in a compassionate dialogue to understand their fears or objections and how these can be addressed or alleviated.

Processing:

- After your internal dialogue, take some time to journal about the experience:
    - Write about the reactions of each part to your future goals. Note any common themes or unique perspectives that emerged from different parts.
    - Were there any parts that were particularly supportive or enthusiastic about your plans? How can their energy and positivity be harnessed?
    - Did any parts express concerns or fears? How might you address these concerns to ensure all parts feel heard and included in your future journey?
    - Reflect on how this exercise might influence your approach to your goals. What insights did you gain about balancing the needs and contributions of all your parts in pursuit of your aspirations?

This exercise aims to harmonize your internal system with your future ambitions. By engaging in open communication with all your parts, you can create a supportive internal environment that aligns with your goals and ensures that every aspect of your being is working in concert towards your envisioned future.

WEEK 9 DAY 6: INTEGRATING TRANSPERSONAL PERSPECTIVES

Objective: Engage in a reflective exercise drawing from Transpersonal Psychology to contemplate future aspirations within the context of the broader universe, focusing on interconnectedness, purpose, and legacy. Reflect on how personal goals align with universal themes and the collective human experience, considering the impact on and contribution to the wider world. Journal about the insights, shifts in perception, and the sense of peace, purpose, or connectedness this broader perspective brings to your vision for the future.

Task:

- Today's exercise involves deeply reflecting on your future, not just as an individual journey but as part of a larger, interconnected universe. This exercise draws upon Transpersonal Psychology, which emphasizes the spiritual and transcendent aspects of human experience.
- Find a quiet and comfortable space where you won't be disturbed. You may choose to sit or lie down in a relaxed posture.
- Begin with a few moments of deep breathing to ground yourself in the present moment.
- Then, shift your focus to your future aspirations, considering them within the context of the broader universe. Think about how your goals and dreams connect to a greater sense of purpose or how they contribute to the world around you.

- Reflect on the interconnectedness of your life with the lives of others and the world at large. Contemplate how your journey of healing and growth extends beyond personal achievement to touch the lives of others and contribute to the collective human experience.
- Ponder the idea of legacy and the impact you wish to leave in the world. How does your envisioned future align with these broader, transcendent goals?

Processing :

- After your reflection, journal about your experience:
  - Describe how viewing your future within a broader, universal context influences your feelings and thoughts about what lies ahead.
  - Does this expanded perspective bring peace, purpose, or connectedness? How so?
  - Reflect on any insights or revelations about how your personal goals are intertwined with more significant themes of human experience and spiritual growth.
  - Write about any shifts in your perception of success, fulfillment, or at peace with yourself and the world.

By integrating a transpersonal perspective into your future planning, you're encouraged to see your journey not only as a path to personal fulfillment but also as a part of a larger tapestry of human existence. This broader view can instill a sense of purpose and connectedness, enriching your vision for the future with deeper meaning and a sense of contribution to the greater good.

| 14 |

Consolidation and Empowerment

Week 10 marks a significant milestone in our journey. It's a time for reflection and to embrace the efforts and dedication invested in the healing process. This week stands as a testament to the remarkable strides made in confronting and overcoming the challenges posed by PTSD. It's a celebration of progress, an acknowledgment of the transformative steps taken, and a moment to prepare for the future.

The past eight weeks have been an intricate tapestry of self-exploration, healing, and empowerment. As we navigate Week 10, the essence of consolidation becomes our central theme. This phase is more than just a review; it's a crucial synthesis of the diverse therapeutic approaches that have guided us along this transformative path.

In these moments of consolidation, we revisit the core principles of Cognitive Behavioral Therapy (CBT). We reflect on how CBT has equipped us with the skills to identify and reshape our thought patterns, empowering us to challenge and alter the negative and distorted narratives that once held sway over our minds. This process of cognitive restructuring has been fundamental in altering our responses to traumatic memories and in managing PTSD symptoms.

Alongside CBT, we revisit the Internal Family Systems (IFS) principles. IFS has provided us with a profound understanding of the multifaceted nature of our psyche. It has allowed us to recognize and embrace the various parts within us – the protectors, the managers, and the exiles – and to understand how these parts have been instrumental in our survival and coping mechanisms. The journey with IFS has been about fostering harmony among these parts, leading to greater self-compassion and inner peace.

Mindfulness, a practice woven into our daily routines, has taught us the art of present-moment awareness. It has allowed us to observe our thoughts and feelings without judgment, offering a sanctuary of calm amid life's turbulence. This grounding in the present has been crucial in managing the symptoms of PTSD and in cultivating a sense of peace and stability.

Transpersonal Psychology has expanded our understanding of self beyond the confines of conventional therapy. It has opened avenues for exploring our spiritual dimensions, our connection to the universe, and the deeper meanings behind our life experiences. This exploration has been essential in shaping a broader perspective on our journey and nurturing a sense of connectedness and purpose.

Solution-focused therapy has provided us with tools to envision a future free from the constraints of our past traumas. It has encouraged us to focus on solutions rather than problems, to set goals, and to envision a future where we thrive and achieve our fullest potential.

Positive Psychology has complemented these modalities by emphasizing the cultivation of strengths, virtues, and positive aspects of life. It has shifted our focus from what's wrong to what's strong, fostering resilience, optimism, and a sense of well-being.

As we combine these diverse therapeutic strands, we create a holistic model for healing and growth. This consolidation is not merely about blending techniques but weaving a narrative of recovery that honors our complexity and resilience. It's about creating a cohesive approach that acknowledges the multifaceted nature of healing from PTSD and offers a robust framework for continued growth and well-being. The journey through Week 10 is thus a testament to the power of this integrative approach and a stepping-stone to a future where we continue to evolve.

As we pause to reflect on the path traversed, a transformation narrative unfolds, marked by significant shifts in thoughts, feelings, and behaviors. From the hesitant first steps to the confident strides of this concluding phase, your journey mirrors a metamorphosis, a profound evolution of the self.

Revisiting each week's journal entries and exercises offers a unique perspective on this journey. It's akin to watching the chapters of a story unfold, each page brimming with insights and reflections. As you leaf through these records, you witness the gradual yet impactful changes. Thoughts that were once dominated by the shadows of trauma now radiate with resilience and hope. Emotions tangled in the past's complexities have found new expressions of peace and acceptance. Coping mechanisms that once seemed foreign or challenging have seamlessly woven into the fabric of your daily life.

Reviewing these entries, you observe the gradual but steady dissolution of old patterns and the birth of new, healthier ways of being. You see how your perspectives have broadened, your understanding of yourself and your trauma has deepened, and a newfound sense of empowerment has emerged. This journey through your own words and reflections is not just a trip down memory lane; it's a powerful reminder of the resilience and strength within you.

Each entry and exercise is a milestone on your path to recovery. They testify to your courage to face trauma, willingness to embrace change, and dedication to healing. This celebration of progress is a crucial component of your journey, as it reinforces the positive changes you've made and solidifies the learning and growth that have transpired.

This phase of reflection and celebration is not merely about acknowledging the end of a journey; it's about recognizing the beginning of a new chapter in your life. It's about understanding that the skills, insights, and self-awareness you've cultivated are now integral to who you are. As you celebrate your progress, you do so with the knowledge that this journey has equipped you with the tools and resilience to face future challenges with strength and grace.

The transformative journey that has unfolded over these weeks goes beyond mere healing from PTSD; it's a profound revelation of inner strength and resilience that you always possessed but may have been obscured by the clouds of trauma. This part of the journey is about acknowledging and embracing your self-efficacy - your belief in your ability to influence the events that affect your life and control your behavior.

As you venture into this phase, it becomes increasingly clear that the tools and insights you've gained are not merely for coping with the aftermath of trauma. They are, in fact, instruments for thriving in the diverse tapestry of life. These tools empower you to face future challenges not with trepidation but with a renewed sense of confidence and capability. You've learned to apply these strategies daily, transforming challenges into opportunities for growth and self-discovery.

This newfound empowerment is a testament to a shift in perspective – from seeing yourself as a passive recipient of therapeutic interventions to recognizing yourself as an active architect of your healing journey. You've become adept at utilizing the skills you've learned, not just in moments of distress but as integral parts of your daily routine. This shift in perception has instilled a sense of control and agency, reinforcing the belief in your ability to shape your life's narrative.

Understanding your self-efficacy is crucial. It's the driving force that propels you forward, knowing that you have the power to implement change, overcome obstacles, and pursue your goals with determination. It's about internalizing that you are the master of your destiny, equipped with a robust set of skills, a deeper understanding of yourself, and an unshakeable belief in your ability to navigate the complexities of life.

This stage of the journey is as much about empowerment as it is about healing. It's about owning your story, recognizing your progress, and stepping into your power. As you consolidate the gains from your therapy and reflect on the synthesis of modalities, you do so with a strengthened sense of self, a confident outlook on the future, and an empowered stance that prepares you to face the world with newfound resilience and optimism.

As we reflect upon the journey thus far, it becomes apparent that the confluence of various therapeutic modalities has been the cornerstone of this transformative process. The synthesis of these approaches forms a comprehensive tapestry of healing and growth, each strand contributing uniquely to the whole.

Cognitive Behavioral Therapy (CBT) has provided you with the tools to reshape and reframe thought patterns. It has taught you to identify and challenge cognitive distortions, replacing them with more balanced and realistic thoughts. This practice has not only alleviated symptoms of PTSD but also empowered you with skills to manage your mental health proactively.

Internal Family Systems (IFS) therapy has offered a profound journey into the depths of your psyche, revealing the diverse and often conflicting parts that constitute your inner world. This modality has facilitated understanding, acceptance, and integration of these parts, leading to a harmonious internal dialogue and greater inner peace.

Mindfulness has brought a transformative awareness to your experience, encouraging a state of presence and acceptance of the current moment. This practice has enabled you to observe your thoughts and feelings without judgment, fostering a sense of calm and equanimity even in the face of stress and anxiety.

Transpersonal Psychology has expanded the horizon of your healing journey, connecting your individual experiences to a broader, more spiritual context. It has helped you explore themes of self-transcendence, connectedness, and the deeper meanings behind your life experiences, offering a sense of purpose and belonging in the grand scheme of existence.

As we approach the conclusion of this program, it is essential to recognize how these diverse therapeutic approaches interlace to support your ongoing journey. They have collectively equipped you with a multifaceted set of skills and insights, each playing a role in your continued path to healing and self-discovery. As you prepare to continue your journey beyond this program, these modalities remain pillars of strength and guidance, each offering unique perspectives and tools to navigate the complexities of life post-PTSD. This synthesis of modalities is a foundation for the past eight weeks and a compass for the road ahead, guiding you toward sustained well-being and personal growth.

As we reach the culmination of this structured program, it's essential to recognize that the journey of healing and personal growth doesn't end here; instead, it transitions into a new phase. This next stage is about crafting a roadmap for the future that outlines how you can continue to nurture and expand upon the progress you've made.

The act of setting new goals and intentions is an empowering step forward. It's about taking the skills, insights, and experiences you've gained and applying them proactively. You might consider incorporating regular mindfulness practices into your daily routine, ensuring a continued connection with the present moment and a heightened awareness. Continued journaling can be a reflective tool, allowing you to document your ongoing journey, celebrate your successes, and navigate challenges with greater clarity and insight.

Setting periodic self-reflections is another vital aspect of this planning process. These moments of introspection can help you assess your growth, recognize areas for further development, and realign your goals as needed. It's a practice that fosters ongoing self-awareness and ensures that your journey of healing and growth is dynamic and responsive to your evolving needs.

This proactive planning is more than just a strategy; it's a commitment to yourself and your well-being. It's an acknowledgment that while the formal structure of the program may conclude your journey of healing, self-discovery and transformation is an enduring process. By embracing this mindset, you ensure that your progress is not just a temporary phase but a foundational part of life.

As we reflect upon the journey of healing, we must embrace the understanding that the path to recovery is not linear but a dynamic process with its natural ebbs and flows. The path of healing from PTSD, or any profound emotional experience, is akin to navigating through a landscape that changes with time and circumstance. Recognizing that there may be setbacks and challenges ahead is a vital aspect of this journey. However, it's crucial to remember that these are not signs of failure but natural components of the healing process.

The tools and skills you've acquired throughout this program provide a robust foundation for dealing with these challenges. Whether employing mindfulness techniques to maintain presence and balance, using cognitive behavioral strategies to reframe unhelpful thoughts, or drawing upon internal family systems to understand and harmonize various parts of your psyche, you now possess a comprehensive toolkit to face and navigate future obstacles.

Moreover, emphasizing self-compassion and patience in your ongoing journey is vital. Healing is a process that requires time, and treating yourself with the same kindness and understanding you would offer others is important. Patience is a virtue that plays a key role here – allowing yourself the space and time to grow, learn, and heal at your own pace.

As you move forward, it's beneficial to routinely acknowledge and celebrate your progress, no matter how small it may seem. These moments of recognition are potent reminders of your strength, resilience, and the distance you've traveled on this path. They also serve as motivators, fueling your journey forward with a sense of accomplishment and hope.

Reinforcing progress is about acknowledging the journey's nature, utilizing your newfound tools and skills to navigate future challenges, and maintaining a compassionate and patient attitude toward yourself. This approach helps consolidate your gains and prepares you to continue your journey with confidence, resilience, and deepened self-awareness.

As we draw this chapter close, it's a moment to pause and embrace a profound sense of accomplishment. The journey you have undertaken is one marked by deep self-discovery, healing, and empowerment. Each step taken, each challenge faced, and each insight gained has contributed to a remarkable transformation, both within and around you.

Looking ahead, you step into the future armed with a rich tapestry of skills, insights, and inner strengths cultivated over these transformative weeks. This arsenal equips you with a newfound confidence and optimism. The journey you've embarked upon doesn't end here; rather, it evolves into a continual process of growth and self-improvement.

Healing, as you've learned, is not a destination but a journey—one that is characterized by resilience, understanding, and compassion. As you move forward, remember that each day is an opportunity to apply the lessons learned, embrace your journey with kindness and patience, and continue growing in ways that nurture your well-being and personal development.

This program may have provided the structure and guidance for your initial steps, but the path ahead is yours to shape and traverse. You carry with you the promise of ongoing growth and transformation, a journey that transcends the confines of these sessions. With each new day, you are equipped to face life's complexities with a grounded sense of self, an open heart, and an empowered spirit.

Week 10 Self-Help Guide

Welcome to the final chapter of our journey, Week Ten, where we focus on the consolidation of all the valuable skills and insights you've gained throughout the first nine weeks. This week is about empowerment and moving forward, equipped with the tools to continue living free from PTSD. Through seven thoughtfully designed homework assignments, we'll celebrate the hard work you've done, reflecting on your growth and the obstacles you've overcome. We encourage further goal-setting to maintain and build upon your progress, emphasizing the importance of self-compassion and resilience. This week is not just a conclusion but a new beginning, marking your continued path toward healing and a future where PTSD no longer defines your experiences. Let's take this time to honor your commitment to healing, acknowledging every step taken as a step toward a brighter, PTSD FREE future.

WEEK 10, DAY 1: REFLECTIVE JOURNALING ON YOUR JOURNEY

Objective: To conduct a reflective journaling exercise that explores your journey through the program, focusing on moments of learning, transformation, challenges overcome, and shifts in perspective.

Task: Today, your task is to embark on a journey of reflection. Take some quiet time to write a journal entry that delves into your experiences throughout this program. Focus on key moments that stand out —moments of learning, transformation, or significant challenges you successfully navigated. Recall the times you felt a shift in perspective, overcame a hurdle, or discovered something new about yourself. Reflect on the exercises and concepts that resonated with you the most and those that presented the greatest challenges.

Processing: As you write, think about how you have changed from the first day you started this program to now. How have your thoughts, feelings, and behaviors evolved? Identify the most significant insights you've gained and how they've impacted different aspects of your life. Consider changes in handling stress, interacting with others, viewing yourself, and approaching challenges. Reflect on the growth in your self-awareness, emotional resilience, and overall mental well-being. This process is about acknowledging change and understanding the depth and breadth of your transformation.

Through this reflective journaling, you're documenting your journey and reinforcing the lessons learned and the strength you've gathered.

In your own words, it's an opportunity to see the path you've traveled and the progress you've made, setting the tone for the next phase of your life post this program.

Journal:

WEEK 10 DAY 2: GOAL-SETTING FOR CONTINUED GROWTH

Objective: To establish specific, achievable goals rooted in the insights and skills acquired during the program, reflecting on personal growth and how these goals align with your values and aspirations across various life domains.

Task: On this day, your focus shifts to the future. It's time to set specific, achievable goals that will guide your continued growth beyond the confines of this program. These goals should be deeply rooted in the insights and learning you've acquired and should resonate with your values and aspirations. Consider different areas of your life where you want to apply the skills you've learned or continue to grow—personal relationships, career, self-care, or spiritual development. Frame these goals to become footholds in your ongoing journey of self-improvement and well-being.

Processing: Once you've set your goals, reflect on them deeply. Consider how these goals are a natural extension of your progress during the program. How do they build upon the changes you've experienced and the strengths you've developed? Think about the strategies you will use to achieve these goals. What specific actions will you take? What resources or support might you need? Also, anticipate potential obstacles or challenges and how you might overcome them. Reflecting on these aspects will solidify your commitment to these goals and prepare you mentally and practically to pursue them.

This exercise is crucial as it ensures that your journey of healing and growth doesn't end with the program but continues to evolve, guided by clear intentions and thoughtful planning. Setting these goals marks the beginning of a new chapter, where you are empowered to take charge of your path forward, armed with the knowledge, skills, and self-awareness you've cultivated.

GOAL(s):

WEEK 10 DAY 3: GRATITUDE AND ACCOMPLISHMENTS EXERCISE

Objective: To engage in a gratitude exercise by listing insights, relationships, breakthroughs, and daily wins experienced throughout the program, along with your accomplishments. Reflect on how recognizing these positive aspects influences your perspective on the journey, fosters a mindset of growth and progress, and impacts your future endeavors. This aims to reinforce progress, celebrate achievements, and cultivate an optimistic outlook for ongoing healing and growth.

Task: Today, you will engage in an exercise focusing on gratitude and recognizing your accomplishments. Begin by listing things you are grateful for from your experiences throughout this program. These can be insights gained, relationships strengthened, personal breakthroughs, or even small daily wins. Alongside, note down the accomplishments you've achieved during your journey. These could range from successfully employing a coping technique to significant shifts in your perspective or behavior. This exercise is about acknowledging and celebrating every step forward, regardless of size.

Processing: After compiling your list, take time to reflect on it. How does acknowledging these positive aspects of your journey influence your feelings about the past nine weeks and your outlook on the future? Consider how recognizing your achievements and the things you're grateful for can shift your perspective from one that is problem-focused to one that appreciates growth and progress. This shift is crucial as it fosters a mindset that recognizes and celebrates progress, fostering a sense of achievement and optimism. Reflect on how this positive out-look can impact your future endeavors and your ongoing journey of healing and growth.

By consciously focusing on the positives and accomplishments, you reinforce your progress and the strengths you've built. This exercise is not just about feeling good at the moment. It's about cementing a positive and empowered mindset you carry forward into your life beyond this program.

JOURNAL:

WEEK 10 DAY 4: CREATING A RESILIENCE RITUAL

Objective: To design and implement a personal resilience ritual that encapsulates the essence of your journey and the resilience cultivated throughout this program. The ritual can range from simple daily affirmations to more elaborate routines, including actions, words, or visits to meaningful places, aimed at fostering empowerment and grounding. Reflect on the emotional impact of the ritual, its symbolic significance, and its role in reinforcing positive changes and focusing on ongoing growth and well-being.

Task: Today's activity involves creating a personal resilience ritual. This ritual should symbolize your journey and the resilience you've built. It can be a simple daily practice or a more elaborate weekly routine. The ritual might involve actions, words, or even a special place you visit regularly. It could be as straightforward as a morning affirmation, nature walk, or specific exercises that make you feel empowered and grounded.

Processing: As you engage in this resilience ritual, be mindful of how it makes you feel. Does it bring a sense of strength, calm, or empowerment? Reflect on the significance of each element in your ritual and how it symbolizes your journey through this program. How does this ritual reinforce the positive changes you've experienced and help you maintain your focus on continued growth and well-being?

JOURNAL:

WEEK 10 DAY 5: CREATING A PERSONAL MANTRA

Objective: To create a personal mantra that encapsulates the essence of your transformative journey and future aspirations, serving as a powerful, guiding phrase that reflects your resilience, growth, and positive changes. Reflect on the mantra's significance, its role as a source of strength and motivation, and visualize its application in overcoming challenges and reminding you of your journey's progress. This task marks a commitment to continuous growth and self-discovery beyond the program.

Task: Today, you will craft a personal mantra that embodies the essence of your transformative journey and your aspirations for the future. This mantra should be a concise, powerful statement that resonates deeply with you. Think of it as a guiding phrase that captures your resilience, growth, and the positive changes you've embraced. This mantra could reflect your newfound strengths, the peace you've found, or the courage you've developed.

Processing: Reflect on the meaning behind your mantra and the journey it represents. Consider how this mantra encapsulates your transformation and how it can be a source of strength and motivation in your everyday life. How does reciting this mantra make you feel? Identify specific situations or moments when this mantra could be empowering or helpful. Visualize yourself using this mantra to overcome challenges, to find peace in difficult moments, or as a reminder of how far you've come.

As you conclude these tasks, you're not just marking the end of a program but embracing a new chapter in your life. Each activity is designed to reinforce the profound shifts you've experienced and prepare you for a future filled with self-awareness, resilience, and a continuous journey of growth and self-discovery.

JOURNAL:

WEEK 10 DAY 6: CAPSTONE ACTIVITY: CREATING YOUR PERSONAL JOURNEY MAP

Objective: To create a Personal Journey Map as a visual representation of your nine-week journey, capturing growth, challenges, insights, and transformations. Utilize various creative mediums to illustrate key moments, breakthroughs, and tools acquired from week one through the end, including significant realizations and emotional shifts. Reflect on the visual impact, themes, significant strides, and challenges of your journey, considering how this map highlights resilience, skills developed, and overall progress. This Capstone Activity celebrates your journey and serves as inspiration for continued growth beyond the program.

Task: Create a Personal Journey Map for your final exercise to visually represent your path through these nine weeks. This map will comprehensively and creatively depict your growth, challenges, insights, and transformations. Use drawings, symbols, words, or any other medium that resonates with you. Start from Week 1, illustrating key moments, breakthroughs, and the tools you've acquired. Journey through each week, capturing the essence of your experiences and how they've contributed to your growth. Include significant realizations, emotional shifts, and how your perspectives have evolved. End your map with where you are now, encapsulating your current state of healing, empowerment, and vision for the future.

Processing: Once your Personal Journey Map is complete, reflect on it. How does seeing your journey laid out visually impact you? What themes or patterns do you notice? How do the different weeks and their specific focuses interconnect and contribute to your overall growth? Identify areas where you've made the most significant strides and parts of the journey that were particularly challenging. Consider how this map can serve as a reminder of your resilience, the skills you've developed, and the progress you've made. Think about how you can use this map to guide and inspire your continued journey beyond this program.

This Capstone Activity is designed to be a powerful culmination of your nine-week journey. It serves as a tangible reminder of the path you've walked, the obstacles you've overcome, and the growth you've experienced. It's a celebration of your journey and a beacon for your continued path forward, filled with hope, strength, and a deeper understanding of yourself.

JOURNAL:

PART III

MOVING FORWARD

| 15 |

Moving Forward

It's time to celebrate and reflect. This chapter is a tribute to your dedication and tenacity throughout this transformative journey. You've navigated the complexities of healing with courage and persistence, and committed to personal growth and well-being. However, this chapter also serves as a gentle reminder of the journey's continuous nature and the importance of remaining vigilant to prevent any backward steps or relapse into old patterns.

Brain plasticity, the remarkable capacity of our neural pathways to reorganize and strengthen in response to new experiences, stands as a cornerstone of recovery and growth. This incredible adaptability underscores the concept that healing and change are ongoing processes grounded in the persistent and diligent nurturing of one's mental landscape.

Understanding and leveraging this neuroplasticity is akin to a gardener who patiently tends to their garden. Just as the gardener prepares the soil, plants the seeds, and provides consistent care through watering, weeding, and protection from the elements, so must you tend to the garden of your mind. The seeds of new thought patterns and behaviors require regular attention and reinforcement to take root and thrive.

The work doesn't end with the initial planting of seeds—meaning introducing new ways of thinking and reacting. Daily cultivation— responding differently to stressors, practicing mindfulness, and re- inforcing positive self-talk—encourages these seeds to sprout and grow. In time, with dedication and care, these new pathways will become well-established routes in your brain, your default mechanisms for navigating the world.

Living mindfully becomes a central theme in this process as you move forward. Mindfulness is the act of attentive watering, giving each thought and emotion its due consideration without allowing the weeds of negativity to overrun the progress you've made. By staying present and aware, you maintain the health of your mental garden, ensuring that the old patterns of PTSD do not reclaim the space you've so diligently cleared for your new growth.

In essence, the healing journey and the prevention of relapse is an active and conscious one. It involves a daily commitment to cultivating your inner world, ensuring that the neural pathways supporting your well-being and resilience are consistently reinforced, allowing you to live mindfully and with intention.

Expanding mindfulness into your post-therapy life is essential for sustaining the progress made in managing PTSD. This practice of mindfulness forms a protective buffer against relapse, empowering you with the ability to remain anchored in the now, even when past traumas threaten to pull you back into old patterns of distress.

The art of mindfulness is rooted in recognizing the ebb and flow of mental states. It teaches you to observe your thoughts and feelings as if they were leaves floating down a stream—present but not permanent, visible but not vital. This perspective allows you to detach from the grip of negative ruminations and anxious projections that are often precursors to PTSD symptoms. By acknowledging the transient nature of thoughts, you minimize their power to dictate your emotional state.

Integrating mindfulness into daily routines can transform mundane activities into deep awareness and connection moments. Practices such as mindful eating, walking, or listening become exercises in attention, each action an opportunity to cultivate presence. This ongoing practice helps recalibrate your response to stress, reducing the likelihood of being overwhelmed and providing a sense of control that PTSD often erodes.

The role of grounding techniques in this mindful approach cannot be overstated. Techniques such as deep breathing, sensory engagement, or mindful observation are not just crisis management tools but daily habits that reinforce your presence in the here and now. They act as immediate responses to dissociative moments or flashbacks, offering a lifeline back to the present and mitigating the power of triggers.

In addition to grounding techniques, regular meditation can deepen your mindfulness practice. It builds your mental resilience, enhancing your ability to observe without engaging with every thought or feeling that arises. Meditation can also improve concentration and reduce the overall stress that can contribute to PTSD symptoms.

Crucially, mindfulness fosters a compassionate self-relationship. It encourages an attitude of kindness toward yourself, recognizing that healing is not a linear process and that patience is key. This compassionate stance is a powerful antidote to the self-criticism and guilt that often accompany PTSD, promoting a healing environment within your mind.

Finally, mindfulness encourages a holistic view of your experiences. It allows you to see your symptoms not as defining features but as one part of a broader human experience. This holistic awareness can lead to a deeper understanding of the interconnectedness of life's joys and sorrows, further preventing the isolation and alienation that can accompany PTSD.

Living mindfully after PTSD therapy is a commitment to ongoing self-awareness and growth. It's about harnessing the power of the present moment to maintain emotional equilibrium, cultivate resilience, and foster a compassionate relationship with oneself. Mindfulness is not just a tool for managing PTSD; it's a pathway to a richer, more engaged experience of life.

Continual self-appraisal and introspection are the cornerstones of maintaining the progress made in overcoming PTSD. This process of self-examination serves as a vigilant guardian, ensuring that unexamined thoughts or unchecked emotions do not erode the advances you've achieved.

Self-appraisal is a deliberate and structured practice of reviewing your thoughts, feelings, and reactions to various situations. It involves stepping back and observing your internal landscape with a curious and non-judgmental eye. This practice encourages you to ask yourself pivotal questions: "Is this thought based on fact or assumption? Are my emotions reflecting the present situation, or are they remnants of past trauma? How are my internal dialogues shaping my perception of myself and the world?"

By engaging in regular self-appraisal, you cultivate a heightened self-awareness that can identify potential triggers or stressors before they manifest as full-blown symptoms. It allows you to catch the subtle signs of stress or distress early, providing an opportunity to apply coping strategies preemptively. This practice also helps debunk any emerging cognitive distortions, ensuring you don't fall back into old patterns of all-or-nothing thinking, overgeneralization, or catastrophizing.

Introspection goes hand in hand with self-appraisal, providing a deeper exploration of your internal world. It is about understanding the 'why' behind your thoughts and feelings. This reflective practice helps you unravel the layers of your psyche and understand the complex interplay of your experiences, beliefs, and identities. It supports the integration process, where insights gained from therapy are intellectualized, felt, and lived.

Moreover, introspection can reveal the strength and resilience you've developed, reinforcing your sense of self-efficacy. It is about acknowledging the distance you've traversed in your healing journey and appreciating the inner resources you've tapped into. By regularly engaging in introspection, you maintain vigilance over potential setbacks and reinforce the positive self-concept that has emerged from your therapeutic work.

You might adopt practices like journaling, meditation, or therapy sessions focused on self-exploration to facilitate self-appraisal and introspection. These practices provide the space and structure needed for effective self-examination. Journaling, for example, offers a tangible record of your thoughts and feelings, allowing you to trace patterns over time. Meditation, conversely, can quiet the mind enough to provide clarity and insight, while therapy sessions can offer professional guidance in navigating the more complex aspects of self-appraisal.

In essence, the practice of self-appraisal and introspection is about nurturing a relationship with oneself rooted in honesty, curiosity, and compassion. It is a commitment to self-knowledge that serves as a bulwark against relapse and enriches your understanding of yourself and your place in the world. These practices are maintenance strategies for post-PTSD life and pathways to a more conscious, deliberate, and fulfilling existence.

The coping strategies and skills acquired throughout this program are your arsenal against life's inevitable challenges. This chapter emphasizes the importance of continuously employing these tools. Whether engaging in cognitive restructuring, practicing mindfulness, or utilizing Internal Family Systems techniques, each skill plays a vital role in maintaining your well-being.

Finally, this chapter calls to embrace your journey with an open heart and mind. It's about recognizing that healing is not a destination but a path of endless learning and growth. With the insights and tools you've acquired, you can face the future with resilience, understanding, and compassion. The journey continues, and you grow stronger and more empowered with each step.

As this chapter concludes, it leaves you with a sense of accomplishment and a hopeful outlook. The journey you've embarked upon has been profound, and the skills you've developed are the foundation for a life of balance, well-being, and continuous growth. The path ahead is yours to shape with mindfulness, vigilance, and the continued application of all you've learned.

ONGOING PROCESSES

Daily Processes:

1. Mindful Start to the Day: Greet each new dawn with a deliberate pause, carving out a sacred space for stillness and presence before the world stirs you into action. Upon awakening, rather than reaching for your phone or diving into your to-do list, allow yourself the gift of ten uninterrupted minutes of meditation. Settle into a comfortable seated position, close your eyes, and draw your attention inward to the rhythm of your breath. Each inhalation and exhalation permits any lingering remnants of dreams or anticipatory thoughts about the day ahead to surface and then drift away like leaves on a stream. Observe them with gentle curiosity, but do not engage or judge. This daily ritual is more than a mere exercise; it's a commitment to starting your day anchored in serenity. It primes your mind and body to approach the forthcoming hours with a sense of calm assurance, ready to meet life's demands from a place of centered clarity. Make this practice a non-negotiable cornerstone of your morning routine, and witness its transformative effect on the rest of your day.

2. Evening Reflections: As dusk settles and the day winds down, take this quiet transition to look inward and pen your thoughts. Create a sanctuary of time, perhaps just before dinner or right before sleep, to open your journal and let the words flow. Start with a reflection on the day's events, turning your focus to instances that sparked gratitude— these could be as simple as a warm smile from a stranger or as significant as overcoming a personal hurdle. Write about the challenges

you faced and how they made you feel, then explore how you navigated them using the tools you've honed. Were there moments when your coping strategies shone? Were there times when they faltered? Contemplate what these experiences teach you about yourself and how they can shape your responses going forward.

This process isn't about critiquing your day but understanding and learning from it. Your journal becomes a testament to your journey, a record of growth, and an intimate dialogue with yourself. Through it, you solidify the day's lessons, savor the sweetness of your triumphs, and gently guide yourself towards even more adaptive strategies for tomorrow. Embrace this reflective practice as an essential nightly ritual, a way to cap off your day with intention and grace, ensuring that every step, no matter how small, is acknowledged and celebrated on your path to continued well-being.

Weekly Processes:

1. Weekly Self-Appraisal: Set aside a calm hour each week—a Sunday evening perhaps, or any time that suits your rhythm—to engage in a deliberate self-appraisal. This isn't just a glance over the days past but a deep, purposeful examination of your experiences. As you sift through your daily reflections, look for emerging patterns and threads that weave through your week. Pay close attention to recurrent thoughts, emotional responses, and behaviors, particularly those that arise during times of stress or when faced with potential triggers.

Evaluate how effectively you've utilized your coping mechanisms and adaptability. Are there strategies that consistently work? Are there responses that could be fine-tuned? Consider the contextual factors that may have influenced your actions and explore alternatives for managing similar situations in the future. This isn't about judgment but strategic planning; it's about ensuring you remain the architect of your mental and emotional landscape.

This weekly introspection is akin to stepping back and viewing a painting in progress: it allows you to appreciate the broader picture, understand the interplay of colors (emotions), and decide which strokes (behaviors) to carry forward. Through this practice, you maintain a vigilant awareness of your mental state and affirm your commitment to an ongoing journey of growth and self-improvement. Each week's dedicated time becomes a cornerstone of your resilience, a ritual that underscores your journey from a place of healing to a flourishing lifestyle.

2. Mindfulness in Motion: Choose a day that marks a pause in your weekly hustle—a midweek break or a leisurely weekend day—to engage in a mindfulness walk. This is more than a stroll; it's a deliberate practice of presence. Find a setting that speaks to tranquility and inspiration, perhaps a verdant park, a serene beach, or a quiet urban sanctuary. As you walk, allow your senses to come alive: feel the texture of the air on your skin, the nuances of the ground beneath your feet, the symphony of sounds near and far, the palette of colors before your eyes, and the scent of life in bloom or earth in rest.

With each step, attune to the rhythm of your breath—let it be the metronome that guides your pace. Observe your thoughts as they arise, not to engage or critique them, but to acknowledge their presence and let them pass like clouds on a windy day. This walk is a journey within as much as a traverse through space.

Engaging in this practice weekly nurtures your physical well-being through gentle, intentional movement and cultivates robust mindfulness that you can carry into the dynamic scenarios of your life. It reinforces your ability to stay centered amidst activity, ensuring that mindfulness is not confined to stillness but is a versatile tool for every moment of your existence. This weekly ritual becomes a sanctuary in time, a space where the clarity of the present moment can unfold in harmony with the movement of life.

These processes are designed to be integrated into your routine as sustainable practices, helping you to stay grounded, mindful, and forward-moving on your path to long-term well-being.

| 16 |

Emotional & Psychological Resilience

As we turn the pages, our narrative journey unfolds into a deeper exploration of emotional and psychological resilience. This chapter celebrates your unwavering commitment to self-discovery and empowerment. Here, we delve into the intricacies of resilience—not merely as a concept but as a lived, dynamic process that you can cultivate and embed into the fabric of your daily life.

Resilience is often thought of as the ability to bounce back from adversity, but it embodies much more than this. It's not just about recovery; resilience is the proactive cultivation of inner resources that enables you to navigate life's inevitable challenges with grace and strength. This quality is akin to a deeply rooted tree that sways in the strongest winds but does not break. It involves building a reservoir of inner strength that empowers you to face life's challenges with endurance and the capability to emerge stronger and wiser from each experience.

Contrary to popular belief, resilience is not an innate trait possessed by a select few; it is a skill that can be developed and nurtured over time. Resilient individuals view challenges not as insurmountable obstacles but as opportunities for growth and learning. They possess an elasticity of the mind and spirit, allowing them to absorb the shock of adverse events, process their emotions effectively, and adapt flexibly.

The essence of resilience lies in maintaining a fundamentally positive outlook on life. Resilient people see difficulties as temporary and surmountable, maintaining hope and finding meaning despite hardship. They approach problems proactively, think critically, make decisions that navigate through adversities effectively, and find creative solutions. Understanding and managing one's emotions is crucial to resilience. It's about recognizing your feelings, allowing yourself to experience these emotions, and finding healthy ways to express and regulate them.

Moreover, no one builds resilience in isolation. Strong, positive relationships are fundamental in providing emotional support, perspective, and practical assistance. Resilient individuals nurture these connections, understanding that shared experiences and support are invaluable in weathering life's storms.

Regular self-care practices and mindfulness help maintain emotional and physical well-being. Activities like meditation, exercise, and hobbies that bring joy and relaxation are essential for replenishing energy and maintaining balance. Resilience also involves accepting the reality of certain situations, particularly those that cannot be changed. This acceptance paves the way for adaptability – the ability to adjust and find new paths forward.

In fostering resilience, you build the ability to withstand adversity and enrich your journey towards emotional and psychological well-being. Resilience is the undercurrent that runs through all aspects of life, providing strength, flexibility, and the capacity for continuous growth and self-discovery. It's a journey that involves embracing life in all its complexity, learning from every experience, and moving forward with a renewed sense of purpose and vitality.

Emotional Intelligence (EI), a cornerstone of resilience, is far more than a buzzword in personal development; it is the essence of how we interact with the world and ourselves. At its core, EI encompasses four fundamental capacities: self-awareness, self-regulation, empathy, and social skills, each vital in navigating life's complexities.

The first pillar of EI, self-awareness, is the ability to recognize and understand your own emotions. This introspective process involves tuning into your feelings, acknowledging them, and discerning their impact on your thoughts and actions. Self-awareness is akin to holding a mirror to your inner world and examining the reflection honestly and openly. It's the practice of asking, "What am I feeling right now?" and "How is this emotion influencing my perception of the situation?" Cultivating self-awareness enables you to navigate your emotional landscape with clarity and consciousness, laying the groundwork for all other aspects of emotional intelligence.

Building on the foundation of self awareness, self regulation in volves managing your emotions in a healthy, constructive manner. It's not about suppression or denial but rather about expressing your emotions appropriately and adapting to changing circumstances. Self-regulation is the skill that enables you to pause before reacting and choose your response rather than being hijacked by fleeting emotions. It encompasses managing stress effectively, adapting to change, and maintaining a positive outlook despite adversity. Techniques like mindfulness, deep breathing, and reflection are powerful tools for enhancing self-regulation.

Empathy, the third element of EI, is the capacity to understand and share the feelings of others. It goes beyond mere sympathy to a deep, emotional resonance with other people's experiences. Empathy allows you to walk in someone else's shoes to perceive the world through their eyes. It fosters a sense of compassion and understanding, which is crucial for building meaningful relationships. Empathy strengthens personal bonds and enhances professional interactions, making it an invaluable skill in all areas of life.

The final aspect of EI is social skills – the ability to navigate and influence the emotional climate of your interactions with others. This includes effective communication, conflict resolution, and inspiring and leading. Social skills are about creating an environment where positive relationships can flourish. They involve not only understanding your own emotions but also recognizing and responding appropriately to the emotions of others. These skills are fundamental in building a supportive network and fostering a sense of community and belonging.

Incorporating EI into daily life is an ongoing practice that begins with mindfulness – being fully present and engaged with the here and now. Mindfulness enhances your emotional intelligence by bringing a heightened awareness of your emotional state at any moment. It allows you to observe your emotions without judgment, creating space to understand and process them effectively. This mindful approach to emotions is a key to self-regulation, enabling you to respond to life's challenges with thoughtfulness and composure.

By incorporating EI into your daily experiences, you enhance your well-being and contribute positively to the lives of those around you. Emotional intelligence is not a static trait but a set of skills that can be cultivated and nurtured over time. It is a continuous learning, growth, and connection journey that fortifies your resilience and enriches every aspect of your life.

The pursuit of emotional and psychological resilience is deeply enriched by the principles of positive psychology and transpersonal psychology, each contributing unique insights and strategies that fortify an individual against the challenges of life, including the reoccurrence of PTSD.

With its strengths-based approach, positive psychology encourages exploring and applying one's innate abilities and virtues. It's about recognizing and utilizing personal strengths, such as resilience, creativity, or empathy, to navigate life's adversities. This approach doesn't ignore life's difficulties but offers a way to approach them with a more constructive and empowered mindset. For instance, leveraging creativity in problem-solving or using empathy to build supportive relationships can transform challenges into opportunities for growth.

Moreover, positive psychology emphasizes gratitude, optimism, and kindness, which isn't just about feeling good. It's about creating a mental environment where positivity can thrive, even in hardship.

Practicing gratitude, for example, shifts focus from what's lacking to what's abundant, fostering a sense of contentment and well-being. Optimism, grounded in a realistic assessment of situations, allows for a hopeful perspective on future outcomes, providing the mental resilience to face and bounce back from difficulties. Similarly, acts of kindness towards oneself and others generate a positive feedback loop of empathy and connection, which is crucial for building a supportive network.

Transpersonal psychology extends the concept of resilience into spiritual and existential understanding. It posits that resilience is about personal strength and a connection to something larger than oneself. This connection, whether to nature, spirituality, community, or a higher purpose, provides a grounding and expansive perspective. It offers a sense of belonging and meaning beyond individual struggles, transforming personal adversities into opportunities for deeper self-understanding and growth.

This transpersonal approach is particularly effective in preventing PTSD relapse. When challenges arise, being part of a larger whole can offer comfort and perspective, reducing feelings of isolation and helplessness. For instance, nature's resilience – seen in a forest regrowing after a fire – can serve as a powerful metaphor for personal recovery and growth. Similarly, engaging in spiritual or community activities can provide solace and a sense of purpose, making individual challenges seem more manageable and less overwhelming.

The integration of positive and transpersonal psychology offers a multifaceted approach to resilience. It's not merely about enduring life's storms but about emerging from them with a deeper understanding of oneself and one's place in the world. By cultivating a mindset that values personal strengths, seeks meaning in adversity, and finds connection in a larger context, individuals can build a foundation of resilience that helps navigate current difficulties and provides a buffer against future challenges.

As we navigate the rest of this chapter, we will explore practical strategies for developing, fostering, and reinforcing emotional and psychological resilience. We will delve into exercises that build emotional intelligence, examine case studies that exemplify resilience in action, and provide guidance on integrating these principles into your everyday life. Each step will give you a deeper understanding of resilience and the practical know-how to embody it.

In the spirit of Positive and Transpersonal psychology, this chapter is not just about individual growth; it's about how your resilience journey can contribute to the collective well-being. It's about recognizing that your transformation has ripple effects extending far beyond yourself, impacting your relationships, community, and, ultimately, the world.

As you continue to build and reinforce your resilience, you do so with the awareness that this journey is not solitary. It's a shared experience, a collective ascent towards greater emotional and psychological well-being. With each chapter and breakthrough, you are transforming your life and contributing to a more resilient, compassionate, and understanding world.

Daily Process: Mindful Emotional Check-In

Task: Start each day with a mindful emotional check-in. Spend 10 minutes each morning in a quiet space, focusing on your emotional state. Close your eyes, take deep breaths, and ask yourself: "How am I feeling today?" Allow any emotion, whether positive or negative, to surface without judgment. Acknowledge and name each emotion you identify.

Processing: Reflect on why you might be feeling these emotions. Consider their sources and how they align with your understanding of emotional intelligence. Write down these emotions and their potential triggers in a journal. This practice will help you become more attuned to your emotional landscape, fostering self-awareness and emotional regulation, which are critical components of emotional intelligence.

Weekly Process 1: Strengths and Gratitude Reflection

Task: Dedicate one day each week to reflect on your strengths and things for which you are grateful. List five personal strengths you've recognized in yourself and five things you're thankful for that week.

Processing: Reflect on how these strengths have helped you in recent situations and how gratitude has impacted your mood and interactions with others. This practice reinforces positive psychology principles, focusing on your capabilities and the positive aspects of your life, thereby enhancing resilience.

Weekly Process 2: Transpersonal Connection Activity

Task: Once a week, engage in an activity that fosters your connection to something greater than yourself. This could be a nature walk, meditation, religious practice, or community service.

Processing: After the activity, reflect on how this connection makes you feel and contributes to your sense of purpose and belonging. Write down these reflections. This practice, grounded in transpersonal psychology, helps to build a sense of interconnectedness and resilience against life's challenges.

Monthly Process: Emotional Intelligence and Resilience Review

Task: Review your emotional intelligence growth and resilience at the end of each month. Reflect on situations where you successfully managed your emotions, showed empathy, or navigated a problematic situation effectively.

Processing: Identify areas where you felt challenged and consider strategies for improvement. Set goals for next month to continue developing your emotional intelligence and resilience.

This monthly review ensures a continued focus on your personal growth and the application of positive and transpersonal psychology principles.

| 17 |

Continuing the Journey

As we reach these final pages of our guide, we find ourselves not at the end but at the beginning of a renewed chapter in life. This concluding chapter is a testament to the resilience, courage, and commitment you've shown in navigating the challenging path to healing from PTSD. It's a chapter that celebrates your successes and sets the stage for a future filled with ongoing growth, self-discovery, and well-being.

The journey of healing is an ongoing process that does not simply end because the pages of this book do. It's a journey that requires continuous attention, care, and nurturing. Just like a garden that needs regular tending to flourish, your mental and emotional well-being requires ongoing care. This involves practicing self-care, making time for activities that replenish and rejuvenate you, and committing to lifelong learning and exploration.

Your dedication to personal growth shouldn't wane with the conclusion of this program. Instead, let this be the catalyst for further exploration of yourself and the world around you. Your growth is a lifelong endeavor enriched by your experiences, learning, and the wisdom you've gained.

It's important to remember that this book is not a substitute for professional psychological or psychiatric care. As you move forward, continue to seek support and guidance from mental health professionals, especially in times of need. If you ever find yourself in a psychiatric or medical emergency, don't hesitate to reach out to emergency personnel. Your journey may have ups and downs, and seeking support is a sign of strength and fortitude.

An essential aspect of your continued journey is the practice of staying present. Each moment offers an opportunity for mindfulness and making decisions that positively impact your future. Living in the present moment allows you to engage fully with life, appreciate its nuances, and make choices aligned with your true self.

The skills and strategies you've learned in this program are not just tools for overcoming PTSD—they're tools for life. They're resources you can draw upon in times of stress, uncertainty, or new challenges. Whether practicing mindfulness, utilizing cognitive-behavioral strategies, or engaging in positive self-talk, these skills are your companions on the journey ahead.

Remember that the healing journey is not linear as you continue to grow and evolve. There will be times of challenge and times of ease. Embrace both with the knowledge that each experience is an opportunity for growth and deeper understanding.

As we conclude, remember that your journey is uniquely yours. It's a journey of continual self-exploration and learning. Embrace it with curiosity, courage, and an open heart. The world is vast, full of experiences and opportunities to further understand yourself and your place in it. Stay open to new experiences, continue to explore your inner world, and let your journey be one of continual growth, learning, and self-discovery.

This chapter, this book, may be ending, but your journey is just beginning. Step forward with confidence, resilience, and a heart full of hope. You have the tools, the knowledge, and the strength to continue growing and thriving in your life's journey.

ABOUT THE AUTHOR

Dr. Dave Ferruolo

ABOUT DR. DAVE

Dr. Dave Ferruolo is the founder, president, and operational director of LifeWorks Counseling Associates, PLLC. He brings a lifetime of entrepreneurial experience, business ownership and leadership to the company. Dr. Dave strives for excellence in everything he does, with a vision for LifeWorks to be a premier counseling agency in New Hampshire and a leader and innovator with the delivery of online TeleHealth counseling services. Each LifeWorks Clinician is hand-picked from literally dozens of qualified applicants, with qualities that align with the core values and high standards expected of a LifeWorks Clinician.

Dr. Dave ran his first business at 15 years-old, and after high school he served our country as a U.S. Navy SEAL. His highly competitive nature aligns with his core character of achieving excellence and continual improvement in all life endeavors. As a lifelong entrepreneur, Dr. Dave has had his share of success and failures, from which he has learned and continues to evolve. His education includes: a technical school certificate in music theory and performance; a Bachelors in Business; a Bachelor in Psychology; a Masters in Clinical Social Work; and a Doctorate of Education in Leadership with a dissertation focus on veteran mental health and reintegration issues. He is an Licensed Independent Clinical Social Worker (LICSW) and Master Licensed Alcohol and Drug Counselor (MLADC). Dr. Dave brings his over 40 years of acquired knowledge, skills, education, experience, and wisdom to *PTSD FREE*.

Certified in various therapeutic modalities-including cognitive-behavioral therapy, mindfulness, trauma-focused therapies, and psychedelic-assisted therapies, Dr. Dave leverages his extensive knowledge to empower those struggling with PTSD toward liberation.

REFERENCES

American Psychiatric Association. (2013). *Diagnostic and Statistical Manual of Mental Disorders (5th ed.)*. Washington, DC: American Psychiatric Publishing.

Anderson, F. G., Sweezy, M., & Schwartz, R. C. (2017). *Internal Family Systems Skills Training Manual: Trauma-Informed Treatment for Anxiety, Depression, PTSD & Substance Abuse*. PESI Publishing & Media.

Bannink, F. P. (2007). Solution-focused brief therapy. *Journal of contemporary psychotherapy, 37*(2), 87-94.

Bannink, F. P. (2015). *1001 solution-focused questions: Handbook for solution-focused interviewing*. New York, NY: Norton & Company.

Barlow, D., & Durand, V. (2009). Abnormal psychology; An integrative approach (5ed.). New York, NY: McGraw-Hill.

Beck, A. T., Rush, A. J., Shaw, B. F., & Emery, G. (1979). *Cognitive Therapy of Depression*. New York: Guilford Press.

Beck, J. S. (2011). *Cognitive behavior therapy: Basics and beyond* (2nd ed.). New York, NY: Guilford Press.

Blonna, R. (2017). *ACT on life not on anger: The new Acceptance and Commitment Therapy guide to problem anger*. New Harbinger Publications.

Brach, T. (2016). *Radical acceptance: Embracing your life with the heart of a Buddha*. New York, NY: Bantam Books.

Brackett, M. A. (2019). *Permission to feel: Unlocking the power of emotions to help our kids, ourselves, and our society thrive*. New York, NY: Celadon Books.

Brackett, M. A., Rivers, S. E., & Salovey, P. (2011). Emotional intelligence: Implications for personal, social, academic, and workplace success. *Social and Personality Psychology Compass, 5*(1), 88-103.

Butler, A. C., Chapman, J. E., Forman, F. M., & Beck, A. T. (2006). The empirical status of cognitive-behavioral therapy: A review of meta-analyses. Clinical Psychology Review, 26 (1), 17-31.

Chödrön, P. (2016). *When things fall apart: Heart advice for difficult times*. Boston, MA: Shambhala Publications.

Clear, J. (2018). *Atomic habits: An easy & proven way to build good habits & break bad ones*. New York, NY: Avery.

Codd III, R. T. (2018). *Effective Techniques for Dealing with Highly Resistant Clients.* PESI Publishing & Media.

Corcoran, J. (2006). Cognitive-behavioral methods for social workers: A workbook. Boston, MA: Allyn & Bacon.

Corcoran, J., & Pillai, V. (2018). *Social workers' desk reference* (3rd ed.). Oxford, UK: Oxford University Press.

Creswell, J. D. (2017). *Mindfulness interventions.* Annual Review of Psychology, 68, 491-516.

Dahl, J., Wilson, K. G., & Nilsson, A. (2015). Acceptance and Commitment Therapy and the treatment of persons at risk for long-term disability resulting from stress and pain symptoms: A preliminary randomized trial. *Behavior Therapy, 35*(4), 785-801.

Davidson, R. J., & Begley, S. (2012). *The emotional life of your brain: How its unique patterns affect the way you think, feel, and live--and how you can change them.* New York, NY: Hudson Street Press.

De Shazer, S. (1985). *Keys to solution in brief therapy.* New York, NY: Norton.

Dillon, C. (2003). *Learning from mistakes.* Belmont, CA: Brooks/Cole

Dindo, L., Van Liew, J. R., & Arch, J. J. (2017). Acceptance and Commitment Therapy: A transdiagnostic behavioral intervention for mental health and medical conditions. *Neurotherapeutics, 14*(3), 546-553.

Doran, J. M. (2015). *The Theory and Practice of Experiential Dynamic Psychotherapy.* Karnac Books.

Duckworth, A. (2016). *Grit: The power of passion and perseverance.* New York, NY: Scribner.

Duhigg, C. (2016). *Smarter faster better: The secrets of being productive in life and business.* New York, NY: Random House.

Ellis, A. (1962). *Reason and emotion in psychotherapy.* New York, NY: Lyle Stuart.

Fava, G. A., & Tomba, E. (2019). *Increasing psychological well-being in clinical and educational settings: Interventions and cultural contexts.* Dordrecht, Netherlands: Springer.

Feldman, C., & Kuyken, W. (2019). *Compassion in the landscape of suffering.* Contemporary Buddhism, 20(1), 143-155.

Flaxman, P. E., Blackledge, J. T., & Bond, F. W. (2016). *Acceptance and Commitment Therapy: Distinctive features.* Routledge.

Fonagy, P., & Allison, E. (2014). The role of mentalizing and epistemic trust in the therapeutic relationship. *Psychotherapy, 51*(3), 372-380.

Forsyth, J. P., & Eifert, G. H. (2016). *The Mindfulness and Acceptance Workbook for Anxiety: A Guide to Breaking Free from Anxiety, Phobias, and Worry Using Acceptance and Commitment Therapy*, Second Edition. New Harbinger Publications.

Franklin, C., Trepper, T. S., Gingerich, W. J., & McCollum, E. E. (Eds.). (2016). *Solution-focused brief therapy: A handbook of evidence-based practice*. Oxford, UK: Oxford University Press.

Fredrickson, B. L. (2013). *Love 2.0: Finding happiness and health in moments of connection*. New York, NY: Penguin Books.

Freud, A. (1936). *The Ego and the Mechanisms of Defense*. London: Hogarth Press and Institute of Psycho-Analysis.

Gabbard, G. O. (2017). *Gabbard's treatments of psychiatric disorders* (5th ed.). Arlington, VA: American Psychiatric Association Publishing.

Gallagher, M. W., Zvolensky, M. J., Long, L. J., Rogers, A. H., & Garey, L. (2019). *The impact of acceptance and commitment therapy on positive psychological outcomes: A systematic review and meta-analysis*. Journal of Contextual Behavioral Science, 14, 379-395.

Gerber, A. J., & Piers, C. (2019). *Neuropsychodynamic psychiatry*. New York, NY: Springer.

Germer, C. K. (2019). *The mindful path to self-compassion: Freeing yourself from destructive thoughts and emotions*. New York, NY: Guilford Press.

Gilbert, P. (2019). *Compassion: Concepts, research and applications*. London, UK: Routledge.

Gingerich, W. J., & Peterson, L. T. (2013). Effectiveness of solution-focused brief therapy: A systematic qualitative review of controlled outcome studies. *Research on Social Work Practice, 23*(3), 266-283.

Goleman, D. (1995). *Emotional intelligence*. New York, NY: Bantam Books.

Grant, A. M., & Greene, J. (2018). *Solution-focused coaching: Managing people in a complex world*. New York, NY: Routledge.

Greenberg, L. S. (2015). *Emotion-focused therapy: Coaching clients to work through their feelings* (2nd ed.). Washington, DC: American Psychological Association.

Gross, J. J. (Ed.). (2007). *Handbook of Emotion Regulation*. New York: Guilford Press.

Haidt, J. (2012). *The righteous mind: Why good people are divided by politics and religion*. New York, NY: Pantheon Books.

Hanson, R. (2015). *Hardwiring happiness: The new brain science of contentment, calm, and confidence*. New York, NY: Harmony.

Hanson, R. (2018). *Resilient: How to grow an unshakable core of calm, strength, and happiness*. New York, NY: Harmony Books.

Harris, R. (2019). *ACT Made Simple: An Easy-To-Read Primer on Acceptance and Commitment Therapy* (2nd ed.). New Harbinger Publications.

Hayes, S. C., & Hofmann, S. G. (Eds.). (2018). *The third wave of cognitive behavioral therapy and the rise of process-based care*. Guilford Press.

Hayes, S. C., & Lillis, J. (2012). *Acceptance and Commitment Therapy*. Washington, DC: American Psychological Association.

Hayes, S. C., Levin, M. E., Plumb-Vilardaga, J., Villatte, J. L., & Pistorello, J. (2013). Acceptance and commitment therapy and contextual behavioral science: Examining the progress of a distinctive model of behavioral and cognitive therapy. *Behavior Therapy, 44*(2), 180-198.

Hayes, S. C., Strosahl, K. D., & Wilson, K. G. (1999). *Acceptance and Commitment Therapy: An Experiential Approach to Behavior Change*. New York, NY: Guilford Press.

Herbine-Blank, T., Kerpelman, D. C., & Sweezy, M. (2016). *Intimacy from the Inside Out: Courage and Compassion in Couple Therapy*. Routledge.

Hofmann, S. G., & Gómez, A. F. (2017). Mindfulness-based interventions for anxiety and depression. *Psychiatric Clinics of North America, 40*(4), 739-749.

Hofmann, S. G., Asmundson, G. J. G., & Beck, A. T. (2018). *The science of cognitive behavioral therapy*. San Diego, CA: Academic Press.

Hofmann, S. G., Asnaani, A., Vonk, I. J., Sawyer, A. T., & Fang, A. (2012). The efficacy of cognitive behavioral therapy: A review of meta-analyses. *Cognitive Therapy and Research, 36*(5), 427-440.

Holmes, T. R. (2015). *Parts Work: An Illustrated Guide to Your Inner Life*. Winged Heart Press.

Kabat-Zinn, J. (1990). *Full Catastrophe Living: Using the Wisdom of Your Body and Mind to Face Stress, Pain, and Illness*. New York: Delta.

Kabat-Zinn, J. (1994). *Wherever you go, there you are: Mindfulness meditation in everyday life*. New York, NY: Hyperion.

Kabat-Zinn, J. (2016). *Mindfulness for beginners: Reclaiming the present moment—and your life*. Boulder, CO: Sounds True.

Kabat-Zinn, J., & Davidson, R. J. (Eds.). (2019). *The Mind's Own Physician: A Scientific Dialogue with the Dalai Lama on the Healing Power of Meditation*. New Harbinger Publications.

Katz, M., Hilsenroth, M. J., Gold, J. R., Moore, M., Pitman, S. R., Levy, S. R., & Owen, J. (2019). Adherence, flexibility, and outcome in psychodynamic treatment of depression. *Journal of Counseling Psychology, 66*(1), 94.

Keltner, D., Oatley, K., & Jenkins, J. M. (2019). *Understanding emotions* (4th ed.). Hoboken, NJ: Wiley.

Kim, J. S. (2008). Examining the effectiveness of solution-focused brief therapy: A meta-analysis. *Research on Social Work Practice, 18*(2), 107-116.

A Nieuwsma, J., D Walser, R., K Farnsworth, J., D Drescher, K., G Meador, K., & Nash, W. (2015). Possibilities within acceptance and commitment therapy for approaching moral injury. *Current Psychiatry Reviews, 11*(3), 193-206.

Ahmadian, A., Mirzaee, J., Omidbeygi, M., Holsboer-Trachsler, E., & Brand, S. (2015). Differences in maladaptive schemas between patients suffering from chronic and acute posttraumatic stress disorder and healthy controls. *Neuropsychiatric disease and treatment*, 1677-1684.

Bedard-Gilligan, M., Zoellner, L. A., & Feeny, N. C. (2017). Is trauma memory special? Trauma narrative fragmentation in PTSD: Effects of treatment and response. *Clinical Psychological Science, 5*(2), 212-225.

Boyd, J. E., Lanius, R. A., & McKinnon, M. C. (2018). Mindfulness-based treatments for posttraumatic stress disorder: a review of the treatment literature and neurobiological evidence. *Journal of Psychiatry and Neuroscience, 43*(1), 7-25.

Brown, L. A., Belli, G. M., Asnaani, A., & Foa, E. B. (2019). A review of the role of negative cognitions about oneself, others, and the world in the treatment of PTSD. *Cognitive Therapy and Research, 43*, 143-173.

Crespo, M., & Fernández-Lansac, V. (2016). Memory and narrative of traumatic events: A literature review. *Psychological trauma: Theory, research, practice, and policy, 8*(2), 149.

De Jongh, A. D., Resick, P. A., Zoellner, L. A., Van Minnen, A., Lee, C. W., Monson, C. M., ... & Bicanic, I. A. (2016). Critical analysis of the current treatment guidelines for complex PTSD in adults. *Depression and anxiety, 33*(5), 359-369.

Eshuis, L. V., van Gelderen, M. J., van Zuiden, M., Nijdam, M. J., Vermetten, E., Olff, M., & Bakker, A. (2021). Efficacy of immersive PTSD treatments: A systematic review of virtual and augmented reality exposure therapy and a meta-analysis of virtual reality exposure therapy. *Journal of psychiatric research, 143*, 516-527.

Ferruolo, D. M. (2015). Psychosocial equine program for veterans. *Social work, 61*(1), 53-60.

Ferruolo, D. M. (2018). *Veteran Focused Equine Facilitated Mental Health*. Plymouth State University.

Fisher, J. (2017). *Healing the fragmented selves of trauma survivors: Overcoming internal self-alienation*. Routledge.

Hamblen, J. L., Norman, S. B., Sonis, J. H., Phelps, A. J., Bisson, J. I., Nunes, V. D., ... & Schnurr, P. P. (2019). A guide to guidelines for the treatment of posttraumatic stress disorder in adults: An update. *Psychotherapy, 56*(3), 359.

Hopwood, T. L., & Schutte, N. S. (2017). A meta-analytic investigation of the impact of mindfulness-based interventions on post traumatic stress. *Clinical psychology review, 57*, 12-20.

Kim, J. S. (2015). *Solution-focused brief therapy: A multicultural approach.* Thousand Oaks, CA: SAGE Publications.

Kirsch, I., Moore, T. J., Scoboria, A., & Nicholls, S. S. (2002). The emperor's new drugs: An analysis of antidepressant medication data submitted to the U.S. Food and Drug Administration. *Prevention & Treatment, 5*(1), 23.

Knox, J. (2015). *Self-Agency in Psychotherapy: Attachment, Autonomy, and Intimacy.* Norton & Company.

Koorankot, J., Moosa, A., Froerer, A., & Rajan, S. K. (2022). Solution focused vs problem focused questions on affect and processing speed among individuals with depression. *Journal of Contemporary Psychotherapy, 52*(4), 347-353.

Lang, A. J. (2017). Mindfulness in PTSD treatment. *Current Opinion in Psychology, 14*, 40-43.

Lebow, J., Chambers, A., Christensen, A., & Johnson, S. M. (Eds.). (2019). *Encyclopedia of couple and family therapy.* Switzerland: Springer International Publishing.

Lemma, A. (2016). *Introduction to the practice of psychoanalytic psychotherapy* (2nd ed.). Chichester, UK: Wiley Blackwell.

Linehan, M. M. (1993). *Cognitive-behavioral treatment of borderline personality disorder.* New York, NY: Guilford Press.

Lloyd, J., & Hertlein, K. M. (2015). *The complete systemic therapist: Integrating systemic approaches in psychotherapy.* Boston, MA: Cengage Learning.

Lopes, P. N., Salovey, P., & Straus, R. (2017). Emotional intelligence, personality, and the perceived quality of social relationships. *Personality and Individual Differences, 107*, 212-218.

Luoma, J. B., Hayes, S. C., & Walser, R. D. (2017). *Learning ACT: An Acceptance and Commitment Therapy skills-training manual for therapists* (2nd ed.). New Harbinger Publications.

Lutz, A. B. (2017). *Learning solution-focused therapy: An illustrated guide.* Washington, DC: American Psychiatric Association Publishing.

Luyten, P., Mayes, L. C., Fonagy, P., Target, M., & Blatt, S. J. (2015). Handbook of psychodynamic approaches to psychopathology. New York, NY: Guilford Press.

Lyubomirsky, S. (2013). *The myths of happiness: What should make you happy, but doesn't, what shouldn't make you happy, but does.* New York, NY: Penguin Press.

MacCann, C., & Roberts, R. D. (2008). New paradigms for assessing emotional intelligence: theory and data. *Emotion, 8*(4), 540.

MacLearn, C. (2008). Use of self in cognitive behavioral therapy. Clinical Social Work Journal, 36 (3), 245-253.

Maguire, L. (2002). Clinical social work: Beyond generalist practice with individuals, groups, and families. Pacific Grove, CA: Brooks/Cole.

Mansell, W., Harvey, A., Watkins, E., & Shafran, R. (2019). Conceptual foundations of the transdiagnostic approach to CBT. *Journal of Cognitive Psychotherapy, 33*(1), 14-33.

Manson, M. (2016). *The subtle art of not giving a fck*: A counterintuitive approach to living a good life*. New York, NY: HarperOne.

Martin, A., Naunton, M., Kosari, S., Peterson, G., Thomas, J., & Christenson, J. K. (2021). Treatment guidelines for PTSD: a systematic review. *Journal of Clinical Medicine, 10*(18), 4175.

McGonigal, K. (2015). *The upside of stress: Why stress is good for you, and how to get good at it.* New York, NY: Avery.

McKergow, M., & Korman, H. (2017). *Inbetween: Neither inside nor outside the therapy room.* London, UK: Solutions Books.

McWilliams, N. (2016). *Psychoanalytic diagnosis. Understanding personality structure in the clinical process* (2nd ed.). New York, NY: The Guilford Press.

Mikolajczak, M., Gross, J. J., & Roskam, I. (2019). Parental emotional regulation: The wider impact on family life. *Emotion Review, 11*(3), 230-243.

Miller, W. R., & Rollnick, S. (2002). Motivational interviewing: Preparing people for change (2nd ed.). New York: Guilford Press.

Neff, K. (2011). *Self-compassion: The proven power of being kind to yourself.* New York, NY: William Morrow.

Neff, K., & Germer, C. (2018). *The Mindful Self-Compassion Workbook: A Proven Way to Accept Yourself, Build Inner Strength, and Thrive.* The Guilford Press.

Nelis, D., Quoidbach, J., Mikolajczak, M., & Hansenne, M. (2011). Increasing emotional intelligence: (How) is it possible? *Personality and Individual Differences, 50*(1), 56-61.

Newport, C. (2016). *Deep work: Rules for focused success in a distracted world.* New York, NY: Grand Central Publishing.

Nezu, A. M., Nezu, C. M., & D'Zurilla, T. J. (2013). *Problem-solving therapy: A treatment manual.* New York, NY: Springer Publishing Company.

Peeters, N., van Passel, B., & Krans, J. (2022). The effectiveness of schema therapy for patients with anxiety disorders, OCD, or PTSD: A systematic review and research agenda. *British Journal of Clinical Psychology, 61*(3), 579-597.

Raes, F., & Williams, J. M. G. (2019). *The power of mindfulness: Mindfulness meditation training in sport (MMTS).* New York, NY: Springer.

Ratner, H., George, E., & Iveson, C. (2012). *Solution focused brief therapy: 100 key points and techniques.* New York, NY: Routledge.

Ryan, R. M., & Deci, E. L. (2017). *Self-determination theory: Basic psychological needs in motivation, development, and wellness.* New York, NY: Guilford Press.

Salzberg, S. (2017). *Real love: The art of mindful connection.* New York, NY: Flatiron Books.

Schnyder, U., Ehlers, A., Elbert, T., Foa, E. B., Gersons, B. P., Resick, P. A., ... & Cloitre, M. (2015). Psychotherapies for PTSD: what do they have in common?. *European journal of psychotraumatology, 6*(1), 28186.

Schultz, D. P., & Schultz, S. E. (2008). *Theories of personality* (9. ed.). Belmont, CA: Wadsworth.

Schwartz, R. C. (1995). *Internal family systems therapy.* New York, NY: Guilford Press.

Schwartz, R. C., & Sweezy, M. (2019). *Internal Family Systems Therapy*, Second Edition. New York, NY: Guilford Press.

Seligman, M. E. P. (2018). *The hope circuit: A psychologist's journey from helplessness to optimism.* New York, NY: Public Affairs.

Shedler, J. (2010). The efficacy of psychodynamic psychotherapy. *American Psychologist, 65*(2), 98-109.

Shulman, L. (2012). The skills of helping: Individuals, groups, and communities (7 ed.). Belmont, CA: Thomson Brooks/Cole.

Siegel, D. J. (2016). *Mind: A journey to the heart of being human.* New York, NY: W. W. Norton & Company.

Sijbrandij, M., Kunovski, I., & Cuijpers, P. (2016). Effectiveness of internet-delivered cognitive behavioral therapy for posttraumatic stress disorder: A systematic review and meta-analysis. *Depression and anxiety, 33*(9), 783-791.

Sinek, S. (2019). *The infinite game.* New York, NY: Portfolio/Penguin.

Smock Jordan, S., Froerer, A. S., & Bavelas, J. B. (Eds.). (2019). *SFBT conversations: The art and practice of solution-focused brief therapy.* New York, NY: Routledge.

Stockton, D., Kellett, S., Berrios, R., Sirois, F., Wilkinson, N., & Miles, G. (2019). Identifying the underlying mechanisms of change during acceptance and commitment therapy (ACT): A systematic review of contemporary mediation studies. *Behavioural and cognitive psychotherapy, 47*(3), 332-362.

Stoddard, J. A., & Afari, N. (Eds.). (2014). *The big book of ACT metaphors: A practitioner's guide to experiential exercises and metaphors in acceptance and commitment therapy.* Oakland, CA: New Harbinger Publications.

Strosahl, K., Robinson, P. J., & Gustavsson, T. (2015). *Brief interventions for radical change: Principles and practice of focused acceptance and commitment therapy.* New Harbinger Publications.

Summers, F. (2016). *Transcending the legacies of childhood abuse: A psychodynamic view.* New York, NY: Guilford Press.

Sweezy, M., & Ziskind, E. L. (Eds.). (2016). *Innovations and Elaborations in Internal Family Systems Therapy*. Routledge.

Taylor, S. (2017). *Clinician's guide to PTSD: A cognitive-behavioral approach*. Guilford Publications.

Twohig, M. P., & Levin, M. E. (2017). Acceptance and Commitment Therapy as a treatment for anxiety and depression: A review. *Psychiatric Clinics of North America, 40*(4), 751-770.

Twomey, C., O'Reilly, G., & Byrne, M. (2015). Effectiveness of cognitive behavioural therapy for anxiety and depression in primary care: a meta-analysis. *Family practice, 32*(1), 3-15.

Vago, D. R., & Silbersweig, D. A. (2012). Self-awareness, self-regulation, and self-transcendence (S-ART): A framework for understanding the neurobiological mechanisms of mindfulness. *Frontiers in Human Neuroscience, 6,* 296.

Van Dam, N. T., van Vugt, M. K., Vago, D. R., Schmalzl, L., Saron, C. D., Olendzki, A., Meissner, T., Lazar, S. W., Kerr, C. E., Gorchov, J., Fox, K. C. R., Field, B. A., Britton, W. B., Brefczynski-Lewis, J. A., & Meyer, D. E. (2018). *Mind the hype: A critical evaluation and prescriptive agenda for research on mindfulness and meditation*. Perspectives on Psychological Science, 13(1), 36-61.

Van Dijk, S. (2018). *DBT made simple: A step-by-step guide to dialectical behavior therapy*. Oakland, CA: New Harbinger Publications.

Villatte, J. L., Vilardaga, R., Villatte, M., Vilardaga, J. C. P., Atkins, D. C., & Hayes, S. C. (2016). Acceptance and Commitment Therapy modules: Differential impact on treatment processes and outcomes. *Behaviour research and therapy, 77,* 52-61.

Wallerstein, R. S. (2015). *Forty-two lives in treatment: A study of psychoanalysis and psychotherapy*. New York, NY: Routledge.

Walser, R. D., & Westrup, D. (2017). *Acceptance & Commitment Therapy for the treatment of post-traumatic stress disorder & trauma-related problems*. New Harbinger Publications.

Watkins, L. E., Sprang, K. R., & Rothbaum, B. O. (2018). Treating PTSD: A review of evidence-based psychotherapy interventions. *Frontiers in behavioral neuroscience, 12,* 258.

Watkins, L. E., Sprang, K. R., & Rothbaum, B. O. (2018). Treating PTSD: A review of evidence-based psychotherapy interventions. *Frontiers in behavioral neuroscience, 12,* 258.

Westen, D., Gabbard, G. O., & Blagov, P. (2015). *Psychodynamic diagnostic manual: PDM-2*. Silver Spring, MD: Alliance of Psychoanalytic Organizations.

Williams, M., & Penman, D. (2015). *Mindfulness: An eight-week plan for finding peace in a frantic world*. New York, NY: Rodale Books.

Wojcik, K. D., Cox, D. W., Kealy, D., Grau, P. P., Wetterneck, C. T., & Zumbo, B. (2022). Maladaptive schemas and posttraumatic stress disorder symptom severity: investigating the mediating role of posttraumatic negative self-appraisals among patients in a partial hospitalization program. *Journal of Aggression, Maltreatment & Trauma, 31*(3), 322-338.

Young, J. E., Klosko, J. S., & Weishaar, M. E. (2003). *Schema Therapy: A Practitioner's Guide.* New York: Guilford Press.

Zayfert, C

www.ingramcontent.com/pod-product-compliance
Lightning Source LLC
Chambersburg PA
CBHW070902120626
46546CB00001B/107